THE ART OF
COSPLAY
AND CREATIVE
MAKEUP

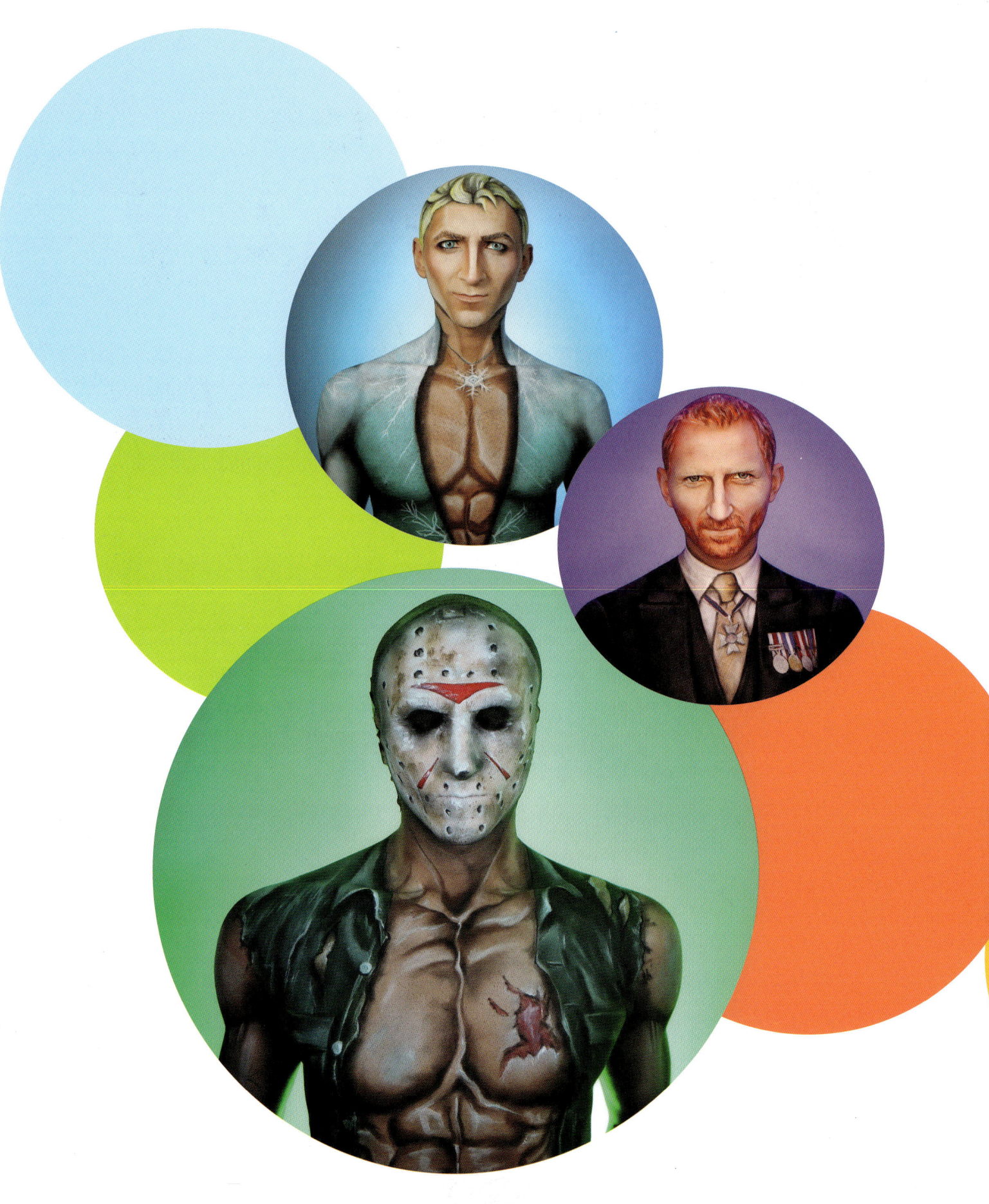

THE ART OF
COSPLAY
AND CREATIVE
MAKEUP

CREATE INCREDIBLE LOOKS WITH SIMPLE
TECHNIQUES AND AFFORDABLE MATERIALS

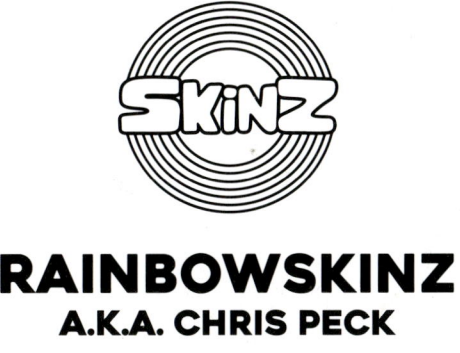

RAINBOWSKINZ
A.K.A. CHRIS PECK

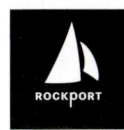

Quarto.com

© 2024 Quarto Publishing Group USA Inc.
Text, Photos, Illustrations © 2024
Rainbowskinz

First published in 2024 by Rockport
Publishers, an imprint of The Quarto Group,
100 Cummings Center, Suite 265-D, Beverly,
MA 01915, USA.
T (978) 282-9590; F (978) 283-2742

Rockport Publishers titles are also available
at discount for retail, wholesale, promotional,
and bulk purchase. For details, contact
the Special Sales Manager by email at
specialsales@quarto.com or by mail at The
Quarto Group, Attn: Special Sales Manager,
100 Cummings Center, Suite 265-D, Beverly,
MA 01915, USA.

10 9 8 7 6 5 4 3 2 1

ISBN: 978-0-7603-8908-9

Digital edition published in 2024
eISBN: 978-0-7603-8909-6

Library of Congress Cataloging-in-
Publication Data

Names: Peck, Chris (Makeup artist), author.
Title: The art of cosplay and creative makeup :
create incredible looks
   with simple techniques and affordable
materials / Rainbowskinz aka Chris
   Peck.
Description: Beverly, MA, USA : Rockport,
2024. | Includes index. |
   Summary: "In The Art of Cosplay and
Creative Makeup, body painter
   extraordinaire Rainbowskinz show you the
fundamental techniques he uses
   to create an infinite number of extraordinary
looks"-- Provided by
   publisher.
Identifiers: LCCN 2024011743 | ISBN
9780760389089 (trade paperback) | ISBN
   9780760389096 (ebook)
Subjects: LCSH: Cosplay--Equipment and
supplies. | Cosmetics. | Beauty,
   Personal. | Social media--Vocational
guidance.
Classification: LCC TT633 .P43 2024 | DDC
646.7/2--dc23/eng/20240402
LC record available at https://lccn.loc.
gov/2024011743

Design and layout: Burge Agency
Photography: Rainbowskinz and Shutterstock

Printed in China

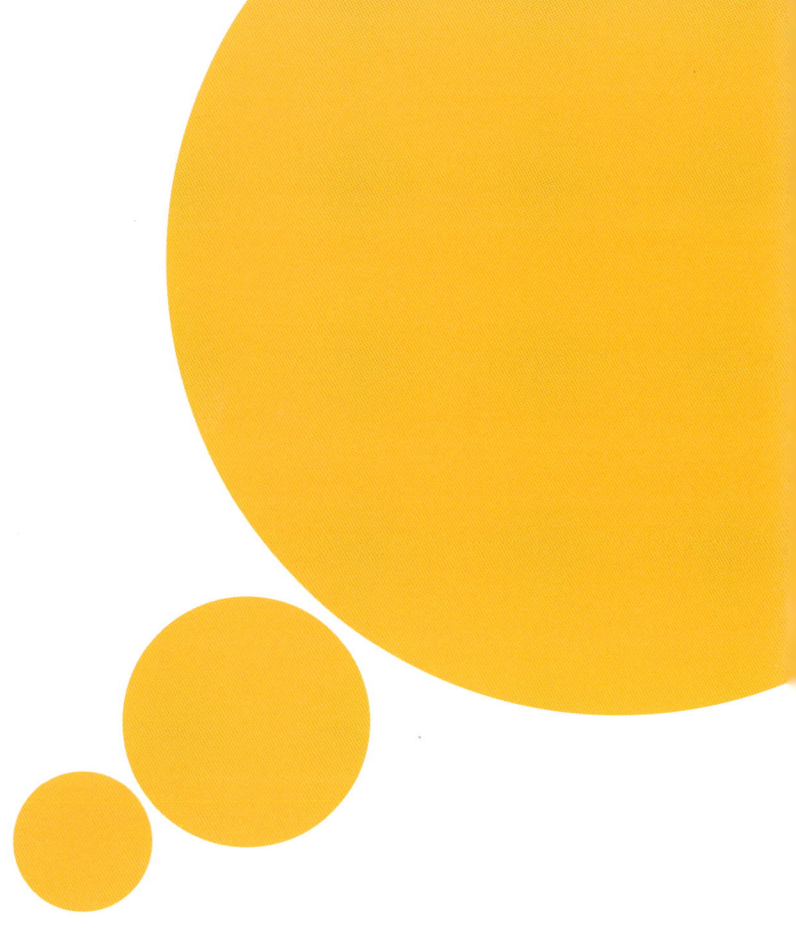

ACKNOWLEDGMENTS

First and foremost, thank you to Michelle Bredeson at Quarto, who has been an absolute dream to work with, guiding me through the publishing process and always being on hand to answer any questions I have. Also, for putting up with my never-ending email and brain dumps! I've fired a lot of questions your way and you've always been super helpful and done so with a smile on your face.

To the project manager on the book, Brooke Pelletier, for shepherding this book through the process and making sure no detail is overlooked.

To the design team and art director, Anne Re, for bringing my vision to life, and for making all the tiny changes I asked for to make the book perfect. You've done an amazing job!

To the models, Kyle, Sarah, Michael, and Matt, for allowing me to use them in the book to demonstrate certain products and painting techniques. I couldn't have asked for better canvases to work on.

To my management at StandBy Talent for supporting me along the way and connecting me with the brands I needed in order to create this book.

To the brands who have kindly donated products and helped promote this book to reach a greater audience.

To my parents, Ian and Caroline, who have always supported me in whatever crazy decision I choose to make, always offering advice and guidance along the way, despite probably thinking I am absolutely mad at the same time. I am forever appreciative to you for you picking up all the late-night phone calls and for all the proofreading you offered to do. Thank you.

To my friends Jack and Joey, despite having zero interest in cosplay and makeup, for listening to me witter on about this book for the past 12 months. Thank you for offering advice when asked and allowing me to run ideas past you.

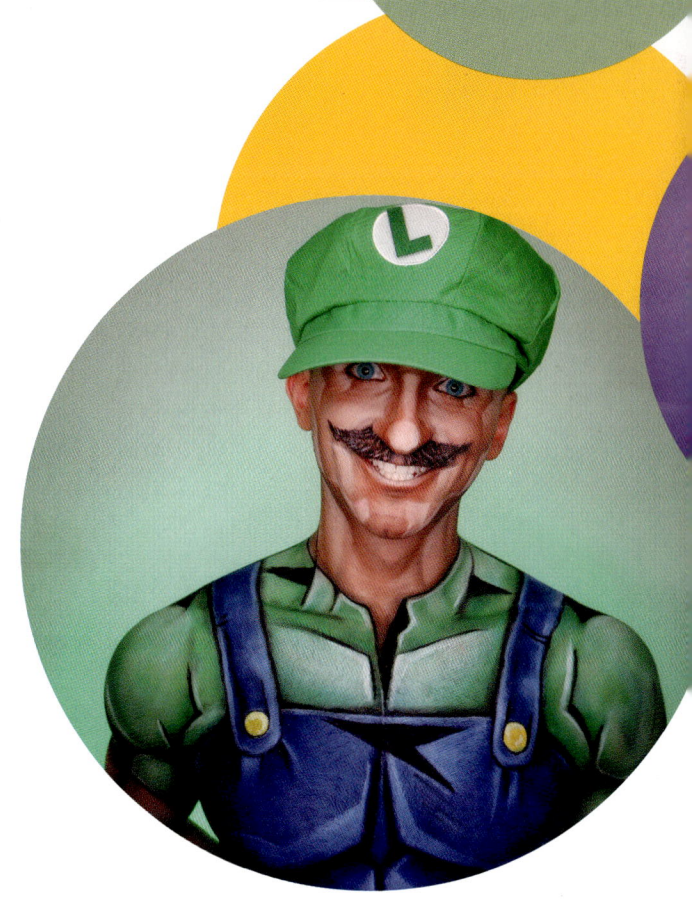

CONTENTS

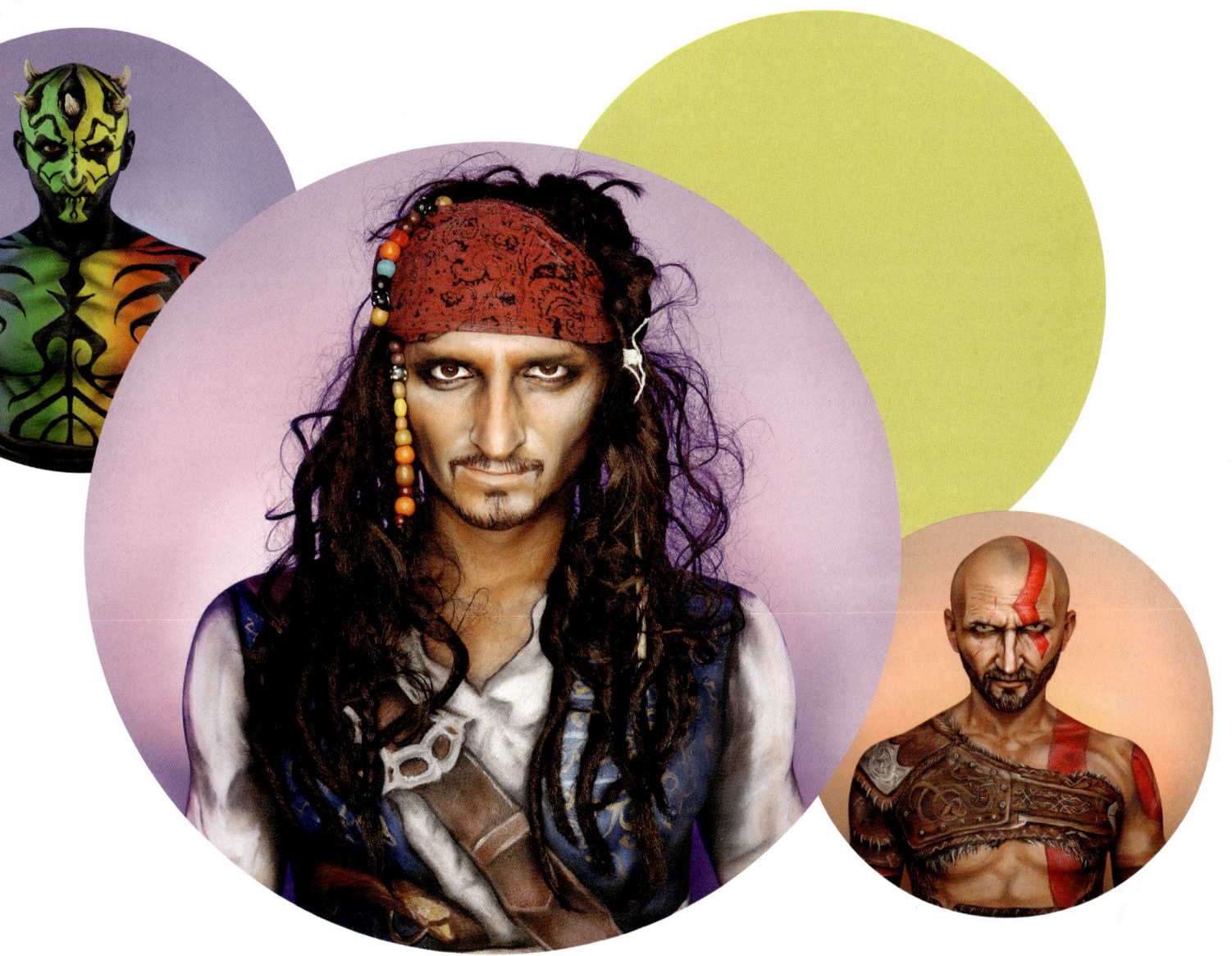

HOW DID I GET HERE?

BELIEVE IT OR NOT MY NAME ISN'T ACTUALLY RAINBOWSKINZ. MY REAL NAME IS CHRIS, AND I GREW UP IN THE UK IN A PLACE CALLED COVENTRY.

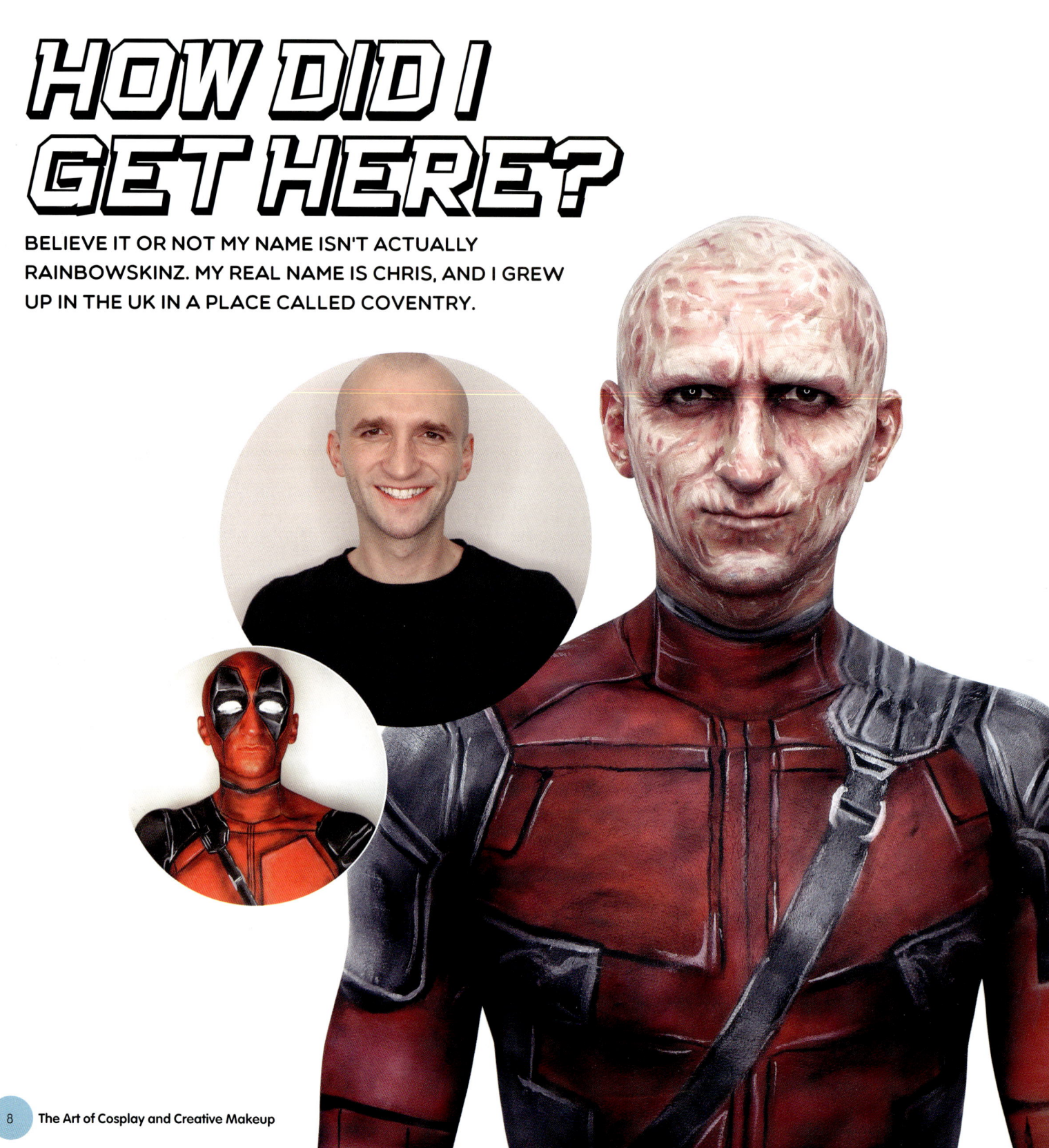

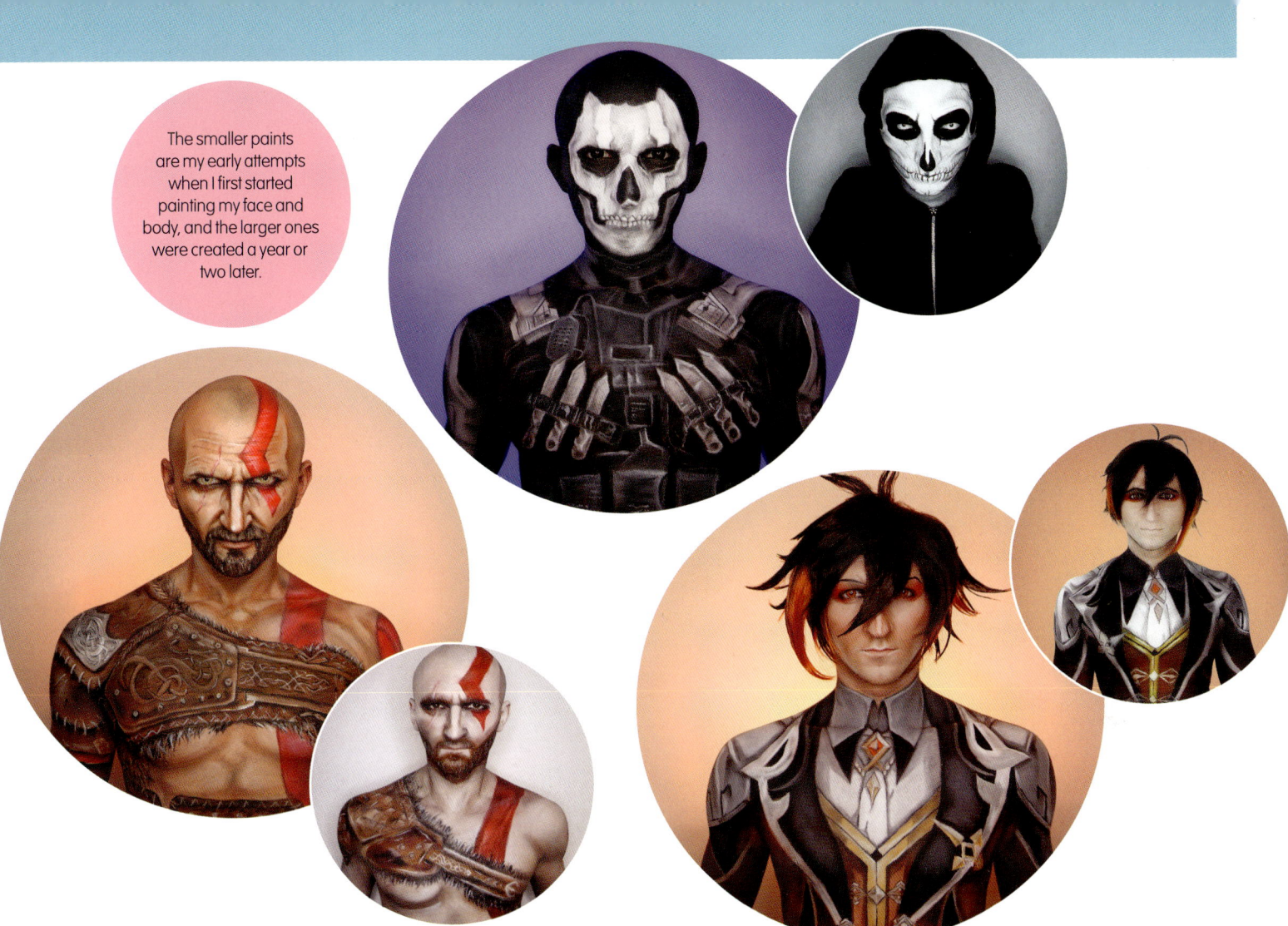

I wasn't a particularly artistic child, but I did enjoy art, so when I was at school I decided to take art for my exams. My teacher didn't want to let me, saying I'd only bring the school's grades down. I took art anyway and I got a B. Nothing groundbreaking, but it wasn't the failing grade my art teacher thought I'd get. Being told I wasn't good enough sparked something in me that made me want to try harder to prove my teacher wrong, and I did.

At university I went to a lot of costume parties. I used to spend ages creating my costumes, painting my face, and painting other people's faces, and I loved it. Other people loved it as well, and I started getting requests from friends to paint them.

A friend suggested I start an Instagram account so I could paint more regularly and have a way of tracking my progress. In 2018 I started Rainbowskinz on Instagram. I never expected it to go anywhere. It was just a hobby I loved doing.

After I finished university, I tried to navigate the corporate world and found that the nine to five lifestyle wasn't for me. I struggled

and found myself stressing all the time, but I *couldn't* give it all up to pursue my dreams of working less, doing something I enjoy, and make a living out of it, right? Well lucky for me, that decision was made for me. But before we get into that, let me take you back to when I joined TikTok.

I joined TikTok just before the first Covid lockdown back in 2020. I started off with painting my face only, and the videos didn't do very well. Someone suggested that I try a half-body paint and my engagement started to increase. I started painting live on TikTok and my first viral videos got over 300,000 views. I was pushing out as much content as my free time allowed while still juggling a personal life and a full-time job. My followers crept up to 400,000 when I was suddenly laid off from my job.

This was quite a shock for me. That comfort of having a monthly income had been taken away instantly. Thankfully, the severance package was enough to tide me over for a few months, so I spent that time building my social media channels.

It was at this point I had my first properly viral video.

It was a Fortnite character called Midas, and 12 hours after posting, going to sleep, and waking up again, the video had over 5M views and 50K hate comments. I distinctly remember feeling like I was at a crossroads: do I give up, or do I keep going and get better?

I remembered when my art teacher told me I wasn't good enough, but I did it anyway and proved her wrong. So, I carried on! I got better, I kept gaining followers, and the more I did, the more people started to appreciate the time, effort, and skill it took to paint myself.

At this point I signed with my first management company, which started bringing in sponsorship work for me. I was able to make money from TikTok and continue to be lucky enough to make a living off painting myself for social media.

It's amazing where a couple of years of hard work and persistence can take you. There isn't a day that goes by that I don't thank my lucky stars I'm able to live this life! Through this book you'll be able to learn some skills, techniques, tips, and tricks to help you get where *you* want to go.

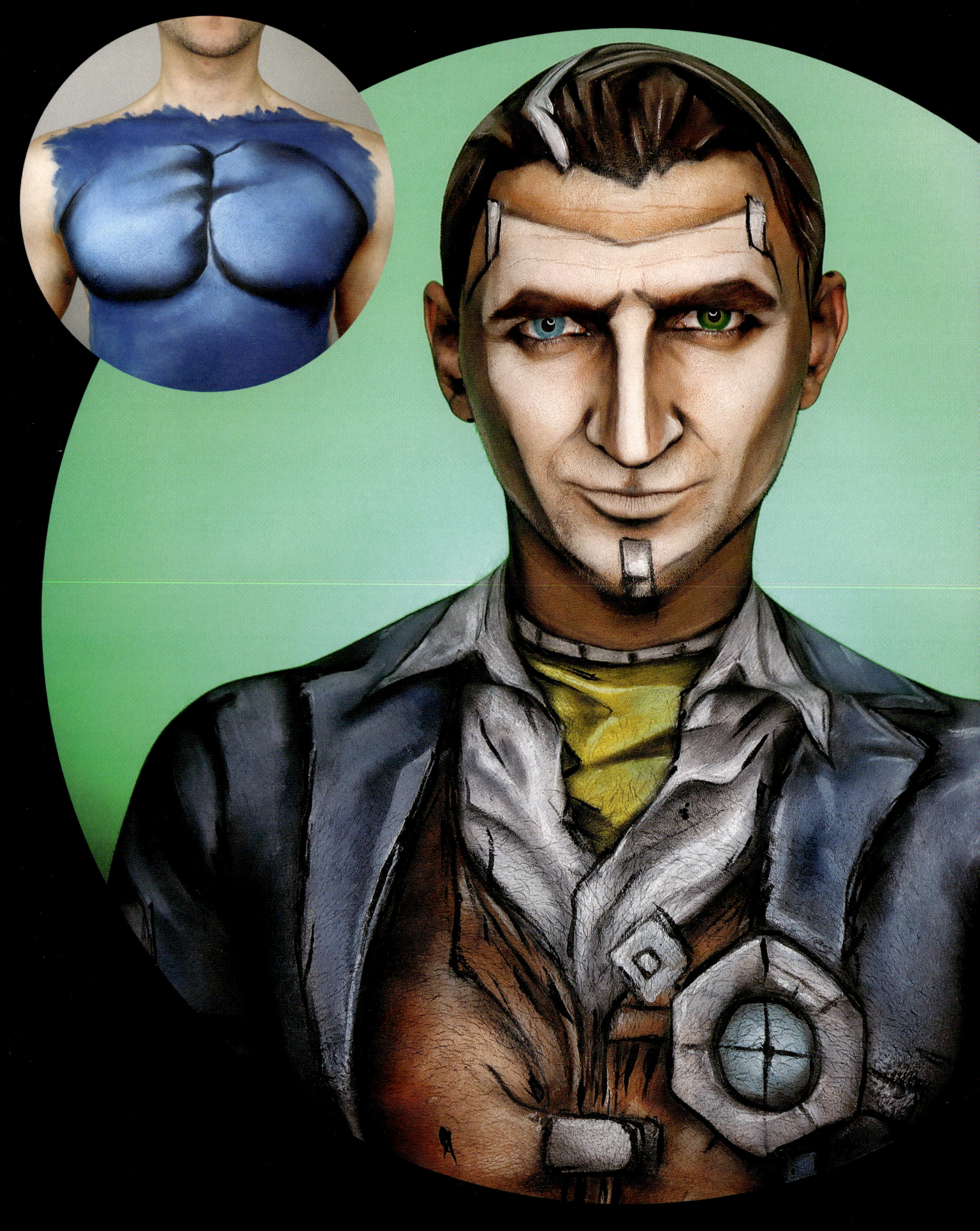

PART 1
PAINTING TECHNIQUES

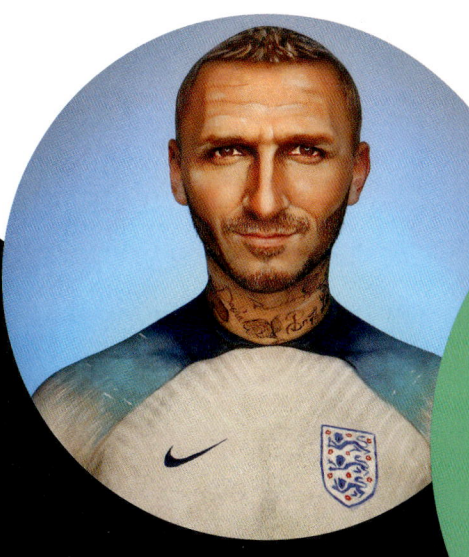

Throughout this section we will spend time learning the basics of painting, how to apply products, and where to apply certain products to create different illusions. There will be some theory and lots of step by step guides but nothing you won't be able to join in and try with me! So pick up a paintbrush and get involved. I want to see you tagging me in all your pictures online!

INTRODUCTION TO FACE PAINTS

If you've never attempted face painting you're probably feeling overwhelmed by the sheer amount of choices there are and have no idea where to start. Well, I'm here to help make sense of it all. There are three main types of paints you'll come across and they all vary in price, purpose, and use.

Water-Activated Paints

These paints are the most common you'll see. They're usually the most affordable and easiest to use and remove. They come in various qualities so be careful when selecting which brand to use. The cheapest store-bought water-activated paints are difficult to work with and enough to put you off facepainting all together. They can be removed with warm water and soap.

Water-activated paints, are a favorite for children's face painters due to their quick drying time and no need for powders to set, or lock-in, the paint. You can create fine detail work and they are the easiest to apply. Usually these paints don't stain, but that depends on the brand you use. Certain colors like yellow, green, and some light blues, are more prone to staining but these won't last longer than a day.

Under the umbrella of water-activated paints, there are two types: glycerin and wax based. Glycerin-based paints dry slower so have more time to blend and are the most common of the two. Brands like Mehron Paradise, Kryolan Aqua color, Snazaroo are all glycerin-based. Wax-based paint feels much thicker than glycerin, dries quicker and is great for line work. If you are just starting out though, it's not a necessity for your makeup kit. I'd stick with the glyercin-based product. Both of these water-activated paints can be applied with a paintbrush or sponge.

Oil, Cream, and Grease Paints

This type of paint is commonly used within the makeup world, usually as a solid base as it is less likely to crack when applying additional layers on top. They are much more difficult to remove, so if you're looking for an all-day application, or if you're going to a concert or club where you are likely to sweat, these are a better option than water-activated paints.

Out of the three, grease paints are the most stubborn, and if set with translucent powder, they are completely waterproof. You'll need a makeup remover that targets grease to remove this, or if you don't have that, your next best option is a hammer and chisel!

Oil and cream paints, while more difficult to remove than water-activated paints, are much easier to remove with makeup removers. While they provide great coverage, these types of paint can be very sticky to work with and do not dry unless they are set with powder. They are very long-lasting, and commonly used for theater and clown makeup.

You can also get greaseless oil-based paints, which are my preference. Mehron does a brilliant Clown White Lite paint which I use all the time to get a vibrant white. This product is also great for blending into water-activated paints to achieve a nice gradient highlight.

Alcohol-Activated Paints

These are by far the most expensive paints out of the lot, and from a glance it doesn't look like you get a lot for your money. These types of paints are not meant to be used for full face coverage but for special effects (SFX) makeup such as cuts, bruises, and small details. They can **only** be activated with 99% alcohol, so if you do decide to use them, make sure you're in a well-ventilated area.

The more alcohol you use the more translucent they get, so they are good for creating effects that look like they're under the skin, like veins. Removal of these products also requires 99% alcohol which means they do not come off with water or sweat. Personally, I've never needed to use these, but if SFX makeup is your thing they're worth the investment.

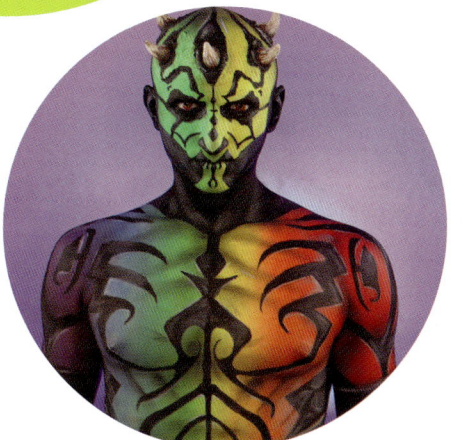

For Rainbow Darth Maul from *Star Wars* I used a range of colorful water-activated paints.

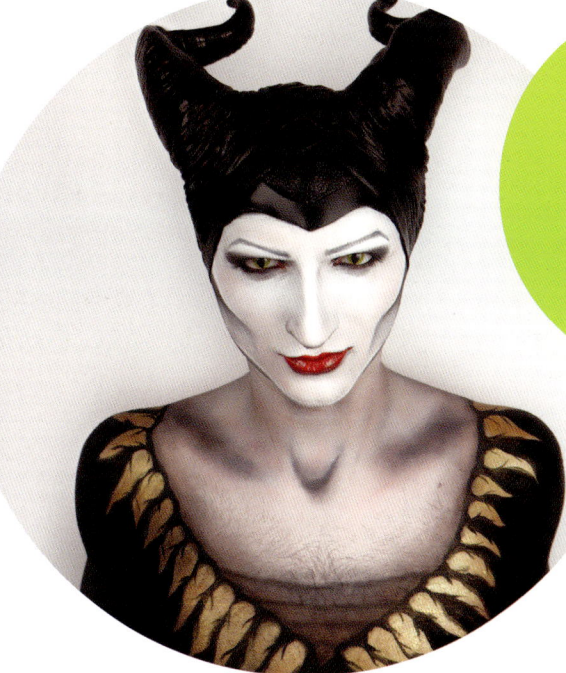

I was able to get Maleficent's stark white skin using Clown White oil-based paint.

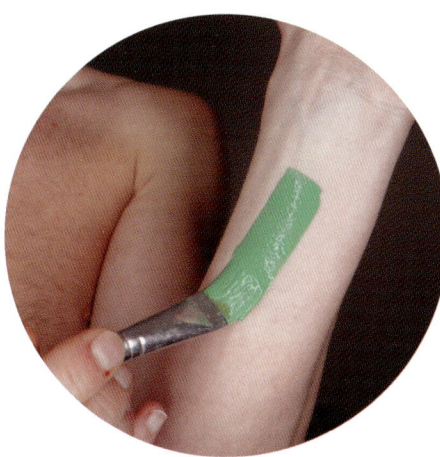

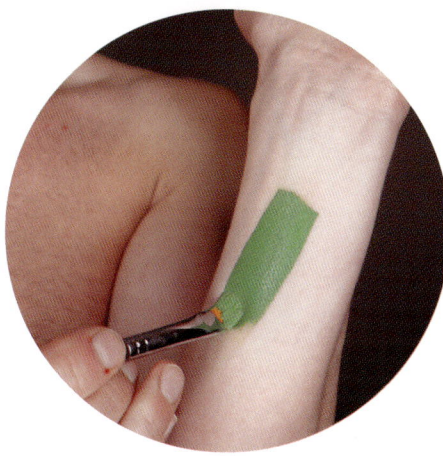

You can see the difference in how water-activated paint (top) and cream paint (bottom) look when first applied.

Face Paint Application Tips

Skin preparation is key! Make sure skin is clean from any dirt or products such as lotion before applying any paint as this will affect the application.

I apply my paints with a thick brush 3.5 cm in width to get the first layer of coverage. While this is quicker when covering larger areas of a body, you are likely to end up with streaks, so I even out the paint with a second layer applied using a sponge.

For finer details, such as outlining, I use a thinner brush. Sets of detail brushes used for painting model figurines come in handy for this. For the smoothest linework, use a long and thin brush.

When applying paint with a sponge, dab, don't scrape. Some water-activated paints need a couple of layers, so wait for each layer to dry before applying the next layer, or you won't get the coverage you need.

The consistency of water also influences the paint. If you apply the paint and it is dripping down the body, then it's too wet. If you apply it and the paint is translucent then this is also too wet. You want enough thickness in the paint to not be able to see any skin under the paint. You might find certain colors, particularly the lighter colors like white, yellow, and sky blue, need multiple layers to get a good coverage. Apply thin layers on top of each other to avoid any cracking. Make sure each layer is completely dry before applying the next.

Try to limit your layers to two to three max.

The key to getting a realistic body paint, with three-dimensional levels is through layering. We'll cover this in more detail later in the book. It includes adding shadows using powders, adding in highlights, and detailed line work. Getting a good base coverage of paint is the first step. When you understand how to effectively apply this, it'll take your body paints to the next level!

When it comes to painting anything symmetrical start with your **least** dominant side. If you're right-handed, start painting the left side of the face despite the natural urge to start with your right. Trust me, you'll find it much easier to match the symmetry of your less dominant side.

HIGHLIGHTING AND SHADING

To understand the next three parts of this chapter, you need to understand the basics of how to create depth. This can be done in numerous ways, but the most common and effective way of creating depth to your work is through paint or makeup alone. To learn how to do this start with adding highlights and shading to your work.

As soon as I got my head around these techniques, it massively elevated my work from barely amateur to super impactful. To this day, it's where most of my time is spent when I am painting myself or someone else. Anyone can lay a color down in the right order, but not everyone understands the power of adding the right highlight and shading to really make your work stand out. The good news is, I'm here to tell you **anyone** can do it, and it's surprisingly much easier than you might expect.

What Is a Highlight?

A highlight is an area of the face you'd like to stand out. It's where the light hits and is created by using a lighter shade of the base color, or in makeup a lighter shade of concealer than your natural shade. Highlights catch the light and draws the attention to that part of the face.

What Is Shading?

Shading is the opposite of a highlight. With a highlight, the light is hitting an object. In shading there is no light hitting the object, and therefore a shadow.

The use of both highlighting and shading is commonly referred to as **contouring**. You'll hear this referred to as facial contouring within the beauty makeup world, but this term can used for body art as well. It's all about manipulating and sculpting the shape of something to enhance and change the natural features. This is how I create the illusion of realistic clothing.

How Light Creates the Illusion of Dimension

To help you understand where to place a highlight, and where to place a shadow, let's think about a real-life example which doesn't involve makeup. Grab two sheets of paper and a light source. On a flat surface, stack these two sheets of paper on top of each other and shine the light on top. Slowly lift the top sheet higher and see what happens. What you should see is that top piece of paper is creating a shadow onto the piece of paper below, and the greater the distance the two sheets are apart, the larger the shadow becomes.

Think about this logic while you're painting clothes. Try to understand where the light would hit that top layer, and where the bottom layer has a shadow cast to it.

Look down at the clothes you're currently wearing. Some parts of your clothes are highlighted but where there is a crease, they'll have a shadow. These are the folds in the clothes you want to recreate with makeup.

Now imagine you want to paint a shirt on your chest. In this example, the shirt represents that top layer of paper fully lit in the light. Your chest is the underlayer of paper that will have the shadow cast against it. So, to create that illusion of the shirt, you need to place a highlight where the shirt ends and a shadow where skin starts.

This basic concept of light and shadows and being able to apply paints to replicate them is all it takes to create dimension and depth to your work.

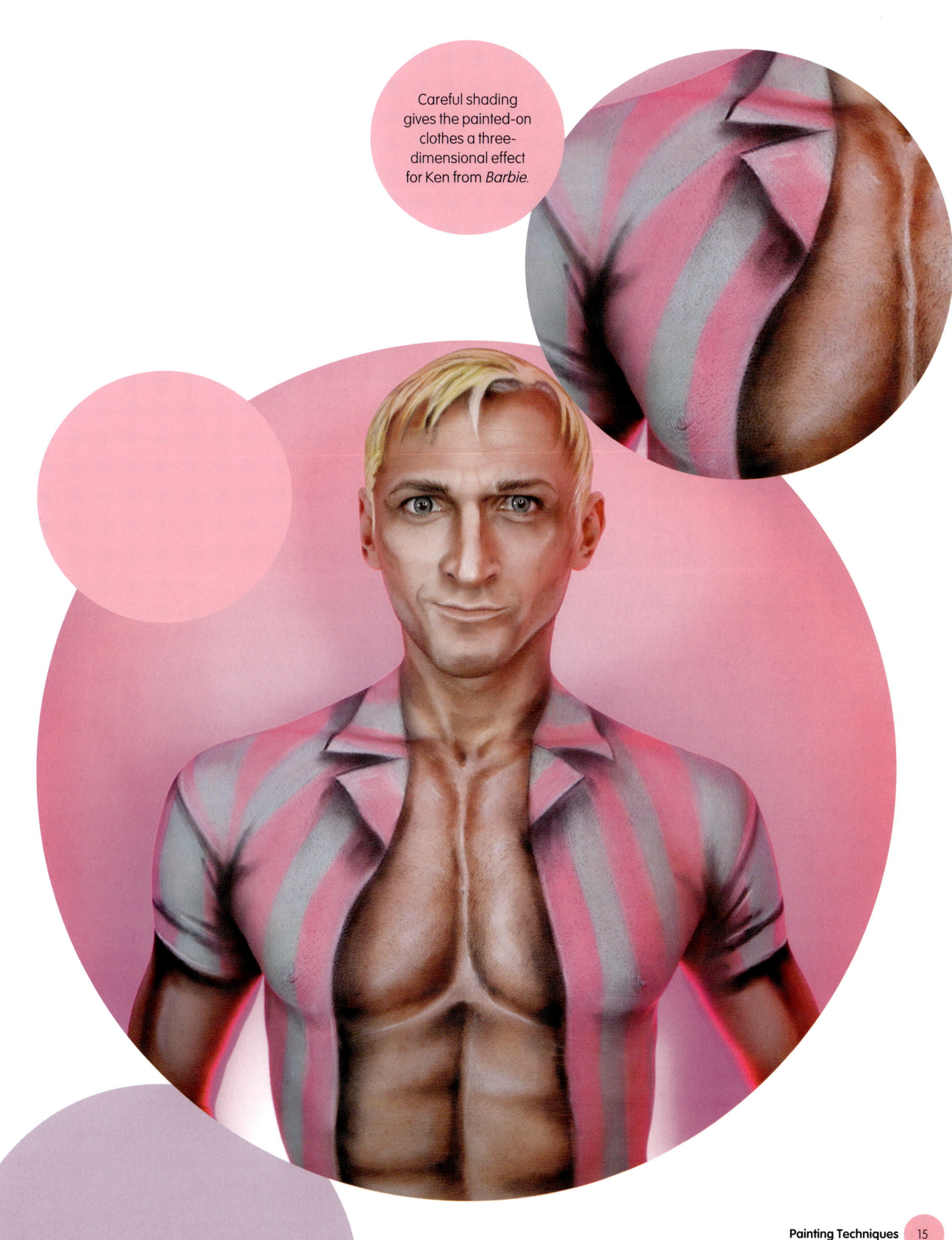

Careful shading gives the painted-on clothes a three-dimensional effect for Ken from *Barbie*.

COLOR THEORY OF CONTOURING

Now we understand the theory behind **where** and **why** to place a highlight and a shadow, it's time to learn **how** to create one. This is a good example of how you can create highlighting and shading using lighter and darker shades of the same color.

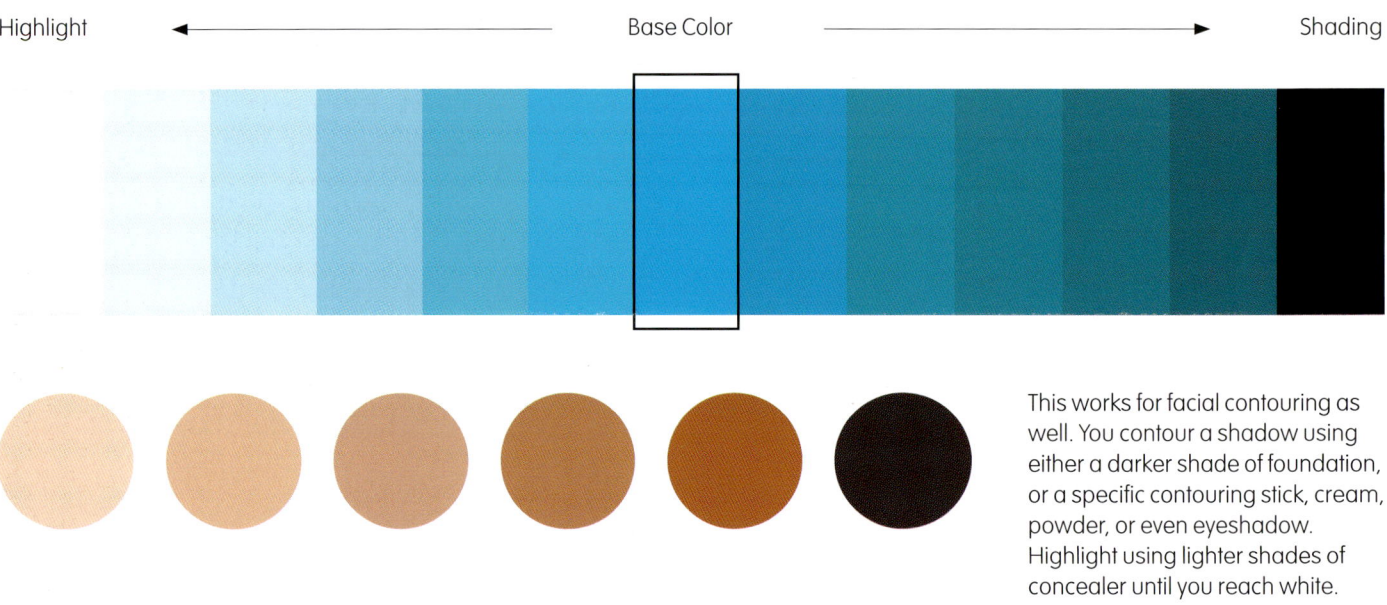

Highlight ← Base Color → Shading

This works for facial contouring as well. You contour a shadow using either a darker shade of foundation, or a specific contouring stick, cream, powder, or even eyeshadow. Highlight using lighter shades of concealer until you reach white.

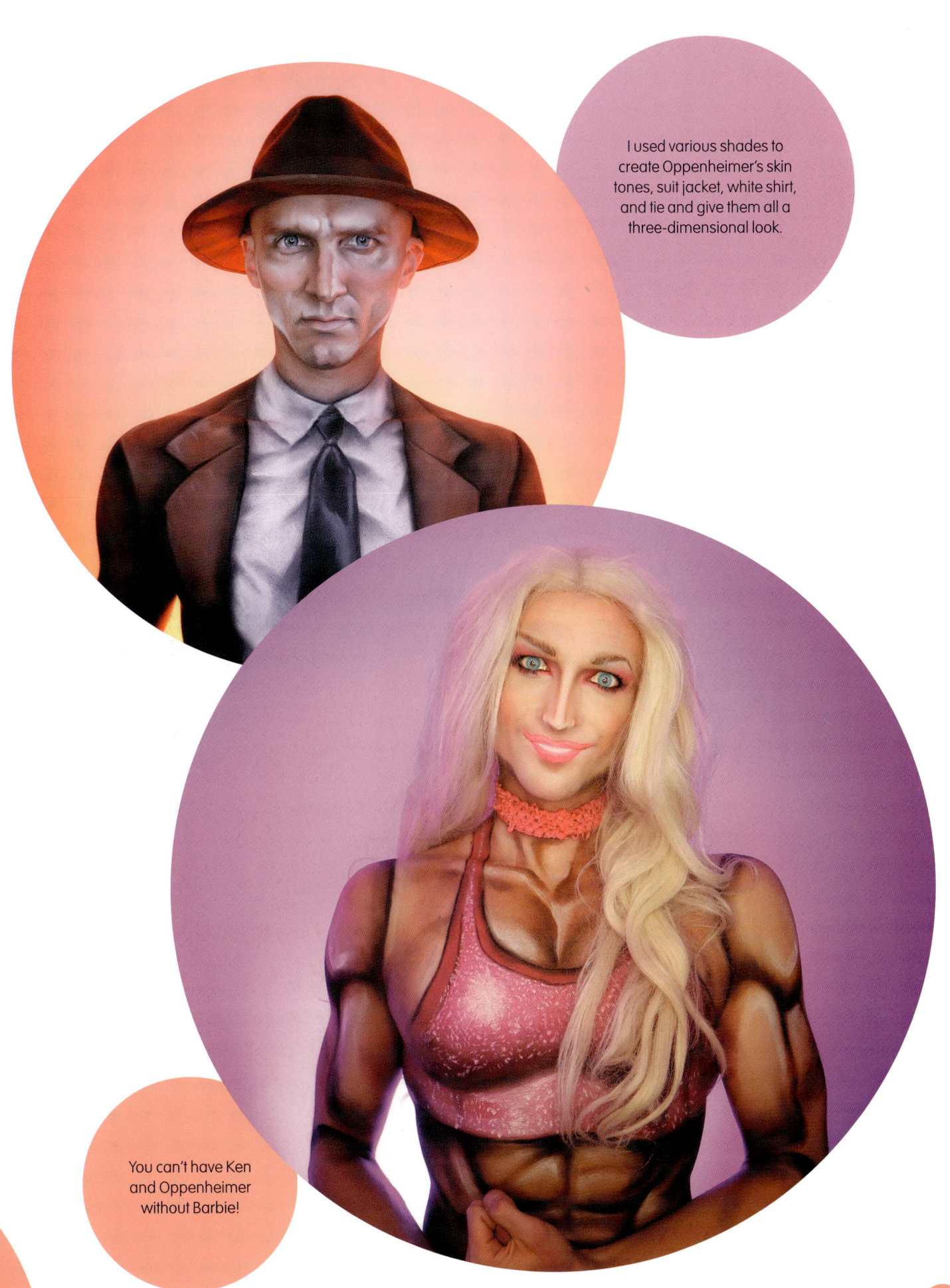

I used various shades to create Oppenheimer's skin tones, suit jacket, white shirt, and tie and give them all a three-dimensional look.

You can't have Ken and Oppenheimer without Barbie!

3D CONTOURING
STEP BY STEP

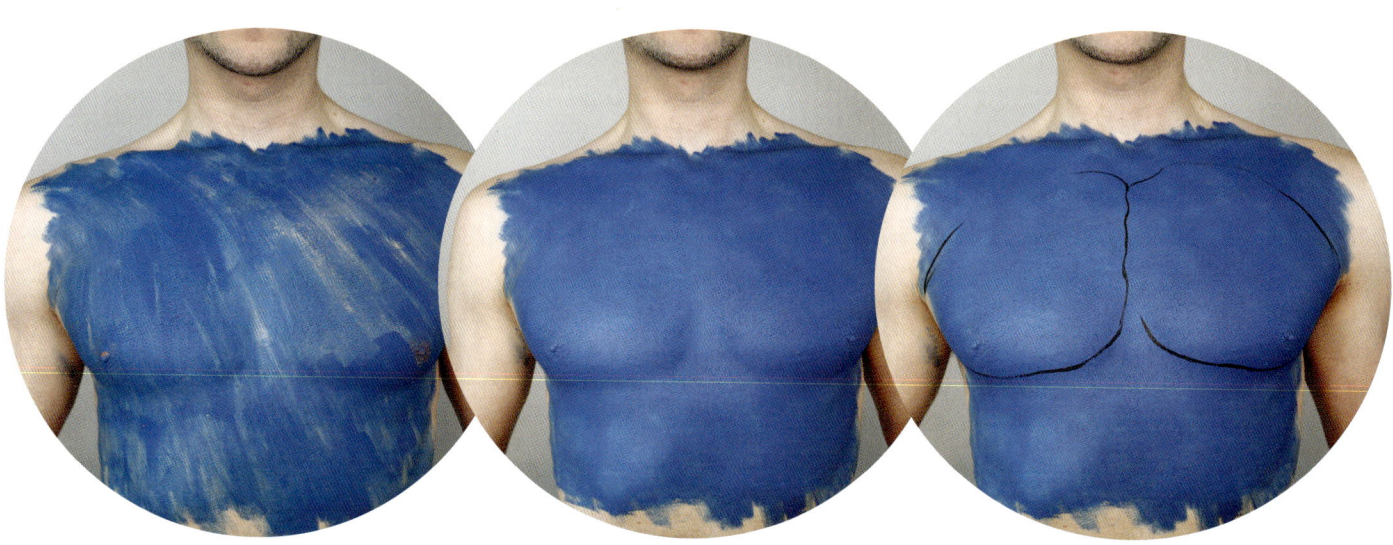

Step 1
Cover the chest in your chosen base color using a brush.

Step 2
Dab with a damp sponge to achieve even coverage.

Step 3
Sketch out the edges of the contour, where the light meets the dark, using black paint or powder.

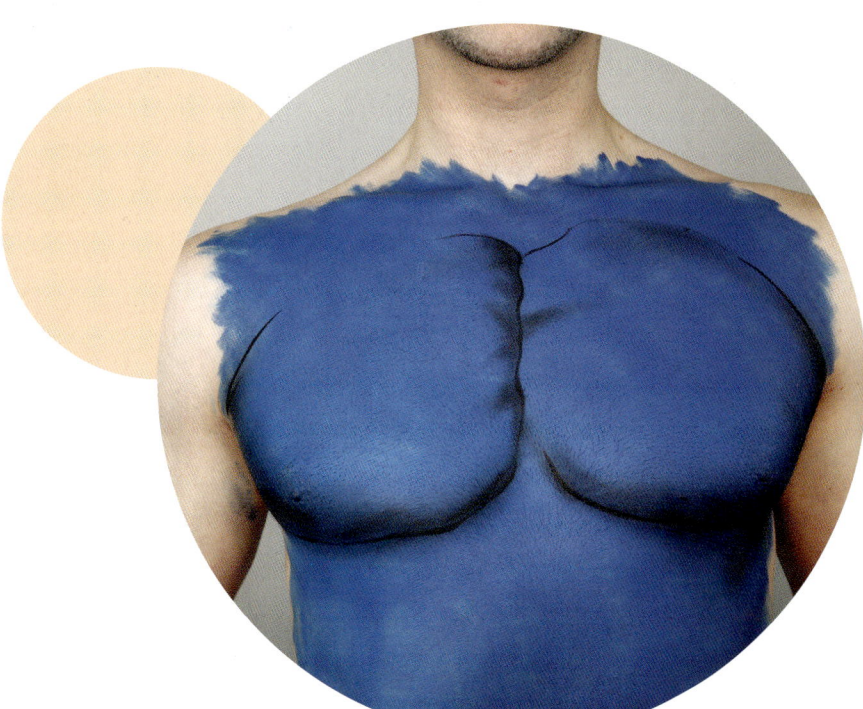

Step 4
Apply more powder and blend this in, adding more powder where you think there will be less light (i.e., more shadow).

Now we're going to see step by step how to use highlighting and shading in your cosplay paints. I'm painting my torso in blue, but the method is the same for natural skin tones. To simplify this example, I'm going to use three colors.

Scan to Watch a Tutorial

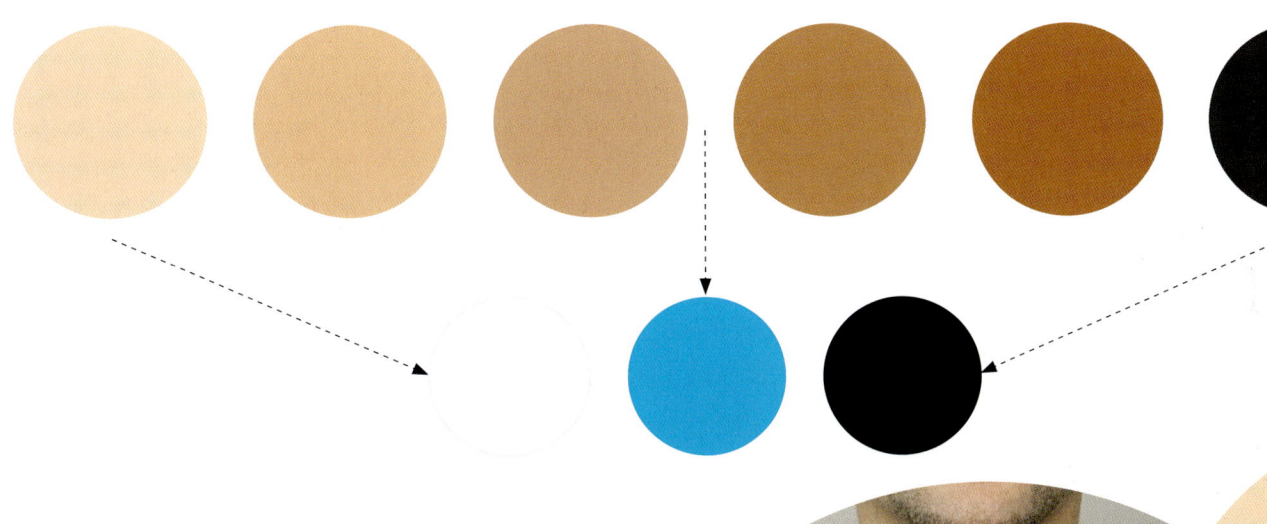

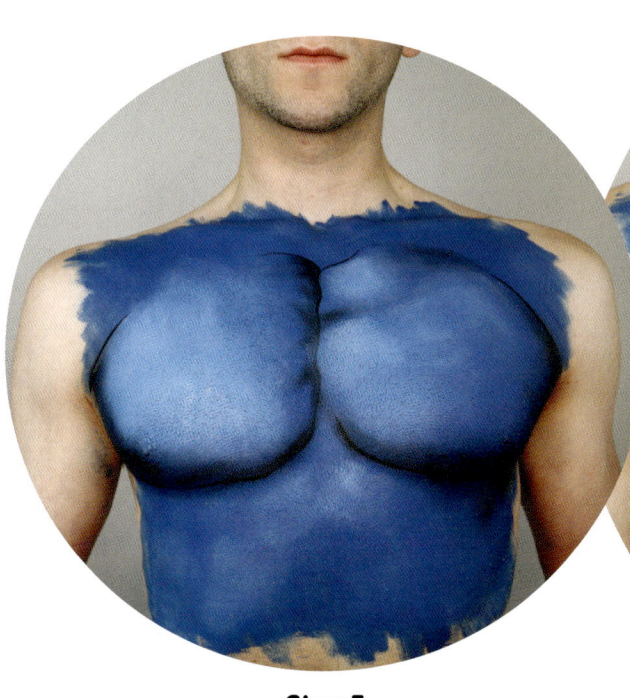

Step 5
Apply white to the areas you want to stand out and that are closest to the light source.

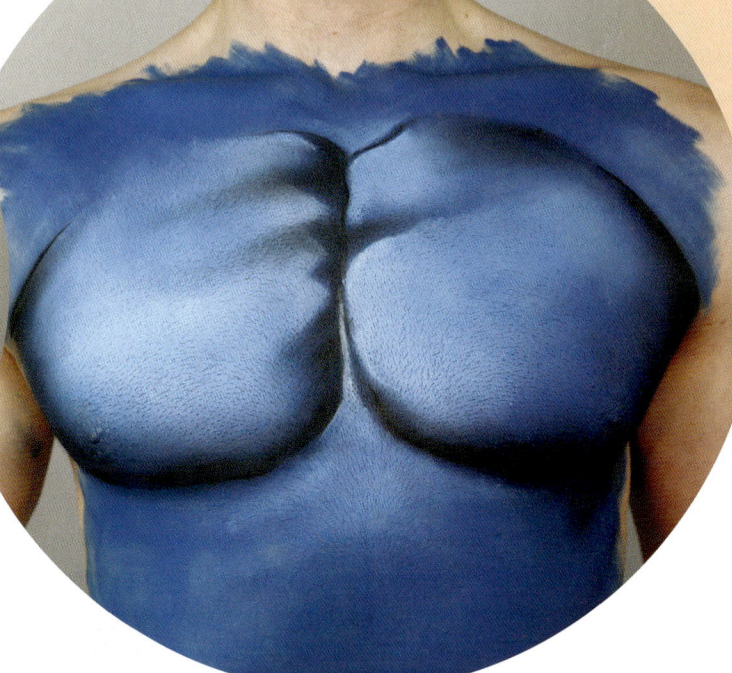

Step 6
Continue to layer until you have a nice even gradient from white to blue to black.

HOW TO CONTOUR A FACE FOR COSPLAY

Contouring in principle is simple: you're applying makeup to help shape and enhance certain parts of your face. However when it comes to transformation into a different person, one size doesn't fit all. What might work on my face, might not work on yours. The best place to apply paints and makeup is heavily dependent on the natural shape of your face. If you search "face contouring" on Google, you'll find ways to contour your face to look something like this.

This is a great guide when it comes to contouring your face to enhance your natural beauty. However, when it comes to contouring your face to transform into a cosplay character you need to be bolder and braver. You might need to fully change your facial structure, like add in cheek bones which aren't there, and that's something these examples won't help with.

There are two different types of contour palettes you can use: powdered contour and cream contour. Powdered contours are much easier to blend but you can achieve the same result with cream ones. So, it comes down to personal preference. I use both and tend to steer more towards cream contours when I recreate harsher looking features which need a clean line finish.

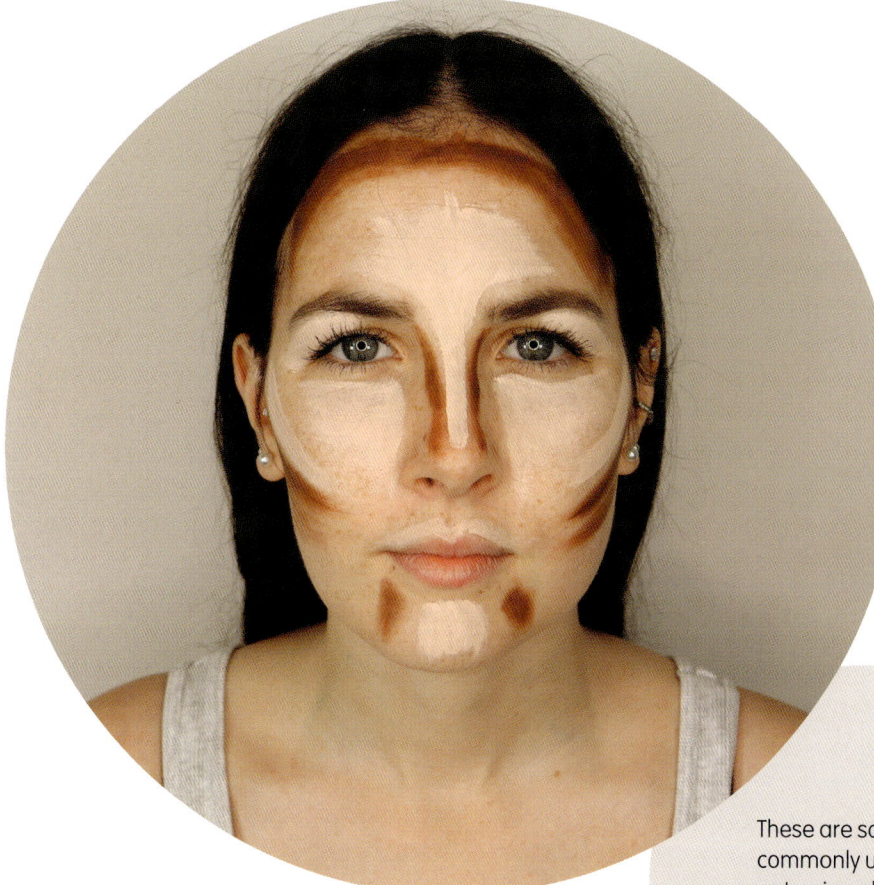

These are some of the commonly used facial contouring placements.

Products You Need

Liquid foundation: to use as a base to be able to blend everything into. You want this in your natural skin color.

Concealer: in shades lighter than your natural foundation color.

A set of makeup brushes and sponges to blend the concealer into the foundation.

Preparation, Tips, and Tricks Before Applying Makeup

To successfully transform your face into someone else, first you'll need multiple reference pictures to see what this person looks like from different angles, and how the light hits different parts of their face.

Second, zoom in on small areas of the face and build it one piece at a time. For instance, if we want to look like the below model, you might choose to start with the lip, really focusing on where you need to apply that contour and where you need to apply the highlight.

Once you've replicated the upper lip, work your way across the whole face bit by bit, remembering to look at your multiple reference pictures. It's the age-old phrase of "trust the process" and you really do need to have a bit of faith with this because it takes a good while to build up the layers enough to start to see a difference.

It's also important to mention this type of contouring can be super effective from *only* one particular angle, so when taking photos be aware of what angle that needs to be. Don't beat yourself up if you can see a resemblance in the phone camera but you *can't* see it as well in the mirror.

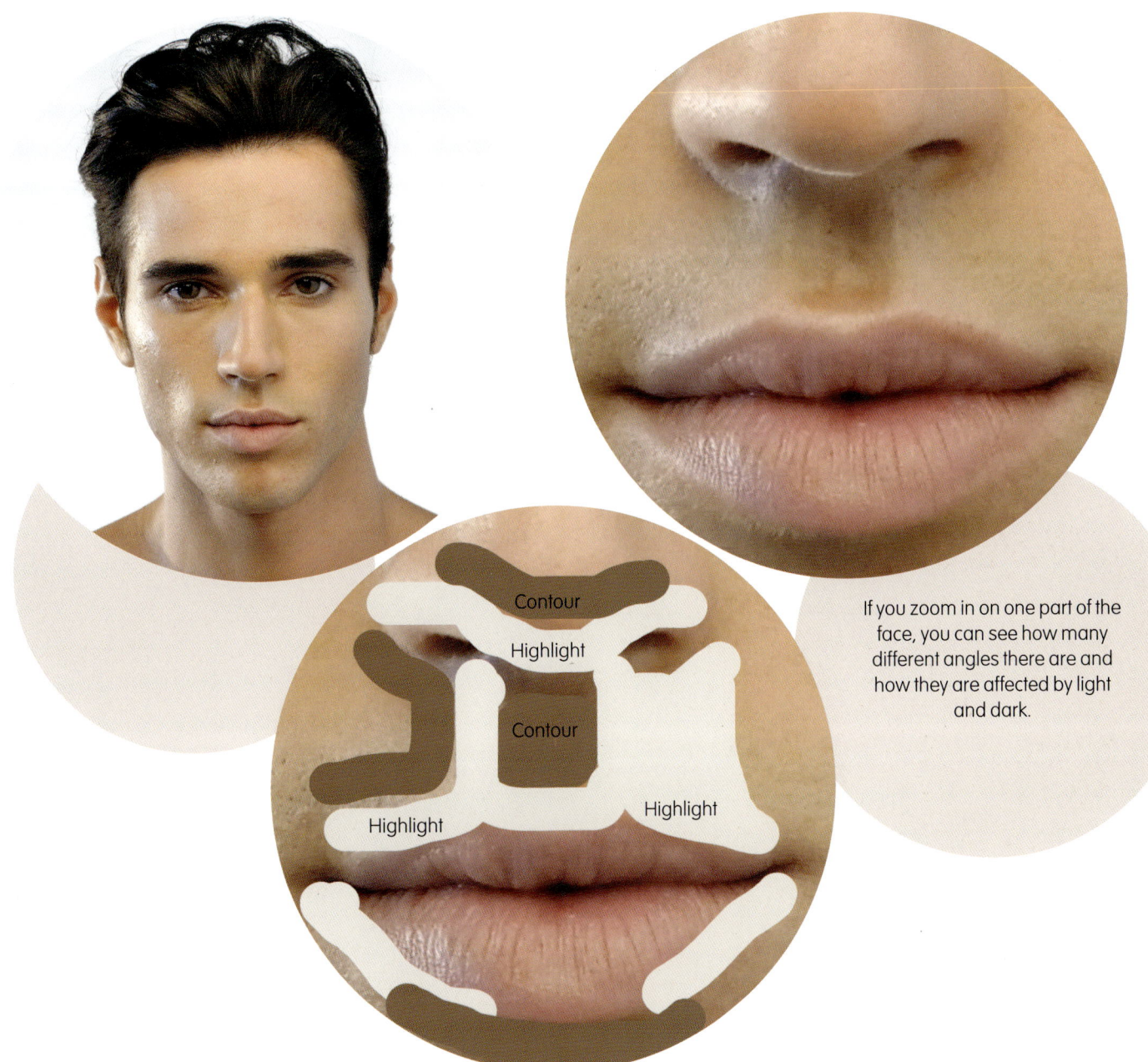

Contour

Highlight

Contour

Highlight

Highlight

If you zoom in on one part of the face, you can see how many different angles there are and how they are affected by light and dark.

Limitations of Facial Contouring

You also need to understand your limitations when it comes to contouring. I tried to turn myself into Elon Musk using just paint, and it did not work in the slightest. Why? Because he has a very large forehead and a very square face. This is a prime example of me not understanding my own facial limitations. My jawline isn't wide enough to be able to replicate Elon's and that isn't something makeup can correct. And as I painted on the hair that ate into the space that could have been allocated to his forehead, so this one was an absolute fail.

While you might find it easy to change the shape of your nose, if you have a naturally narrower and rounder face, like me, and are trying to transform into someone who has a wider, more square face, like Elon Musk, you will probably struggle.

Remember any new skill is a learning process. Chances are the first time you try this it won't be perfect, and that's okay. Even I still mess up! The more you practice, the easier it will get, and you'll see your creations improve by leaps and bounds.

There are gradients of color in this process with brown for contour and cream for highlight. If you look closely at a face, there will still be parts of the face which are lighter even within the same highlight, and vice versa. Here I would use a bit of white, or a tiny bit of black powder to create a gradient.

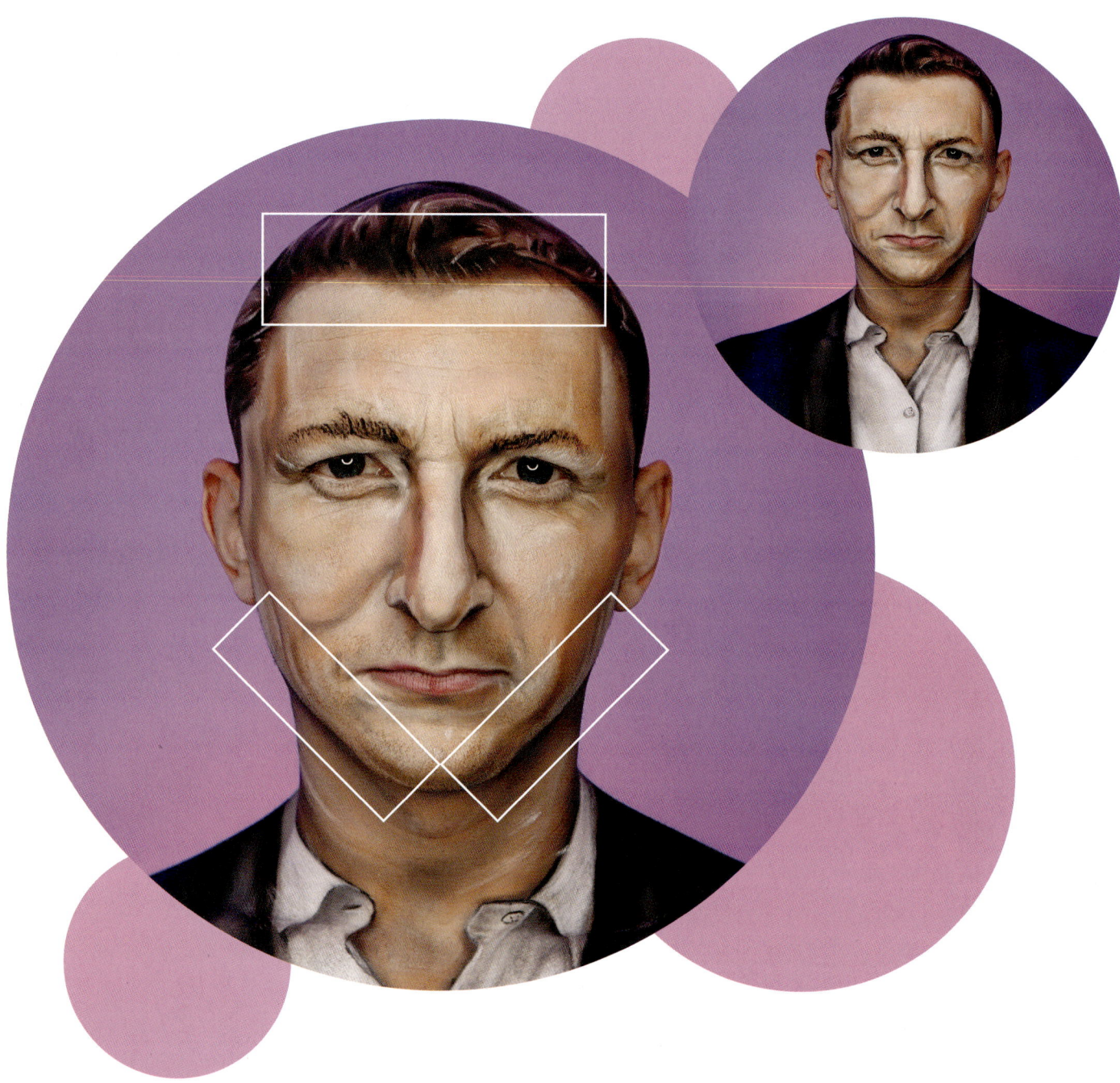

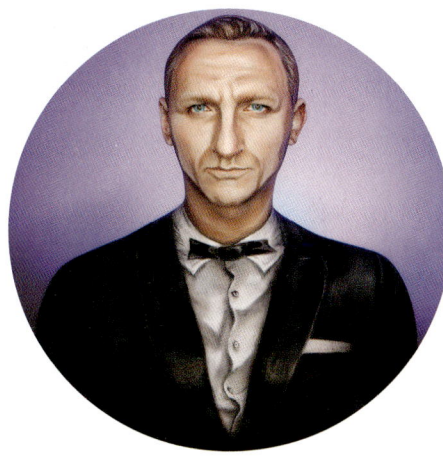
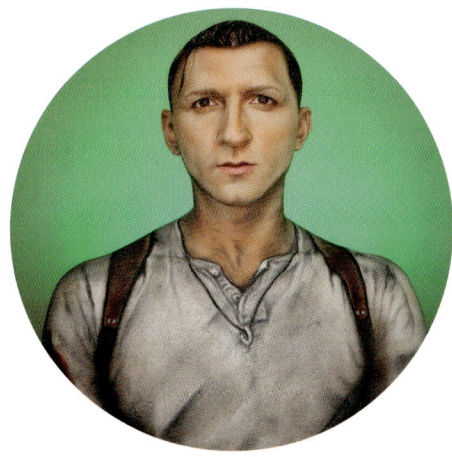
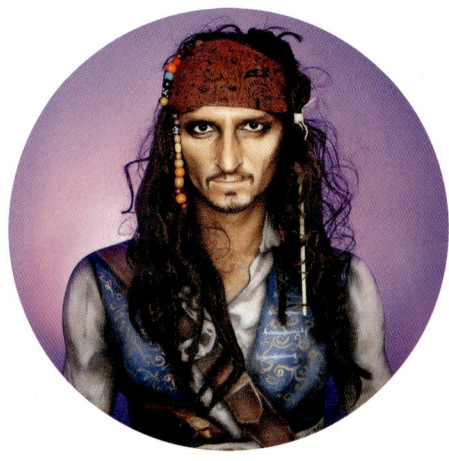

Some successful transformations. Left to right: Daniel Craig as James Bond, Tom Holland, and Johnny Depp as Captain Jack Sparrow in *Pirates of the Caribbean*.

You can see from the comparison below how contouring different parts of the face can help create a completely different look. With Daniel Craig, to elongate his face I brought

the highlight right down to his jawline, whereas for Tom Holland, I subtly rounded his cheeks with a bit of contour. With Jack Sparrow I created a much sharper cheek using a harsher contour.

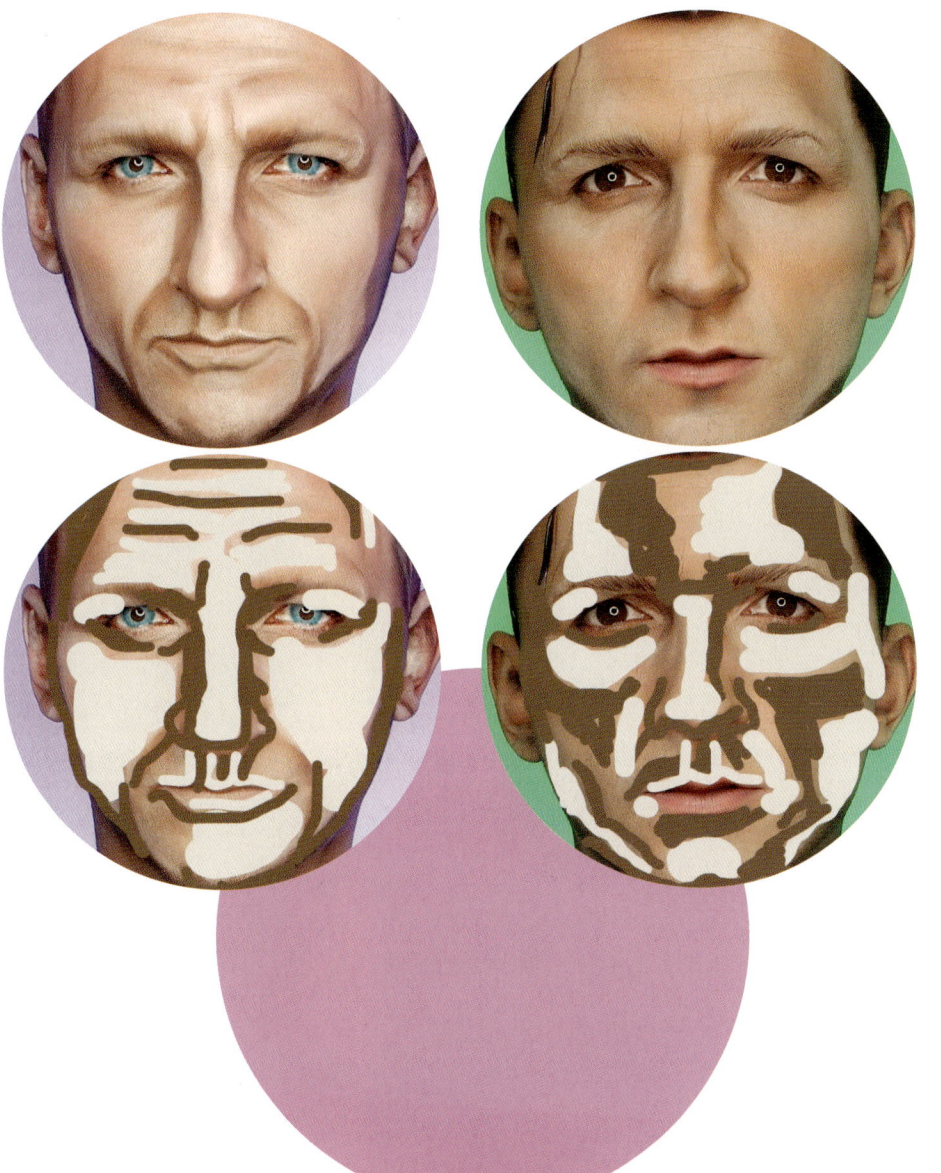

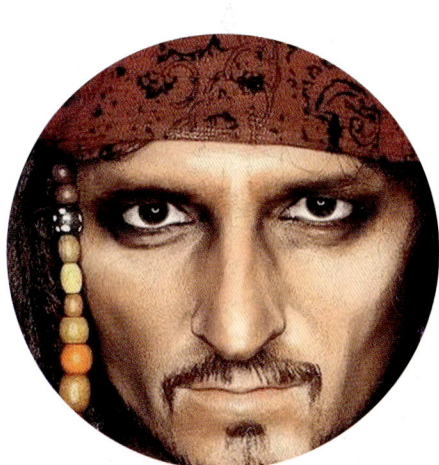

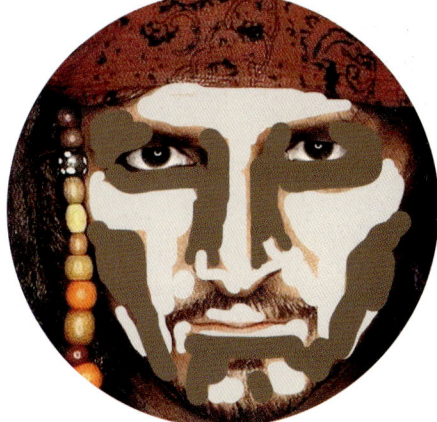

PAINTING MUSCLES

Being able to paint on muscles can really elevate your cosplay from good to great!

You might be thinking this section isn't for you, and how you should be comfortable in your own skin and not feel pressured to conform and look a certain way to be able to cosplay. And yes, I agree with all that, and you can feel free to skip this part of the book. I also know how empowering painting muscles on can feel from a personal perspective but also through painting many people. So, let's explore why people might want to do this.

Outside of cosplaying, this type of makeup could be used within theater, whether that's dancing or acting, the clubbing scene for an exotic dancer, the modeling world for fashion shows and shoots, or for social media.

In this section, I explain how to create a set of abs, muscular arms, shoulders, legs, and torsos.

I will be demonstrating with intense makeup to highlight the extremes you can go to, to create muscles. If you're planning on using these techniques in public you may choose to tone them down to ensure a more seamless and realistic finish.

These products are the same ones we used to contour the face in the previous section.

Now that we understand the basics on how to create a 3D illusion using paints, and we've covered how to contour the face using makeup, we can take what we've learned from both sections and extend this to create muscles on the rest of the body.

In this section, I'll be creating the muscle illusion using makeup rather than paint for that more realistic effect. But the same principles apply if you're using paint.

If you're painting a male, refer to page 18 for a reminder on how to create a 3D chest, but use your contour palette and concealer rather than blue paint.

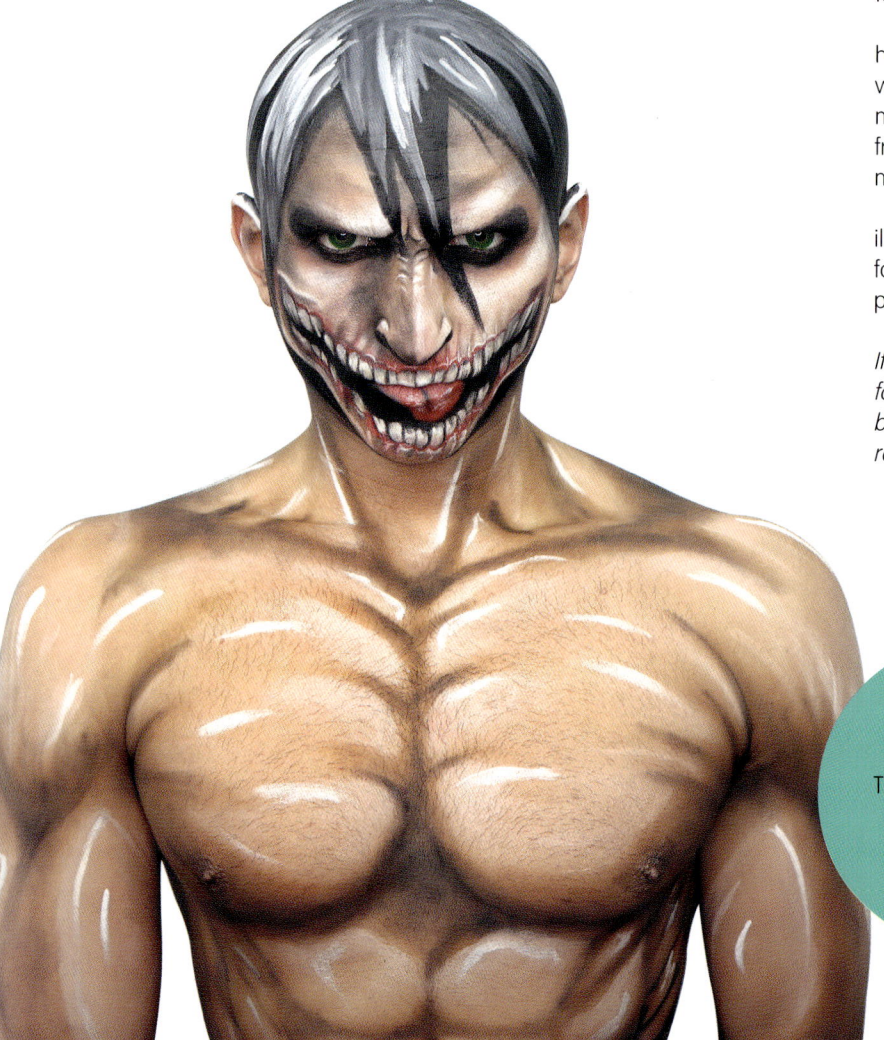

The Attack Titan from *Attack on Titan*

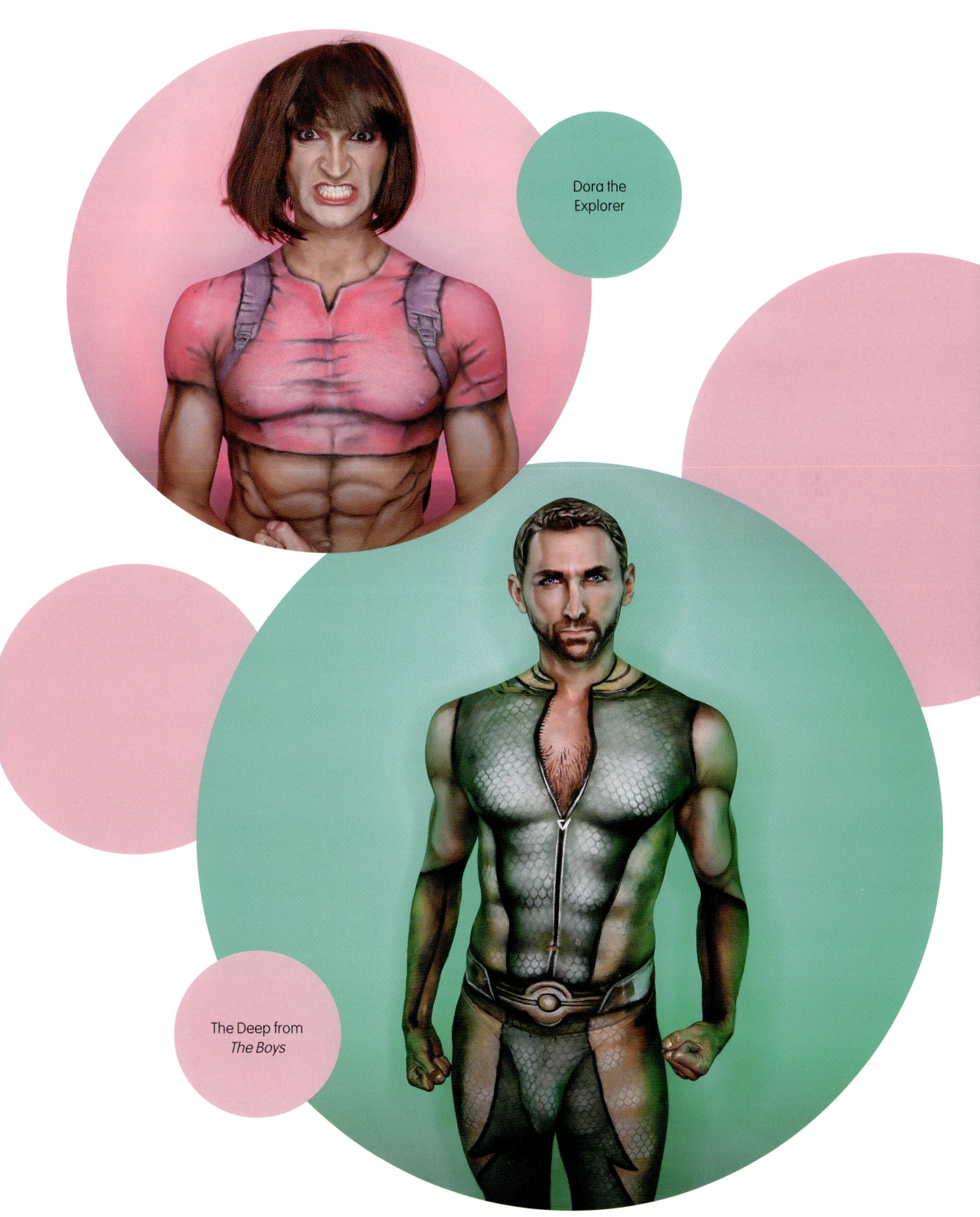

Dora the Explorer

The Deep from *The Boys*

HOW TO PAINT ABS
STEP BY STEP

You can hit the gym and do thousands of crunches to get six-pack abs, or you can just paint them on!

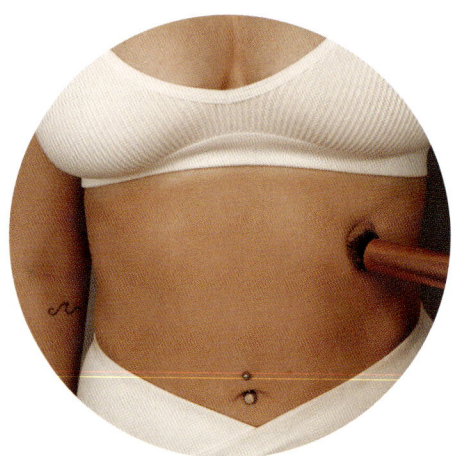

Step 1
Apply a base layer of foundation. (Not a necessity; I just find it easier to blend products into.)

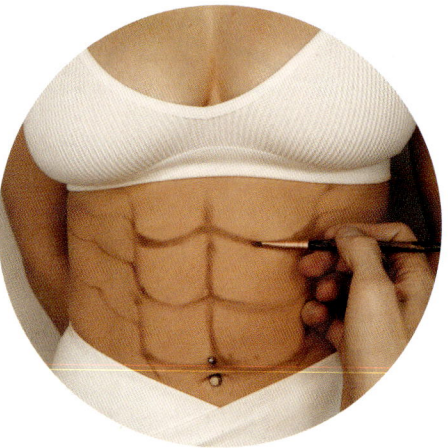

Step 2
Mark the basic outline of the abs using a contour palette.

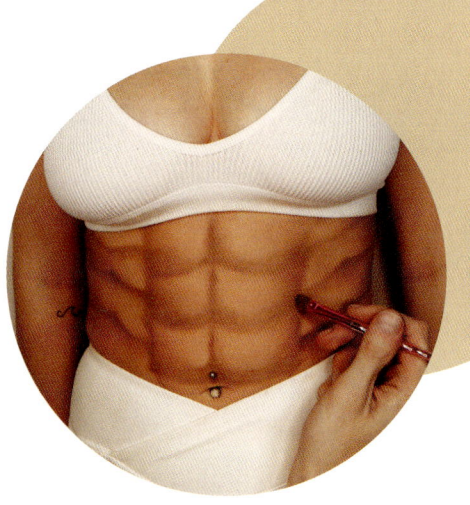

Step 3
Blend out the contour around the bottom corners of each ab.

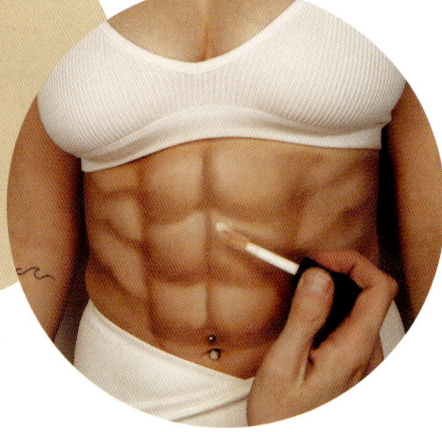

Step 4
Apply concealer to the upper areas of the abs to highlight these areas.

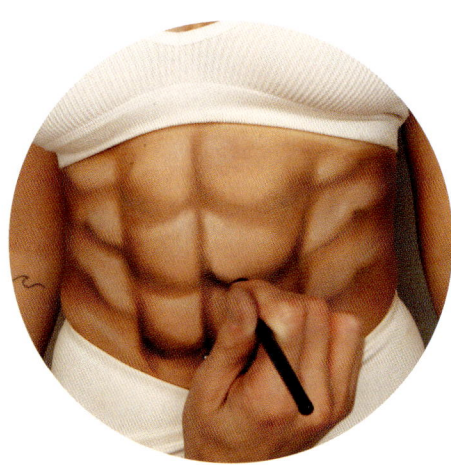

Step 5
Apply black powder to areas that are most indented and white concealer to areas that stick out most.

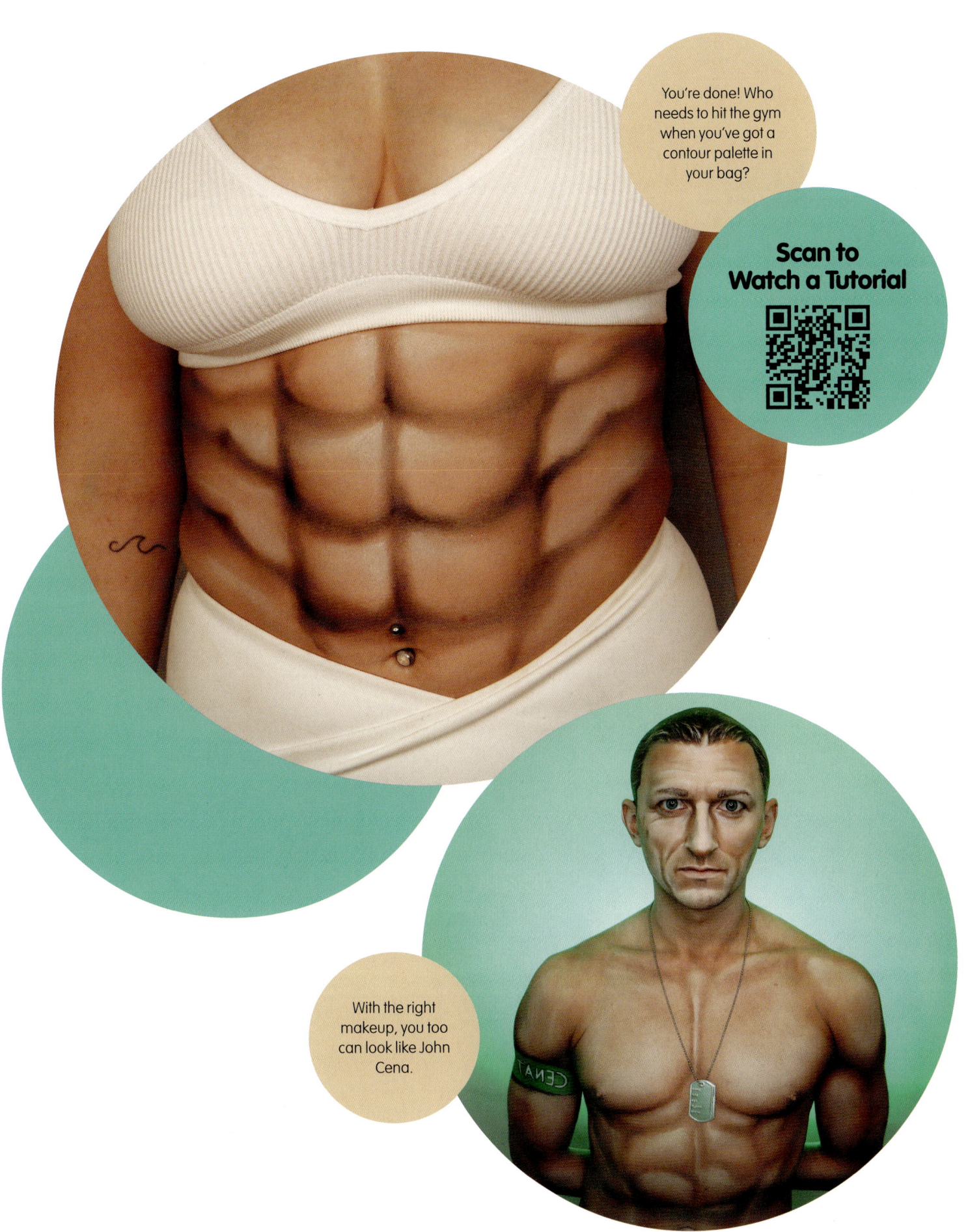

Scan to
Watch a Tutorial

You're done! Who needs to hit the gym when you've got a contour palette in your bag?

With the right makeup, you too can look like John Cena.

HOW TO PAINT A TORSO
STEP BY STEP

Now we've got our abs created we can work on the upper torso.

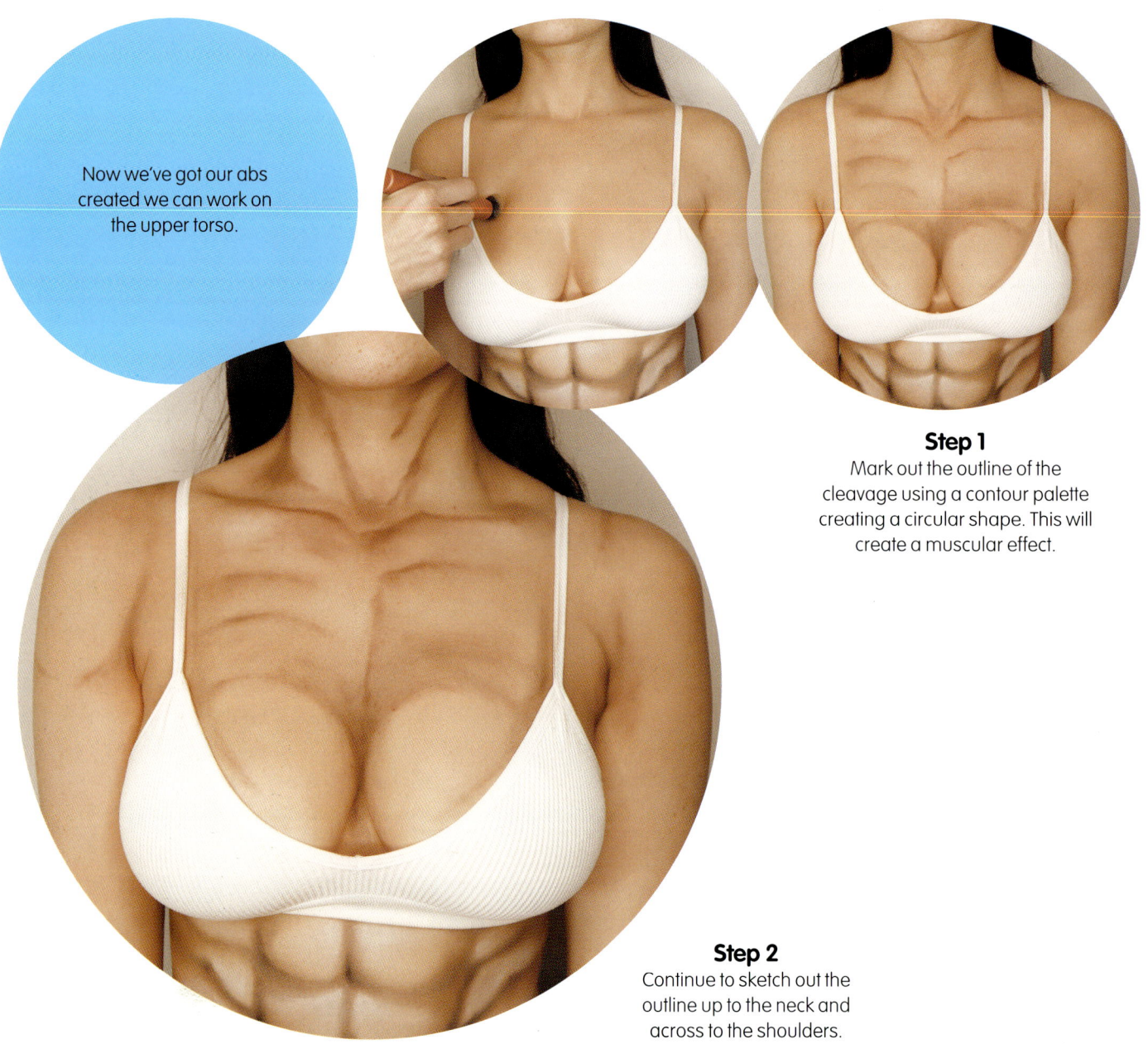

Step 1
Mark out the outline of the cleavage using a contour palette creating a circular shape. This will create a muscular effect.

Step 2
Continue to sketch out the outline up to the neck and across to the shoulders.

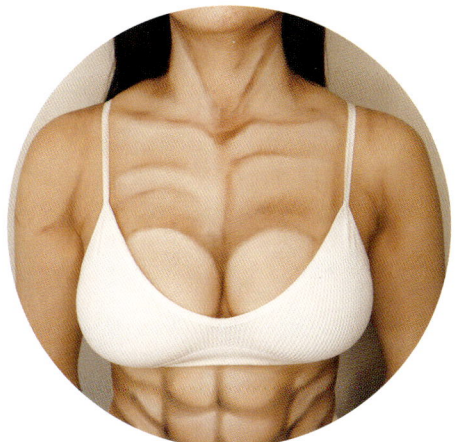

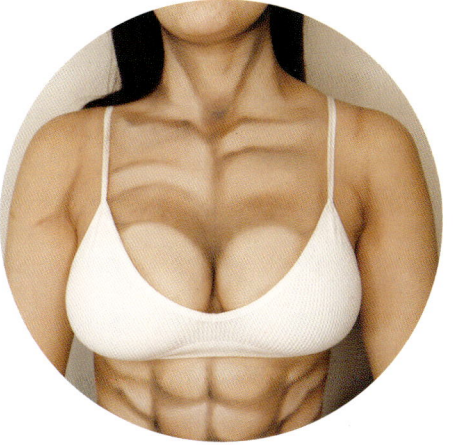

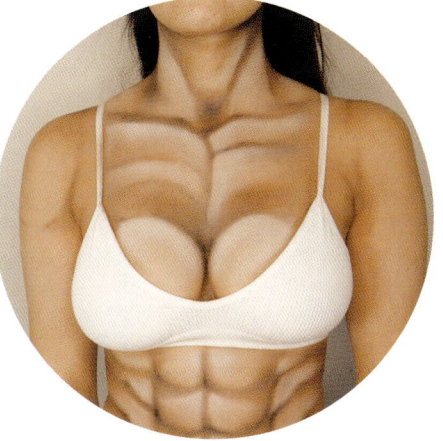

Step 3
Apply a layer of concealer to the areas you want to highlight.

Step 4
Apply black powder to areas that are most indented.

Step 5
Apply white concealer to areas which stick out most.

Tip: Add More Black!

Don't be afraid to really layer this up with black powder. You might feel like you will ruin it if you add too much, but just try it and see. If you do apply too much, then you will know for next time to hold back on the powder. Don't be afraid to make mistakes when you're learning to paint. I've made thousands and still make mistakes now! It's all part of the learning process.

When I first started painting muscles, I would apply brown contour and thought it looked fine. Then when I started applying black, I realized how effectively it added extra depth to the muscles.

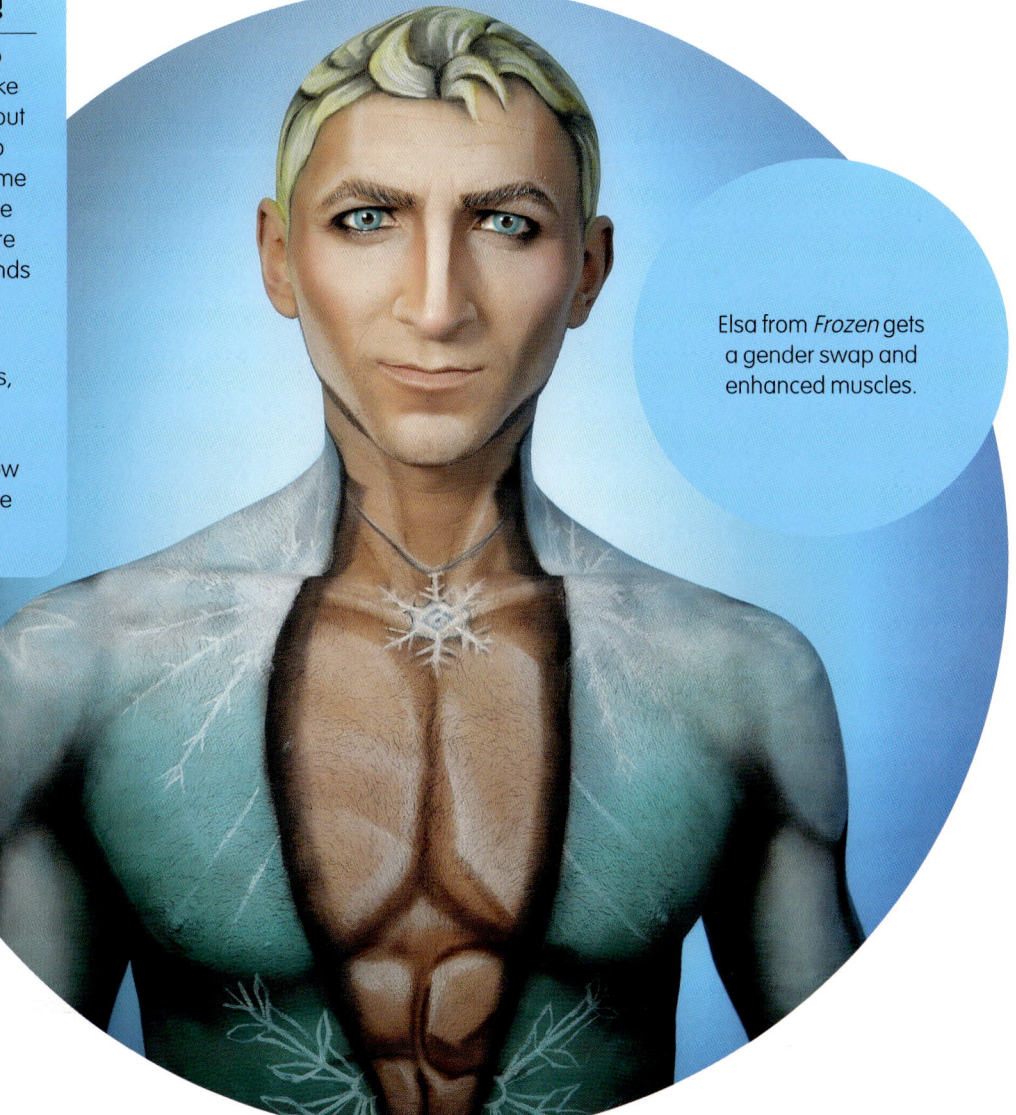

Elsa from *Frozen* gets a gender swap and enhanced muscles.

HOW TO PAINT MUSCULAR ARMS
STEP BY STEP

Muscular arms are essential for superheroes, action figures, and many other characters. Check out these guns!

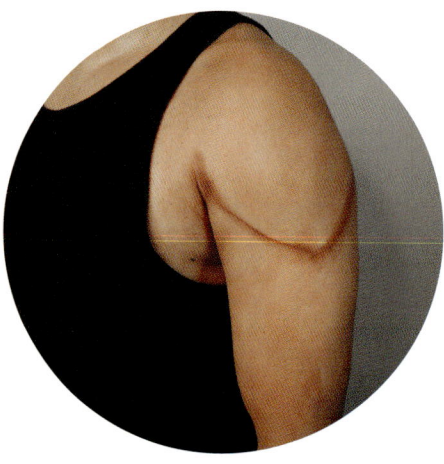

Step 1
Create a V shape where your shoulder meets your arm.

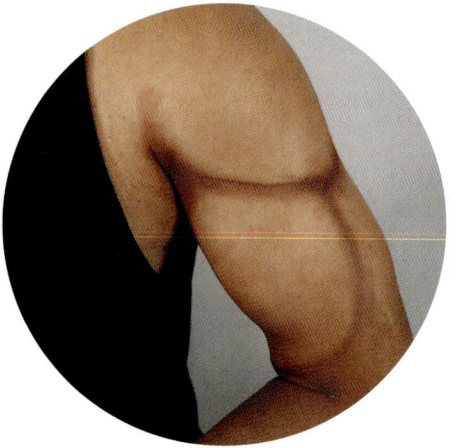

Step 2
Carve out the shape of the bicep using contour on both sides of the arm.

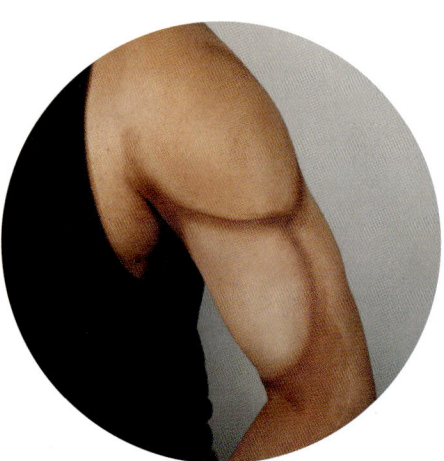

Step 3
Apply the concealer on the inside of the bicep itself.

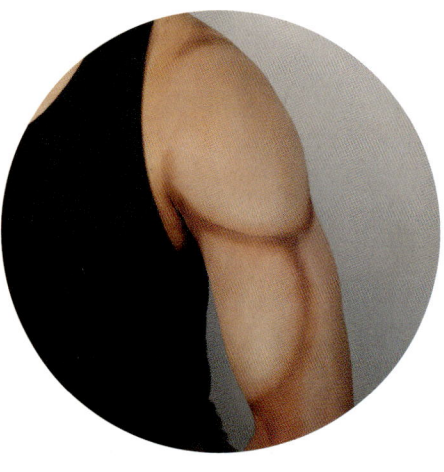

Step 4
Apply the concealer on the top of the shoulder and around the tricep.

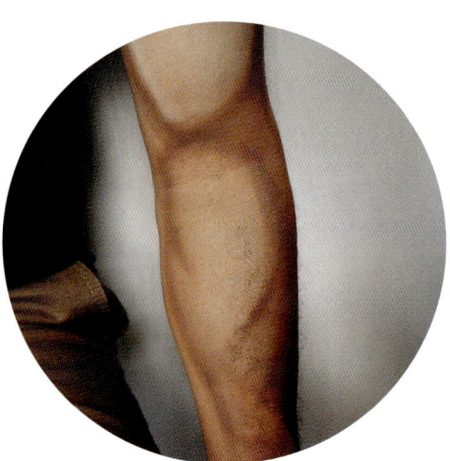

Step 5
Contour outline on the forearm.

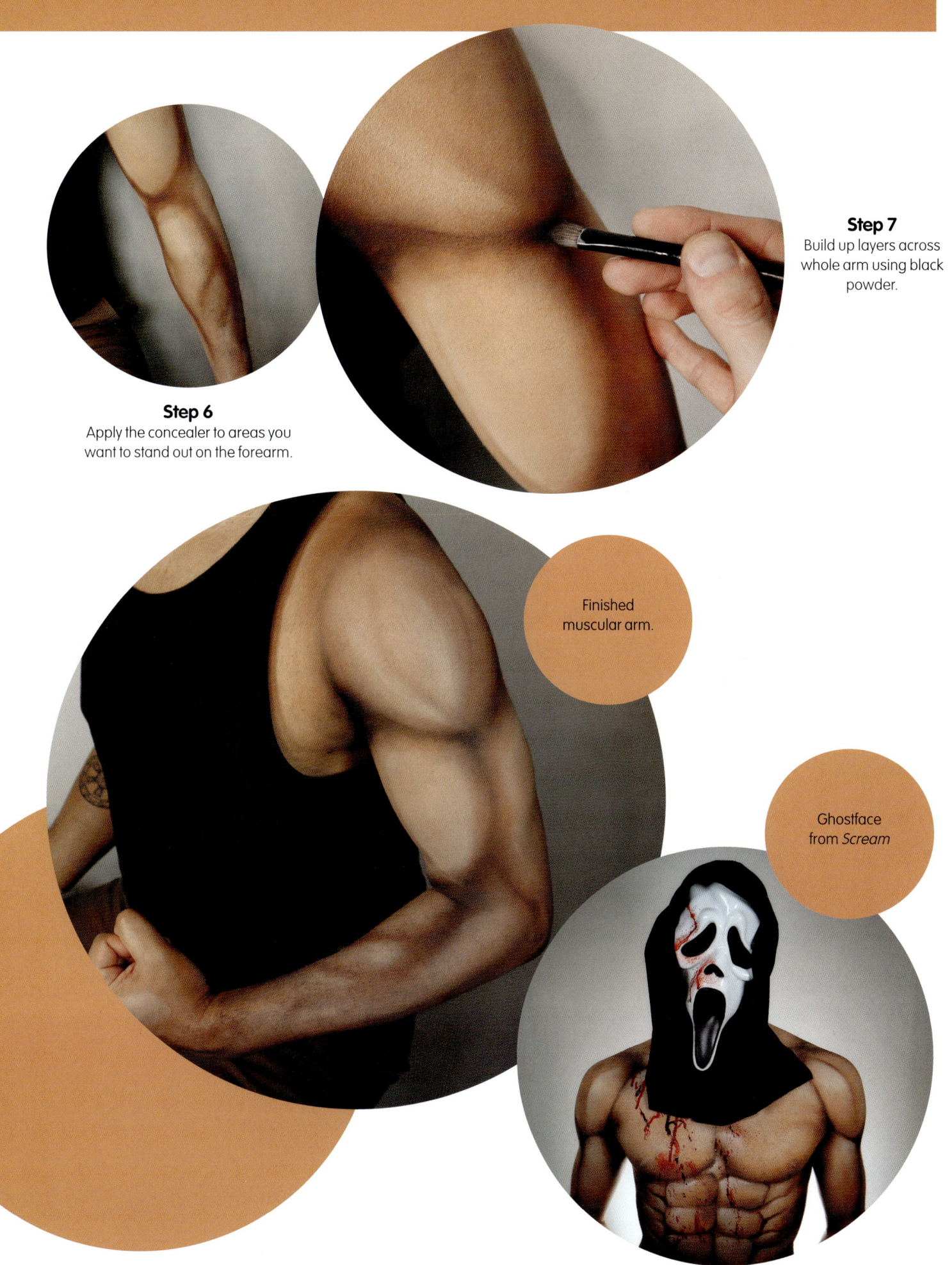

Step 7
Build up layers across whole arm using black powder.

Step 6
Apply the concealer to areas you want to stand out on the forearm.

Finished muscular arm.

Ghostface from *Scream*

HOW TO PAINT MUSCULAR LEGS
STEP BY STEP

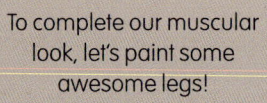

To complete our muscular look, let's paint some awesome legs!

Step 1
Apply a base layer of foundation.

Step 2
Follow a reference picture and mark out the outline of the quads using a contour palette.

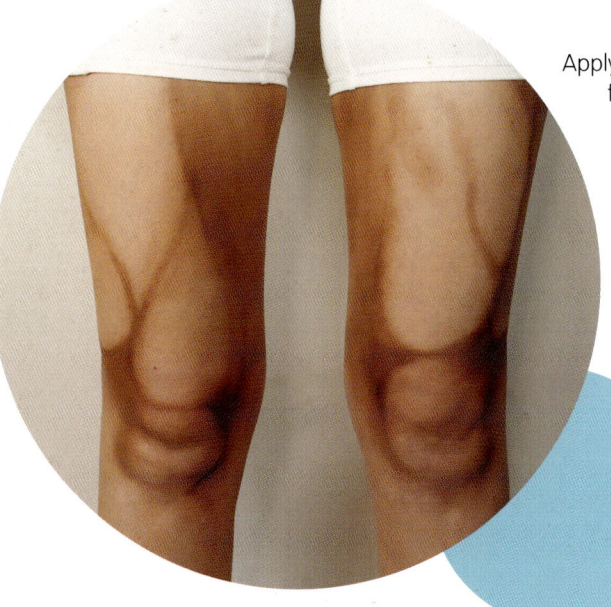

Step 3
Apply a thick shadow around the inner thigh and the outer leg.

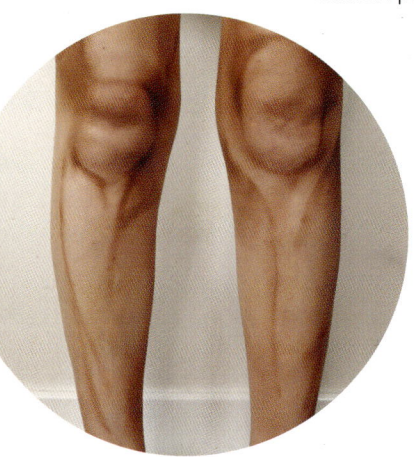

Step 4
Follow your reference picture to apply an outline for the bottom half of the legs.

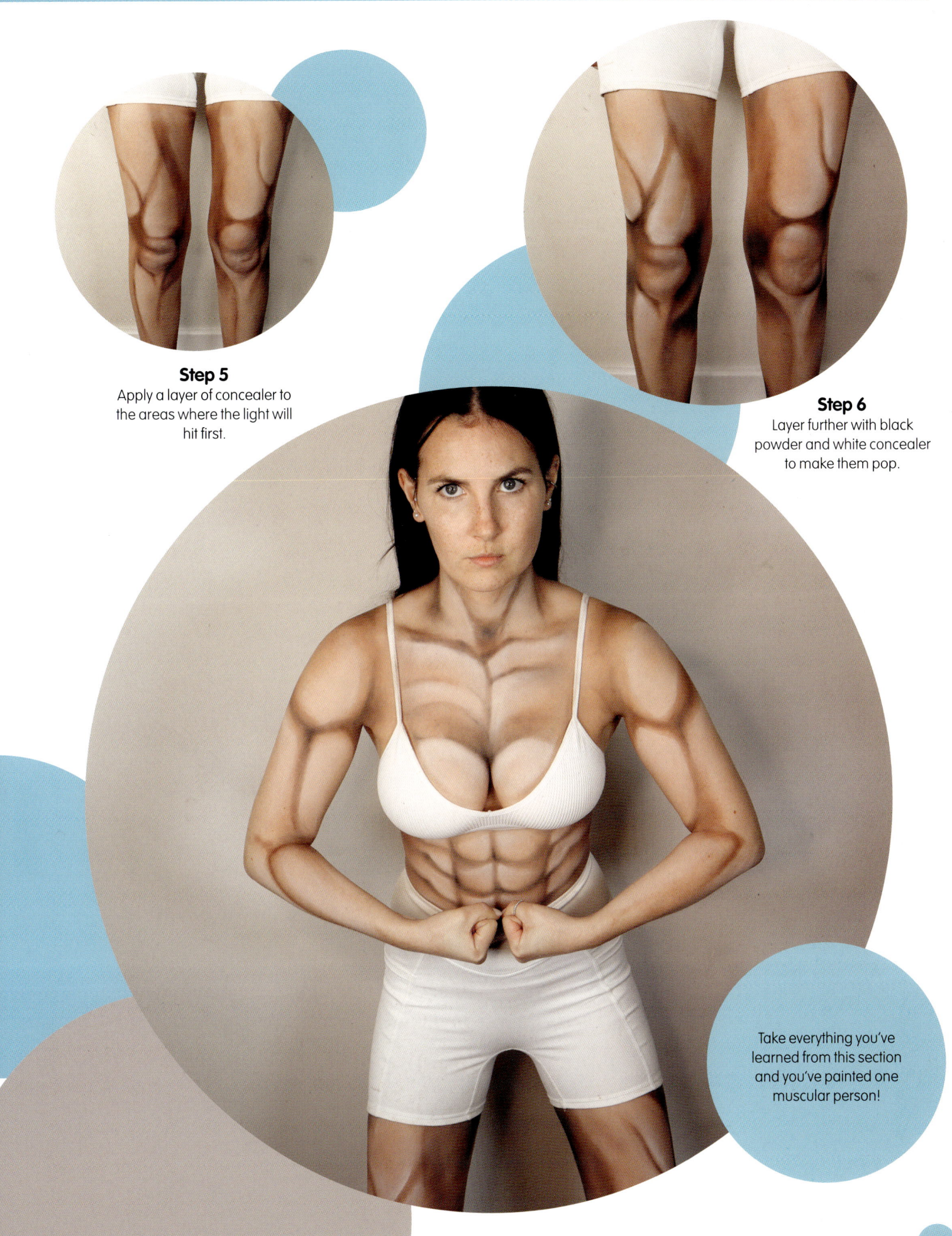

Step 5

Apply a layer of concealer to the areas where the light will hit first.

Step 6

Layer further with black powder and white concealer to make them pop.

Take everything you've learned from this section and you've painted one muscular person!

Here are some more examples of paints where using highlighting and shading to create defined muscles really took the looks to the next level, whether the character is wearing clothes or not.

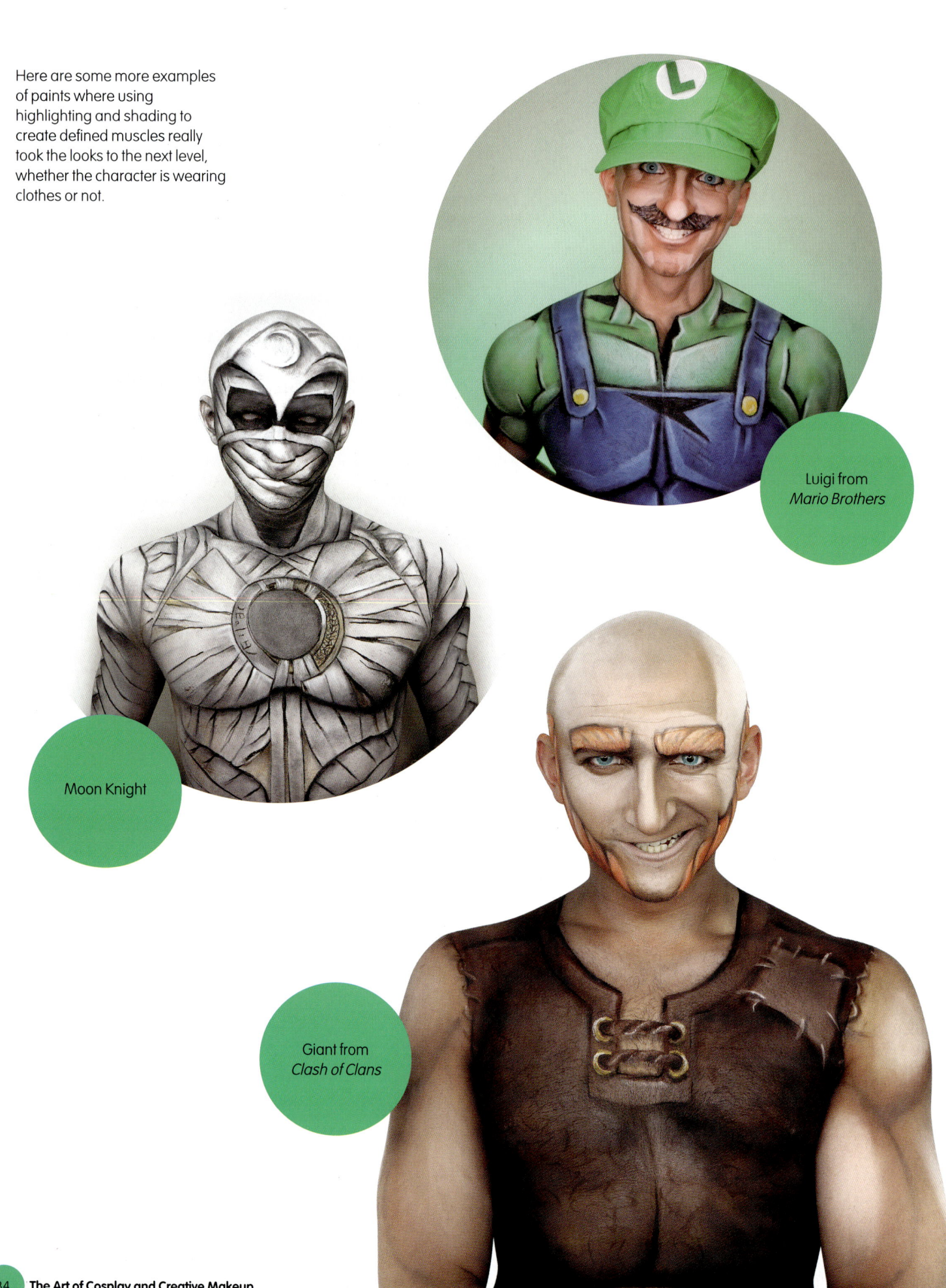

Luigi from *Mario Brothers*

Moon Knight

Giant from *Clash of Clans*

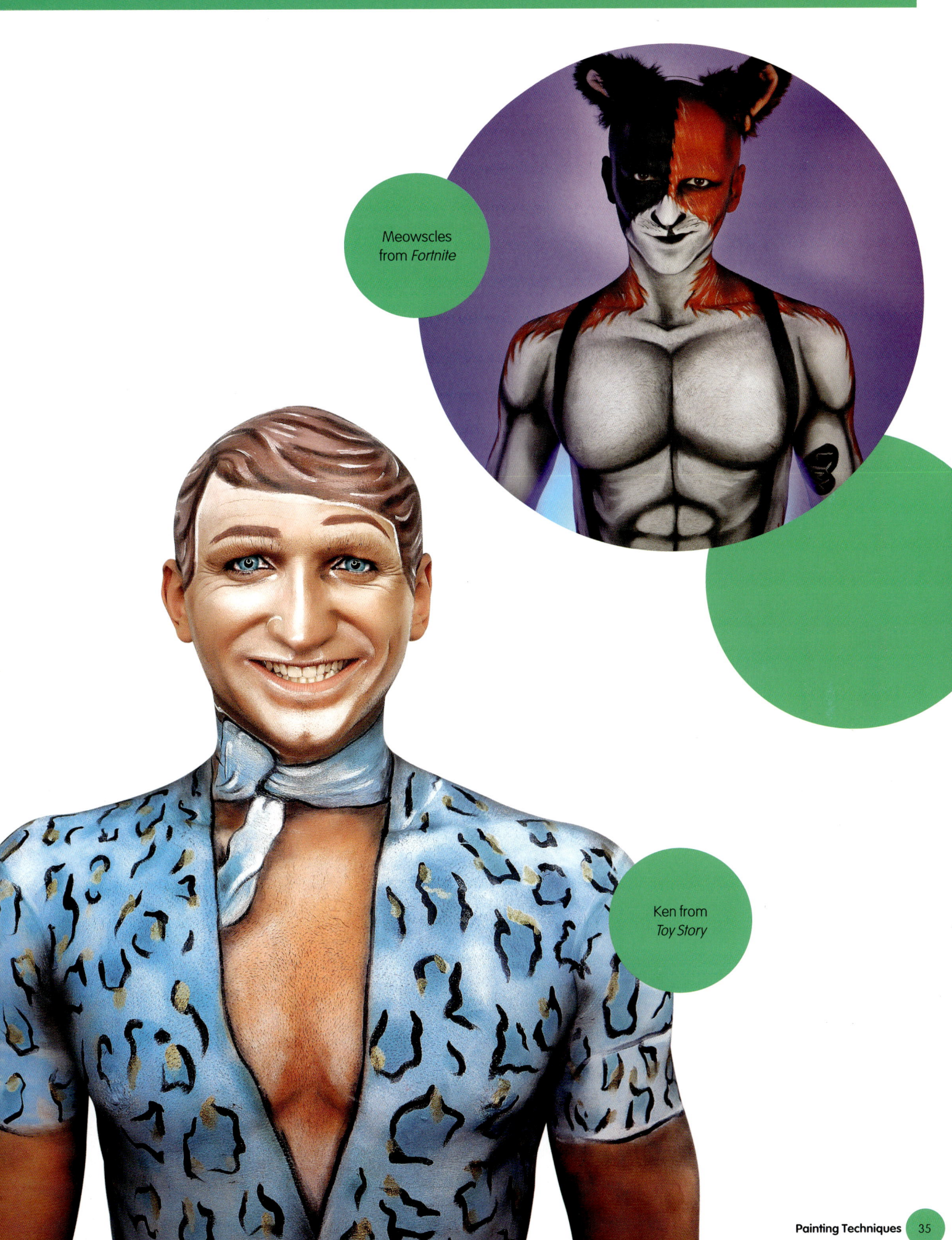

Meowscles from *Fortnite*

Ken from *Toy Story*

PAINTING HAIR

I paint hair on my head in most of my looks as I have none! Some people love it, some people hate it, but it's my USP, or unique selling point, so it's here to stay! That being said, one of the most frequent questions I get is, "How do you paint hair and make it look realistic?" I appreciate that a majority of the population will never need to paint hair on their head, so for these demos, I'm going to focus on how to create a realistic beard, eyebrows, and chest hair using paint. The basic techniques are the same.

First, understand that something can look very different in real life versus on camera. That is why I have both a mirror in front of me as well as my selfie camera for the application process so I can check how it looks on camera.

Painting hair can be time consuming especially to get that realistic look because you need to build it up with singular strands one by one. I incorporate different colors, usually a brown, a black, and a white, to replicate how light can hit a beard or chest hair differently. It also helps separate the individual hairs so it doesn't look like a big glob of paint.

Once you've built up all the different layers of hair, you can go in with some eyeshadow to help shape the beard. This technique also works when painting hair on your head. Add a simple shadow where your hair meets your head for a 3D effect.

Remember there are limitations when it comes to painting on hair and beards. For instance, you won't ever be able to paint a really bushy beard. You can only create the illusion of a beard as far as your face is long.

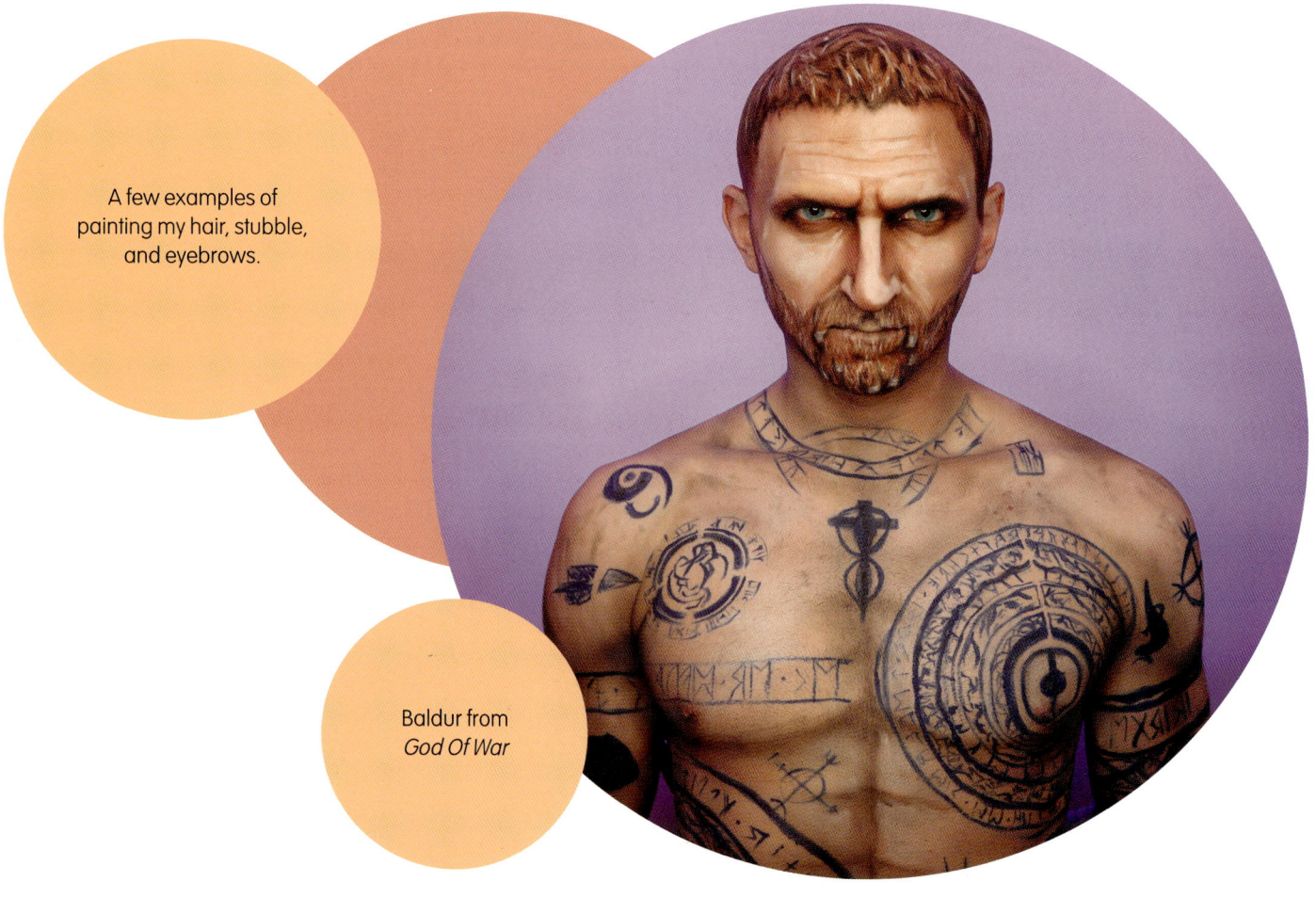

A few examples of painting my hair, stubble, and eyebrows.

Baldur from
God Of War

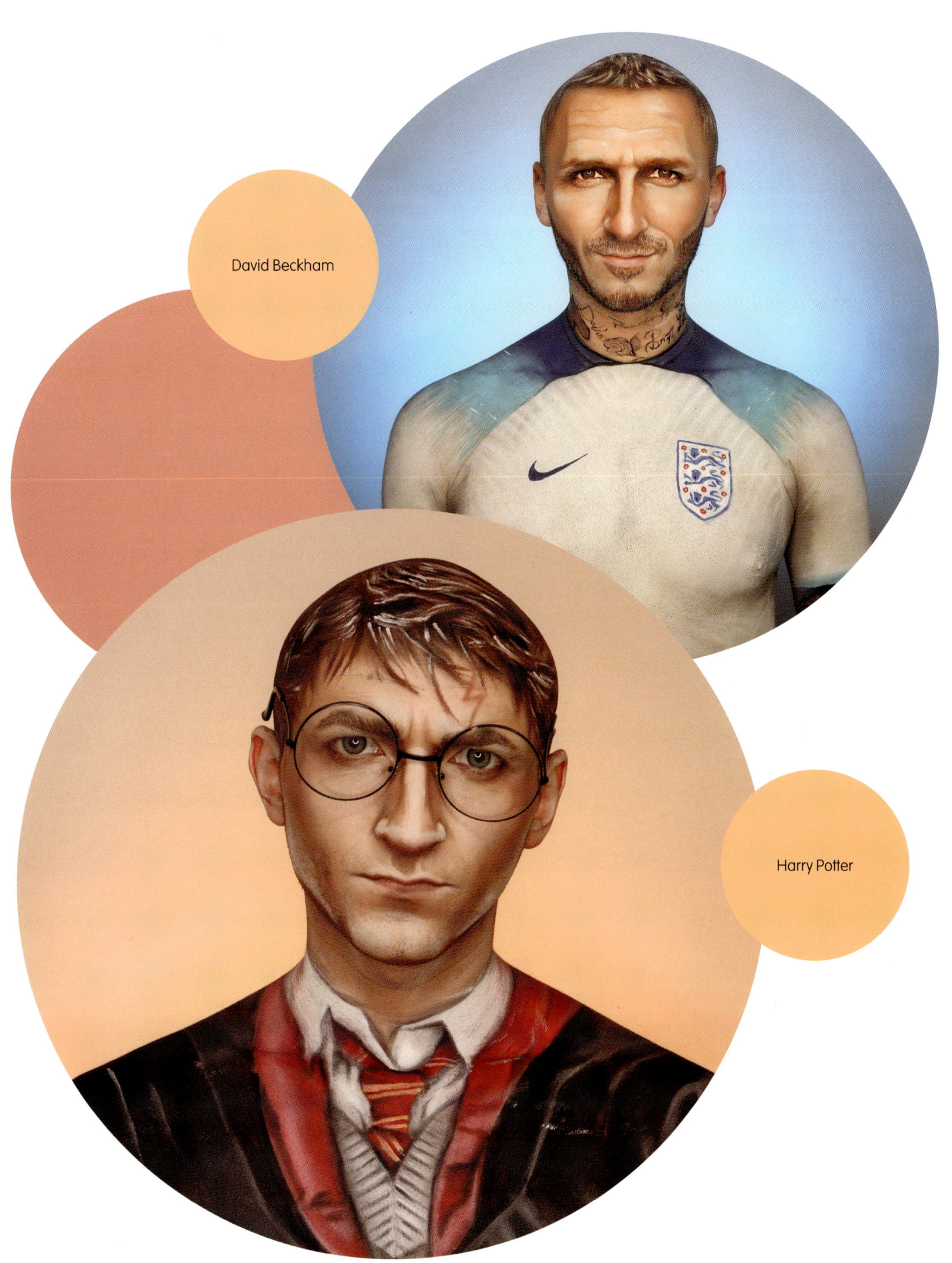

David Beckham

Harry Potter

PAINTING A BEARD
STEP BY STEP

Painting on your beard has multiple purposes. It can be used within the cosplay world, but it's also a technique that can be adopted in real life. For instance, if your beard is a bit patchy, you might choose to color it in to make it look fuller. In this section, I will walk you through how to paint on a full beard.

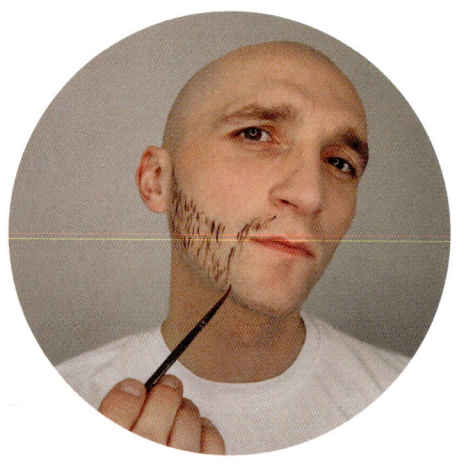

Step 1
Shave your real beard if needed. It's very difficult to paint on top of actual hair. Go in with the base color of your beard and apply individual lines with a detail paintbrush.

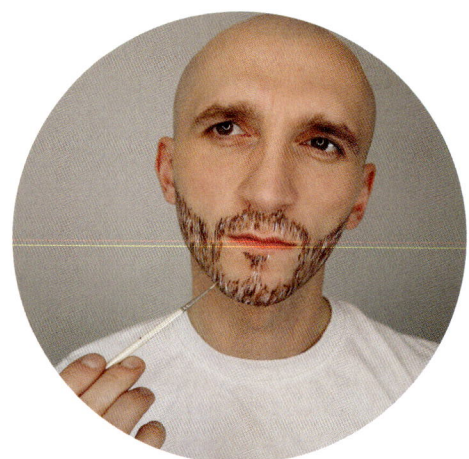

Step 2
Continue until your face is covered and the desired shape has been created. Paint on a second layer with white. This is to create separation between the base color and strands of hair.

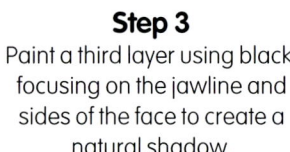

Step 3
Paint a third layer using black, focusing on the jawline and sides of the face to create a natural shadow.

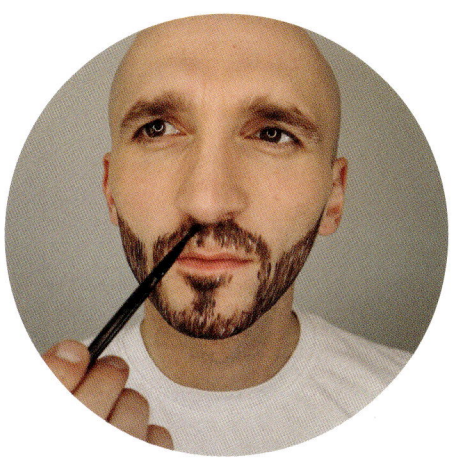

Step 4

Paint a final layer of paint with your base color to help blend everything in. Apply some brown and black eyeshadow to fill in any spaces left without paint and to accentuate the shadows.

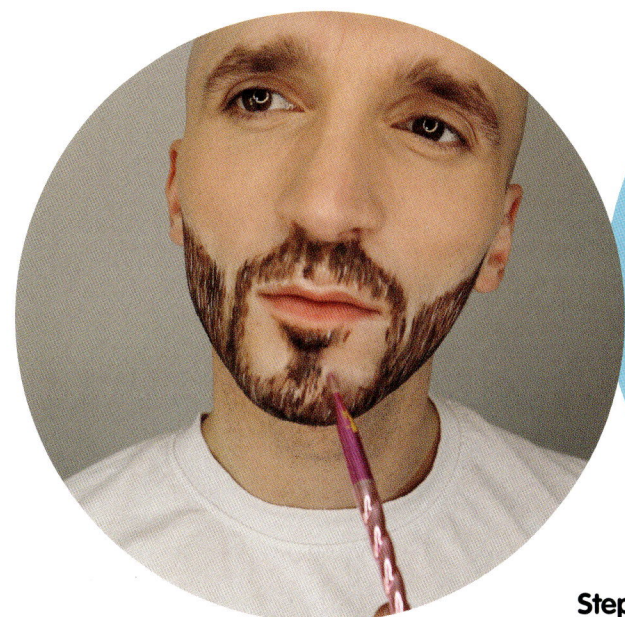

Step 5

Apply a lighter concealer where the beard meets the cheek and under the lip to create a three-dimensional effect.

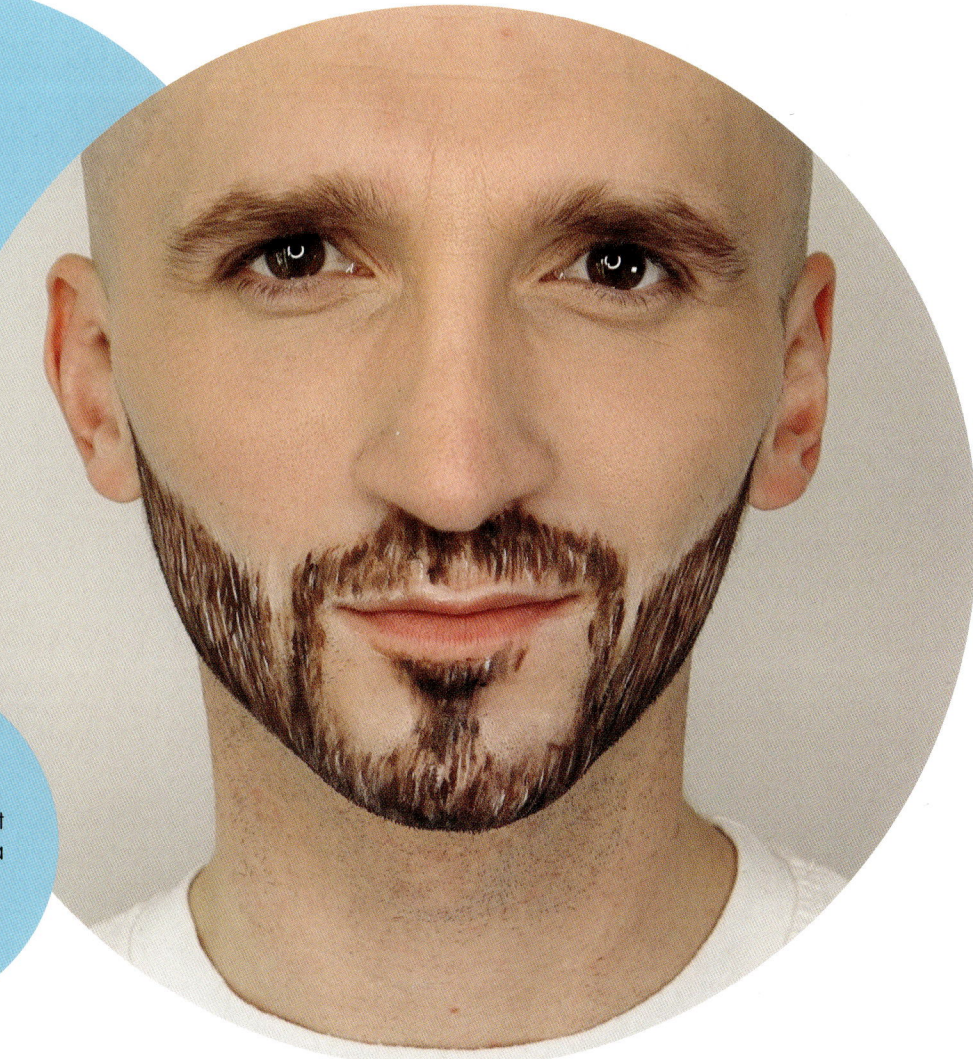

There you have it: a semi-realistic beard that could fool people from a distance.

HOW TO GLUE DOWN EYEBROWS
STEP BY STEP

Glueing down your eyebrows is a technique that has been used in makeup for years! This technique is commonly used by drag queens to cover up their natural eyebrows to give them a blank canvas to apply extravagant eye makeup. Because my eyebrows curve down my face, I usually need to glue them down and shape them higher to imitate a person or character. If your eyebrows are particularly thick, you may need to layer on more glue.

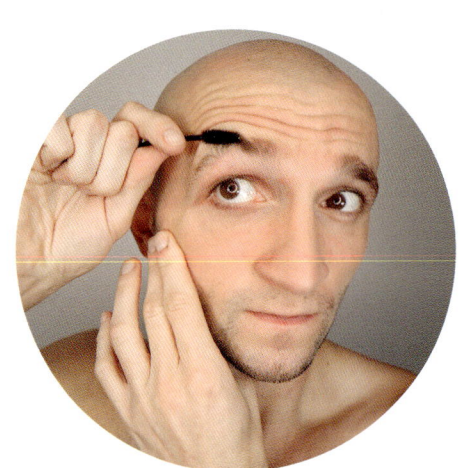

Step 1
Brush your brows upward using an eyebrow spoolie brush.

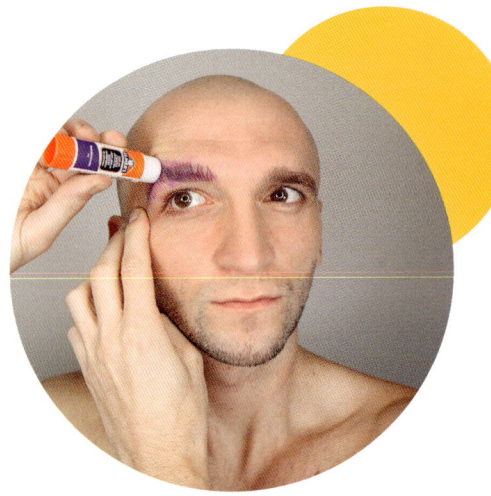

Step 2
Apply a thick layer of water-soluble glue over the entire brow.

Step 3
Go back in with the spoolie and brush the hairs upward again.

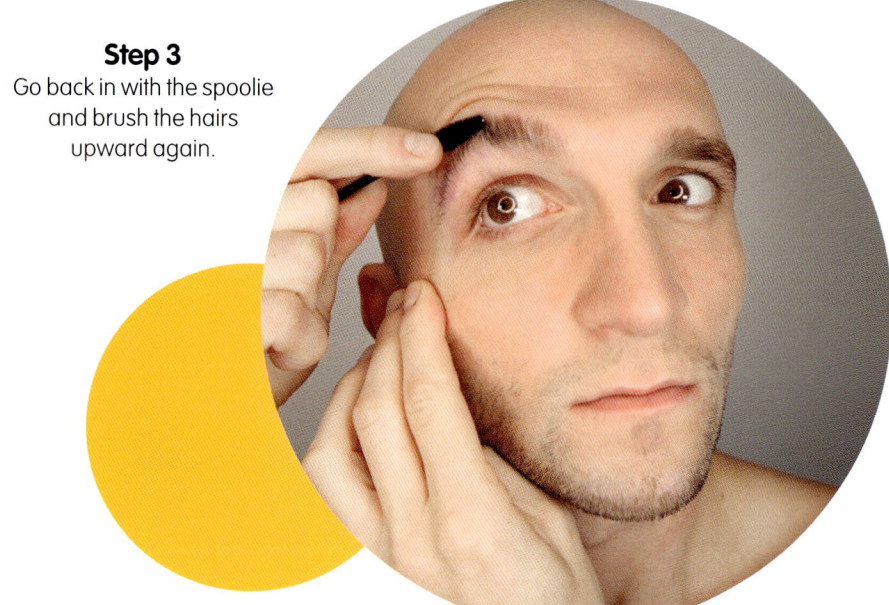

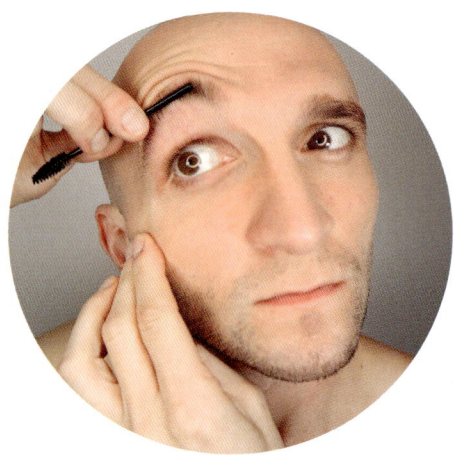

Step 4
Use the opposite end of the spoolie to push the eyebrow flat to the face and squeeze out any excess glue.

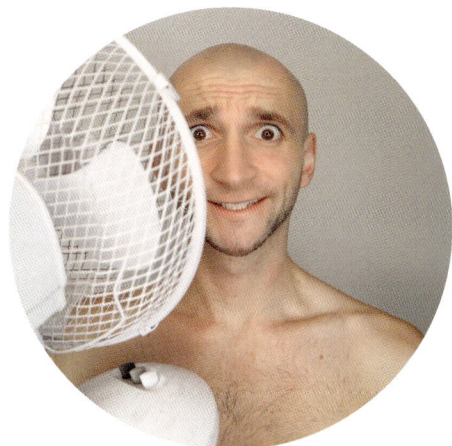

Step 5
Let this layer dry. If you don't own a hairdryer use a fan.

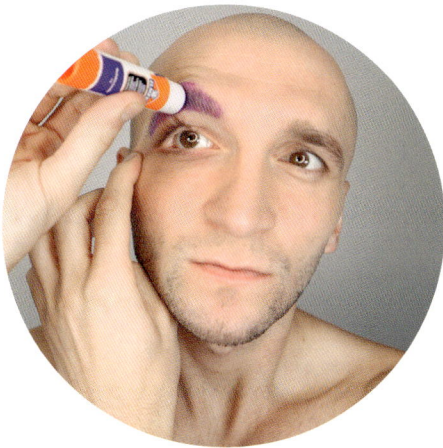

Step 6
Apply a second layer of water-soluble glue making sure to leave no gaps.

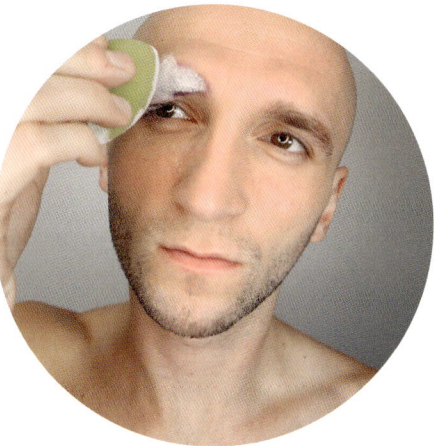

Step 7
While the glue is still wet, apply a generous amount of loose powder over the entire eyebrow.

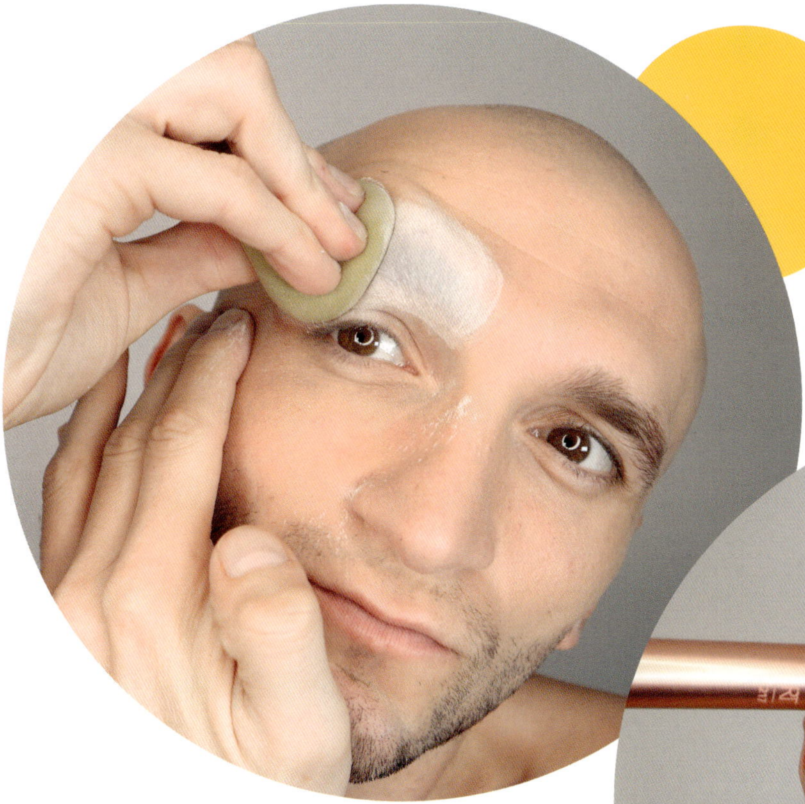

Step 8
Firmly push that powder into the eyebrow and then remove any loose powder.

Scan to Watch a Tutorial

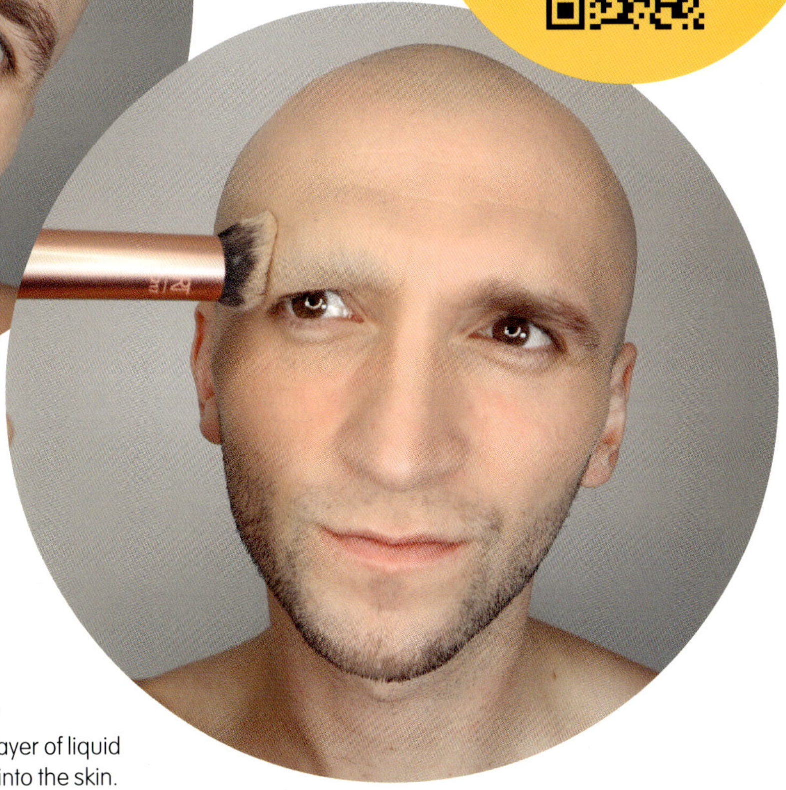

Step 9
Cover eyebrow in a layer of liquid foundation to blend into the skin.

HOW TO PAINT EYEBROWS
STEP BY STEP

Now that you've glued your eyebrows down, you need to paint them back on in the desired shape. Note that this is more of a natural eyebrow example as opposed to what you would see if you were watching a drag queen, for example, draw on their eyebrows.

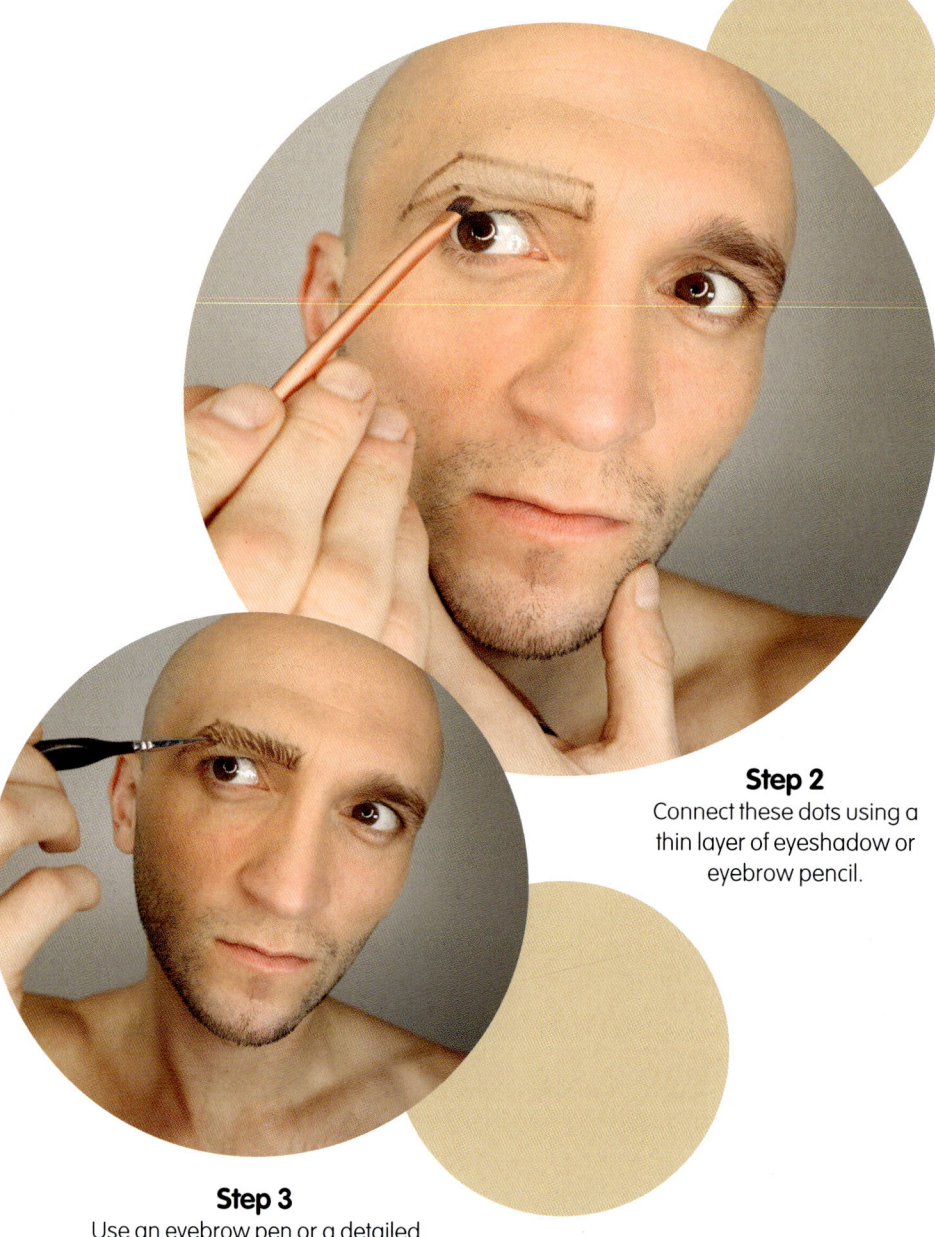

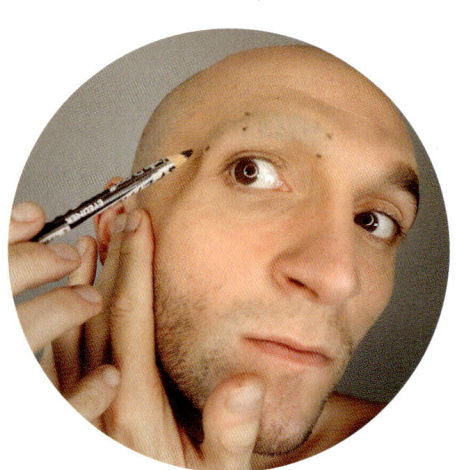

Step 1
Place five dots on your face to mark out the desired shape of the eyebrow.

Step 2
Connect these dots using a thin layer of eyeshadow or eyebrow pencil.

Step 3
Use an eyebrow pen or a detailed paintbrush with face paint to draw on individual hairs.

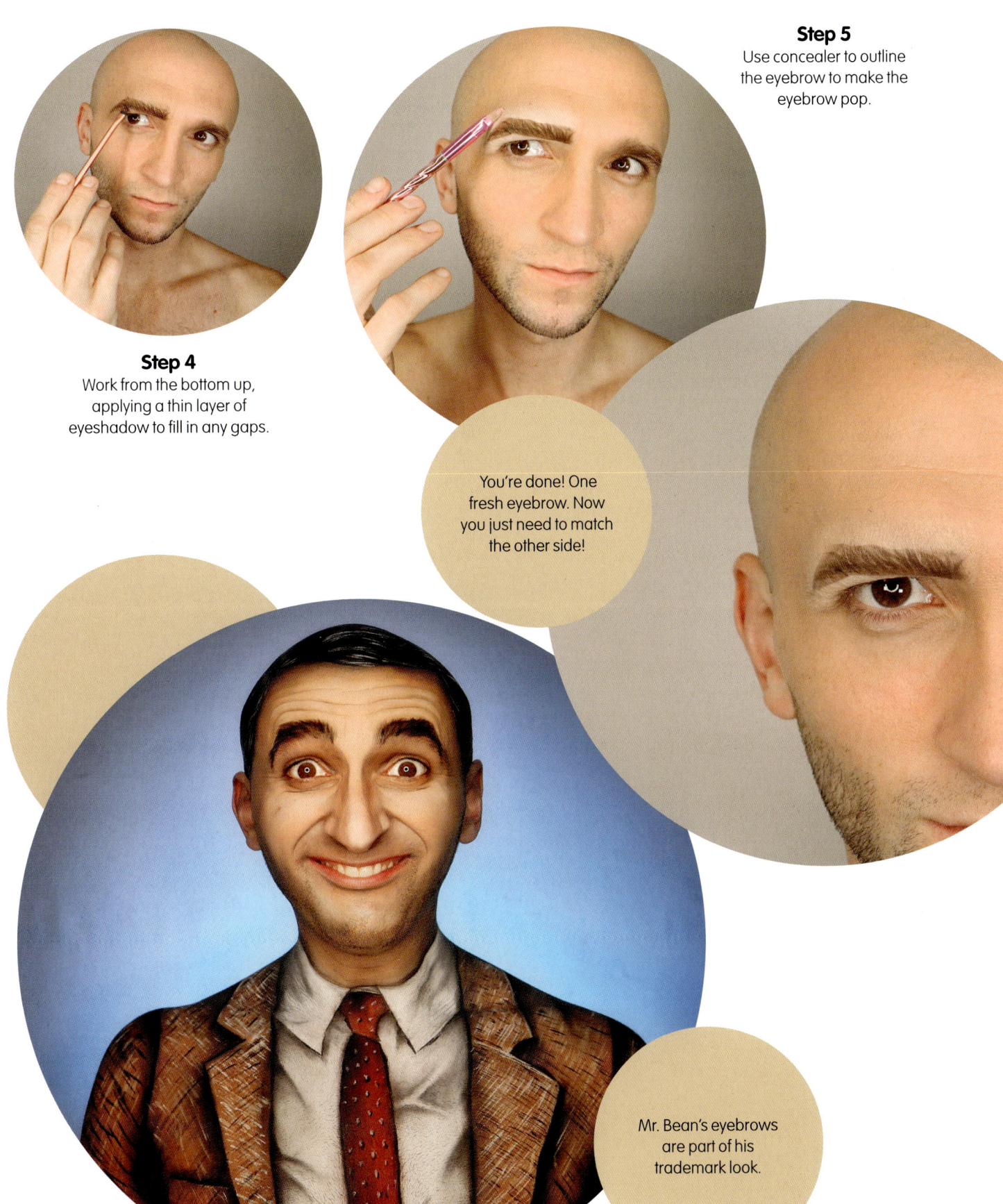

Step 4
Work from the bottom up, applying a thin layer of eyeshadow to fill in any gaps.

You're done! One fresh eyebrow. Now you just need to match the other side!

Mr. Bean's eyebrows are part of his trademark look.

HOW TO PAINT CHEST HAIR
STEP BY STEP

Moving on to chest hair. If you're lucky enough to be able to grow a full chest of fur you can skip over this part, but for those who can't and are looking to elevate their cosplay looks, I'll talk you through how I would do it.

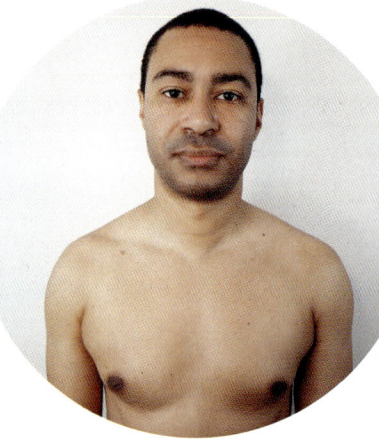

Step 1
If necessary, shave your chest.

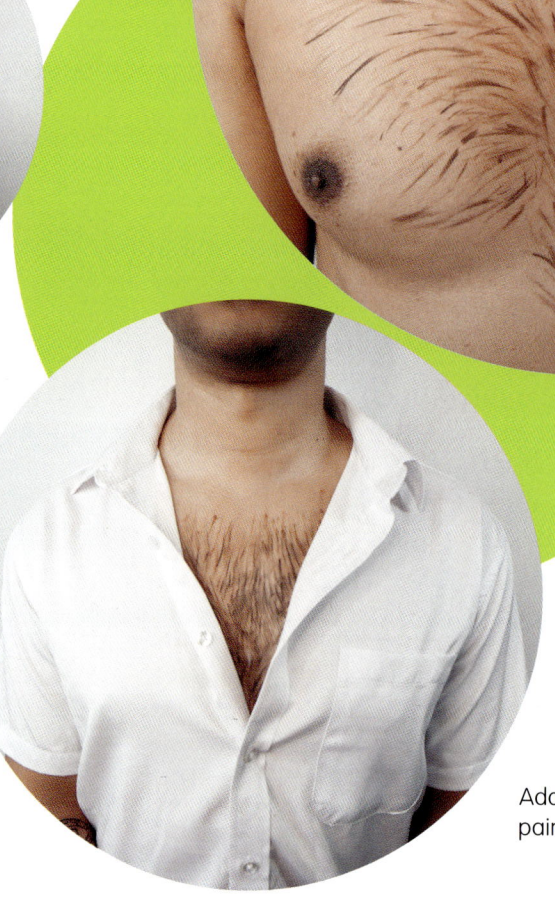

Step 2
Build up individual hairs in the natural direction the chest hair grows.

Step 3
Add in white and black paint to create depth to the hair.

HOW TO PAINT STUBBLE/SKIN FADE

STEP BY STEP

We've already covered how to paint on a beard, but painting on stubble can be just as effective, and it's as simple as using one product. If you're looking to fill in a patchy beard, this is how I would recommend you do it.

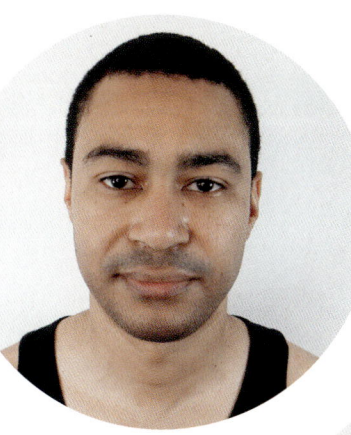

Step 1
Shave your face if you need to.

Step 2
Using eyeshadow or black powder, lightly and smoothly apply to face to create the desired shape.

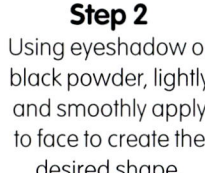

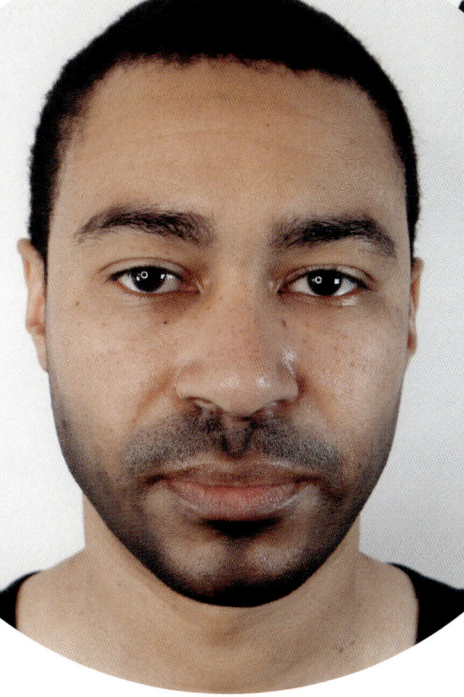

Step 3
Build up a thicker layer of powder where the hair might be thicker.

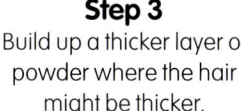

The Limitations of Painting Hair

At close range, it won't look realistic. Distance can work wonders.

Remember the camera can be very forgiving. We're creating the illusion of a beard so it will never be 100% realistic.

You can't make a beard look thicker than your face. You're working with a limited canvas so you won't be able to achieve a full bushy beard.

CEL-SHADING

Cel-shading (also known as toon-shading) is not terminology commonly bandied around amongst makeup artists. It actually refers to a technique used with computer animation. It is commonly used for anime, comic books, and video games to make what was previously a 3D object look flatter and appear more cartoonish.

When trying this technique for the first time it might feel unnatural. You're going to be placing lines where your brain is telling you they shouldn't be! But trust the process and follow your reference pictures closely. Just remember in the back of your mind, it's not meant to look smooth.

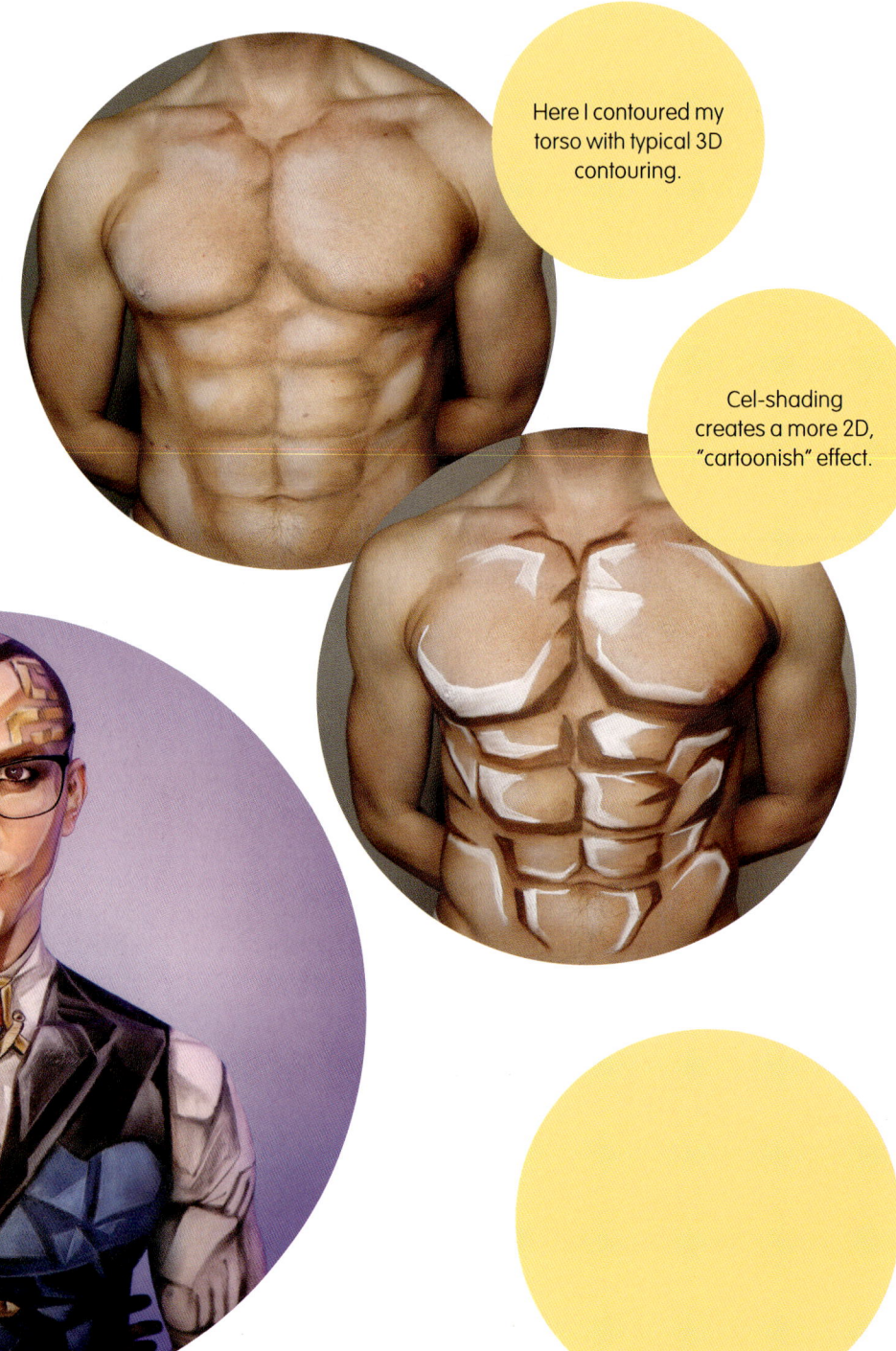

Here I contoured my torso with typical 3D contouring.

Cel-shading creates a more 2D, "cartoonish" effect.

Chamber from *Valorant*

Products to Use for Cel-Shading

To achieve the distinct effect needed for cel-shading, most of the products we're using are the same as for contouring. As always, it's good to start with a base of liquid foundation, so you have even coverage to work from.

When it comes to contouring and highlighting, I've added a few paints and removed the powdered contouring palette. It's much easier to get a defined line using cream contour than powder and we're going for an even coverage in blocked shapes, so there is no need to blend these products. If you wanted to complete the whole look using just paints, it is possible. However, you will need various gradients of paint from brown to black or flesh-colored to white.

Application-wise you can use beauty blender sponges or makeup brushes to apply to cream contour. I find it slightly easier to apply with a makeup brush, and then dab with a beauty blender to even out any harder application marks. If you're using paints, use paintbrushes.

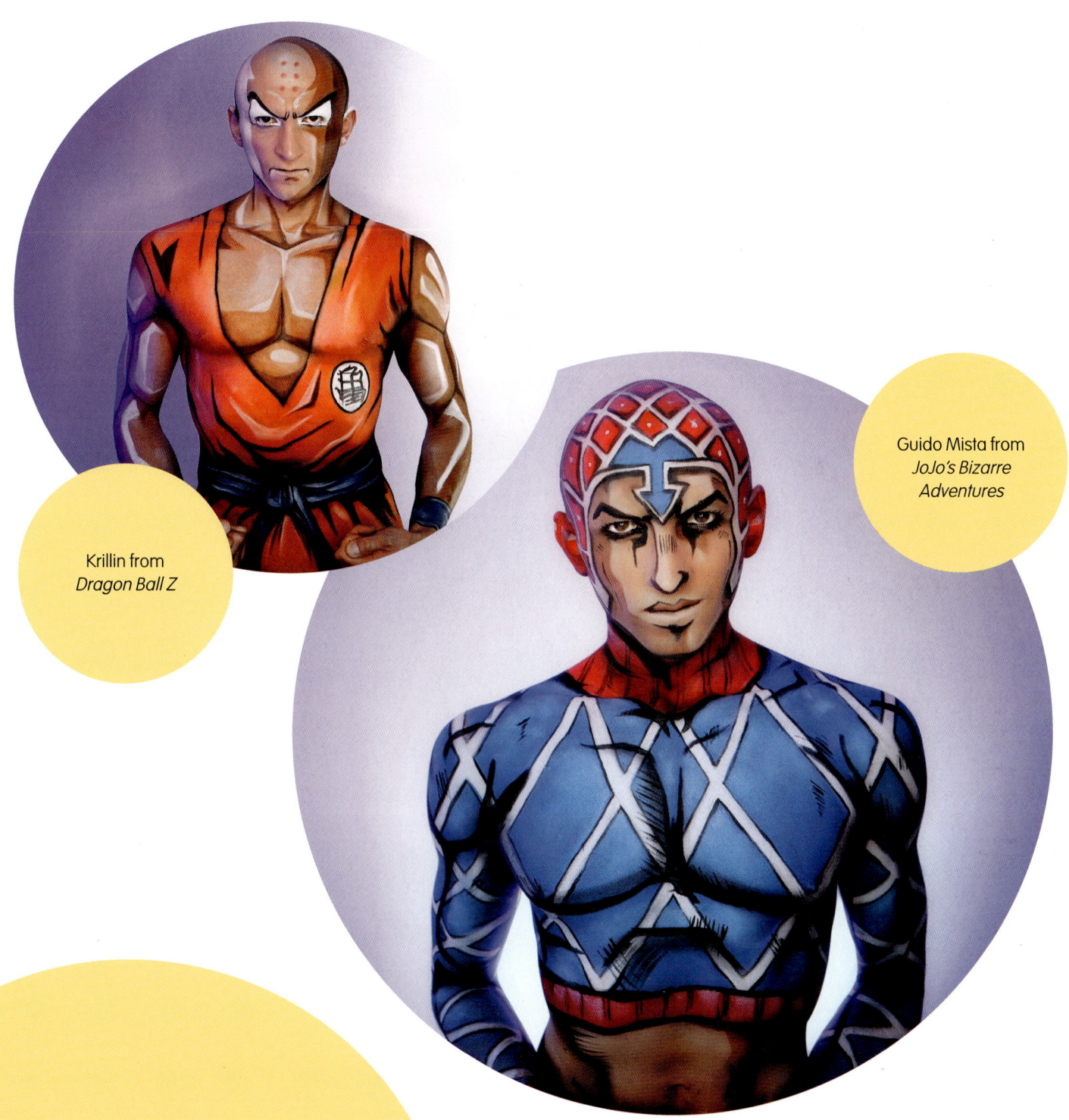

Krillin from
Dragon Ball Z

Guido Mista from
JoJo's Bizarre Adventures

CEL-SHADING
STEP BY STEP

This is an extreme example for demonstration purposes. You can go much subtler with this and still achieve a cartoon-like finish. Remember, you want sharp edges with no curves. Don't be afraid to use black!

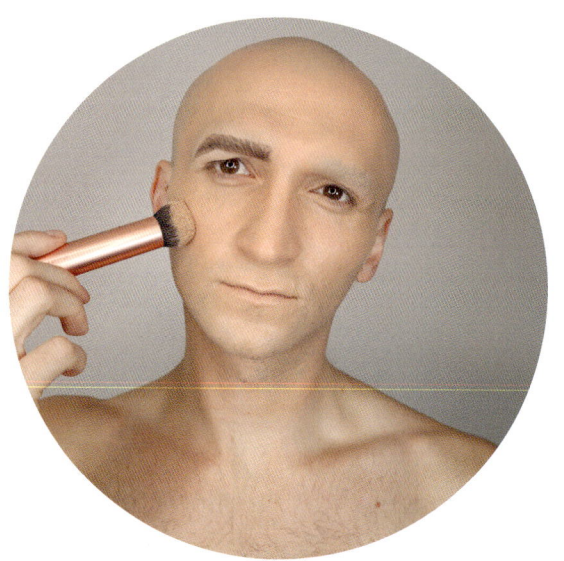

Step 1
Cover your face in liquid foundation so you're starting with an even base.

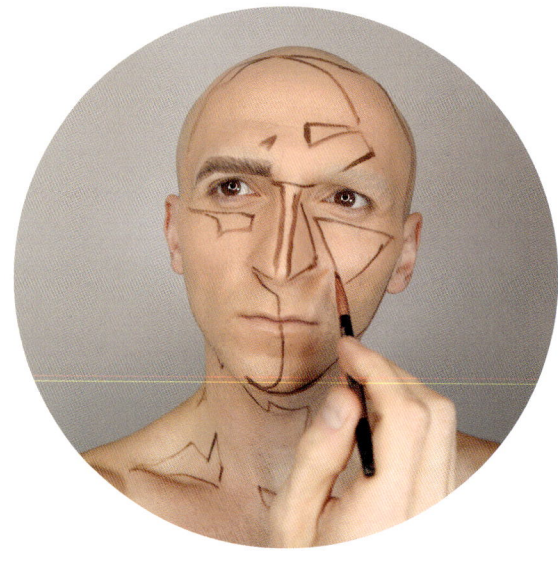

Step 2
Sketch out your line work with a cream contour pencil to create a sharp edge. It's easiest to start with the darkest shade first. (I'll say it again: don't be afraid to use black!)

Step 3
Use different shades of contour pencil to create the illusion of gradual shadow and block and fill in these boxes with that color.

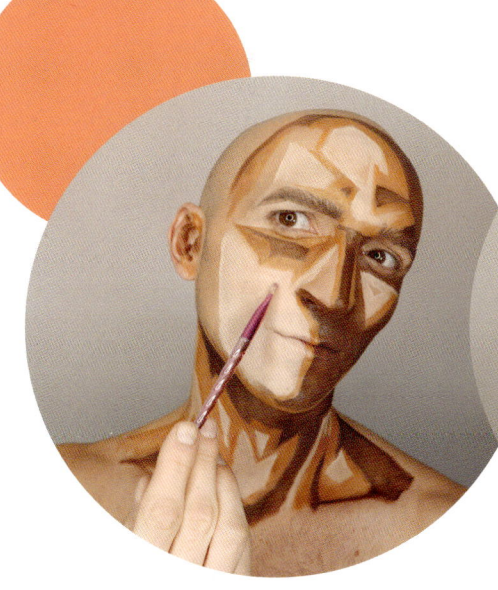

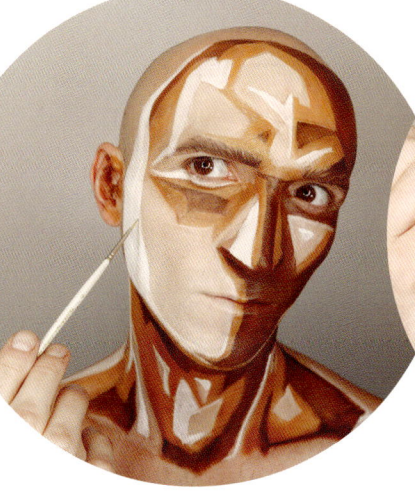

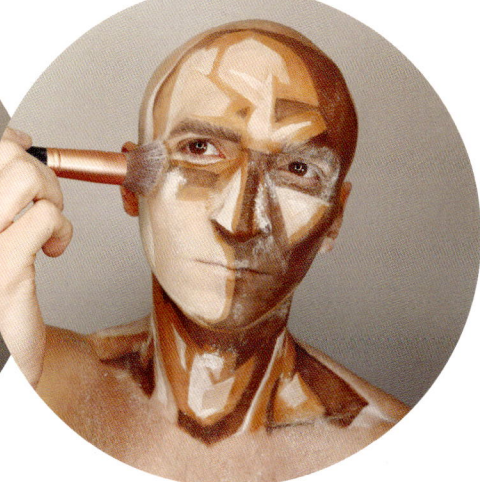

Step 4
Sketch out the highlights with concealer or a cream contour pencil.

Step 5
Mark out the lightest parts of the face with white concealer or paint.

Step 6
Use color-setting powder to dry out all the cream-based products.

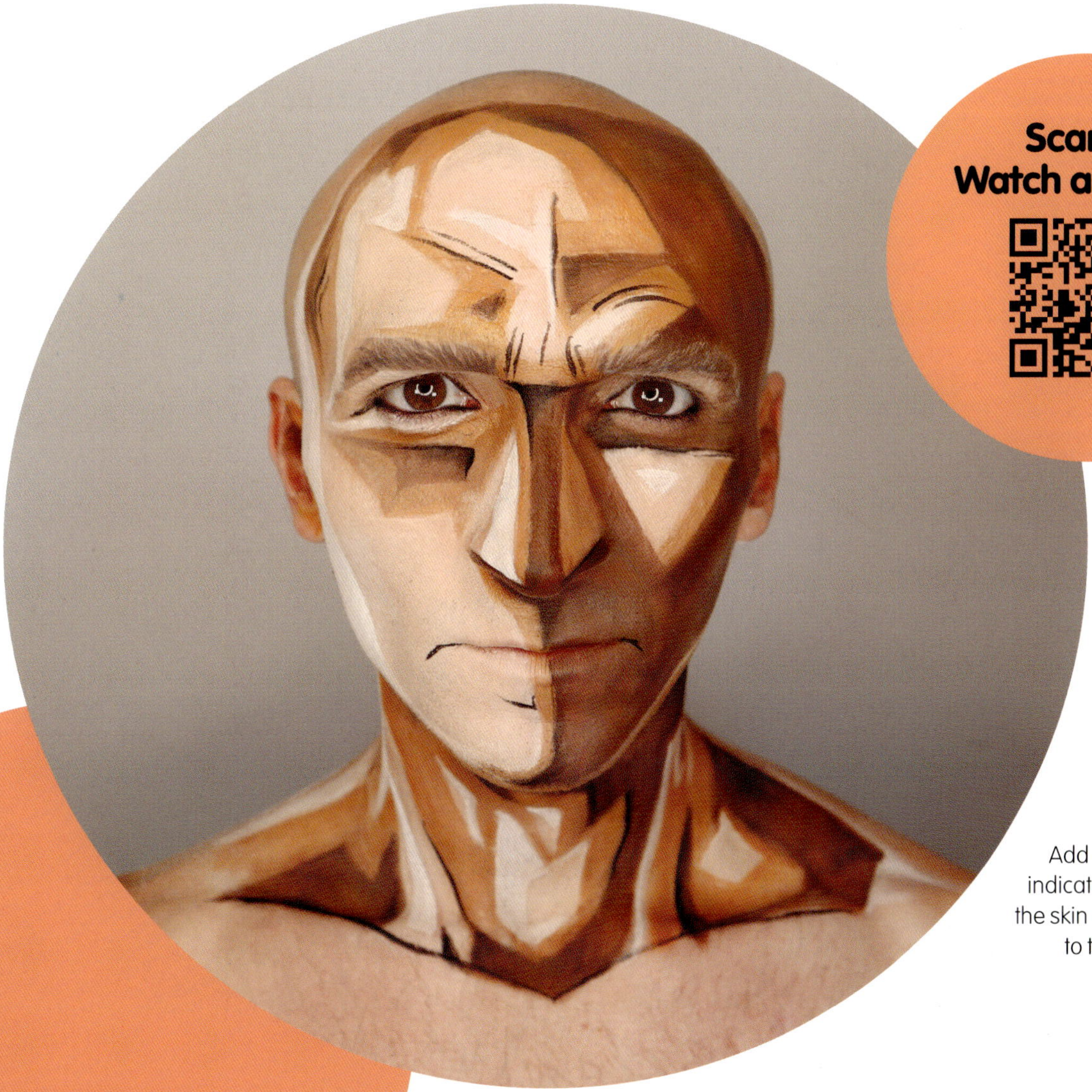

Scan to Watch a Tutorial

Step 7
Add a few black lines to indicate wrinkles/creases in the skin and mouth and to add to the cartoon effect.

PAINTING DIFFERENT TEXTURES

Painting different textures can really help elevate your look, but if you're painting these on freehand it can be very time consuming and monotonous, so I always think it's important to work smarter not harder. There are a variety of tools that can help.

Stencils

Using stencils is a great way to bring different textures into your body painting, with minimal effort. You can either make your own or buy a bunch of ready-made stencils. All you need to do is place the stencil flat against your chest or wherever you want the design to be, take a sponge with your chosen paint, and lightly dab the sponge against the stencil. Wherever there is a hole in the stencil, the paint will take.

To create your own stencils, all you'll need is an X-Acto knife, a cutting board, and some cardstock. Draw out the design you'd like onto the piece of cardstock, then take the knife and cut out each segment so you're left with a stencil. You'll probably get two or three uses out of them before the card will start to rip or become soggy, especially if you're using water-activated paint. If you're looking for a more permanent and waterproof DIY stencil, draw your design out on a piece of paper, laminate that piece of paper, and then cut out the design.

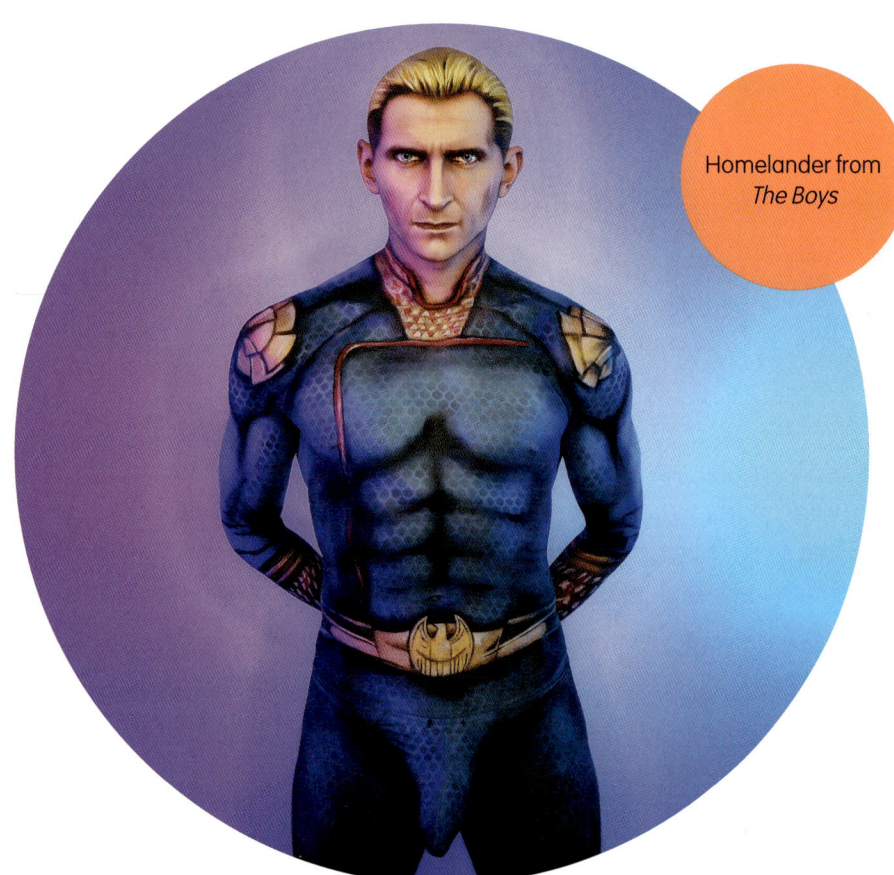

Homelander from *The Boys*

Downloadable Stencils

I have created some stencils you can use. Scan this QR code to download and print them.

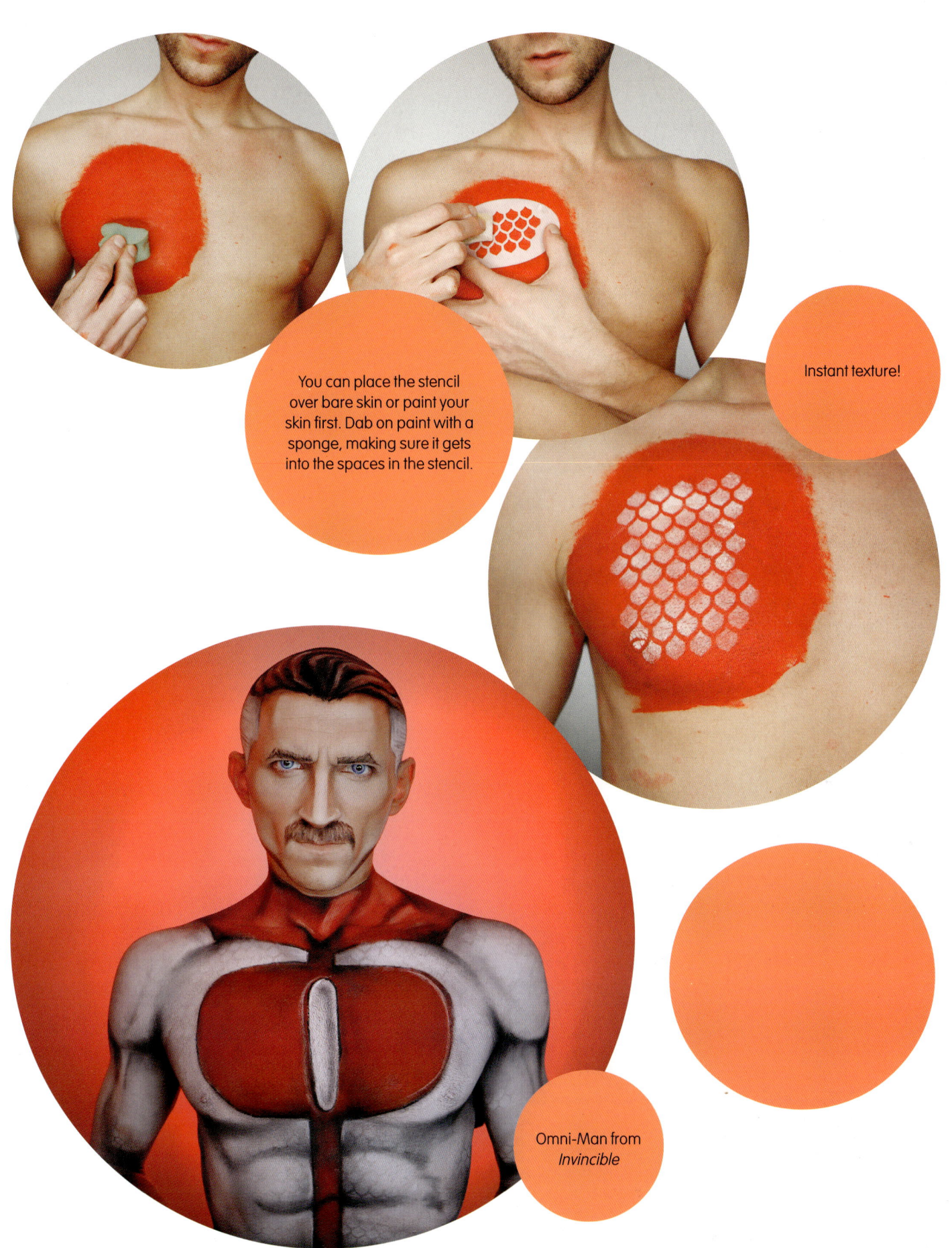

You can place the stencil over bare skin or paint your skin first. Dab on paint with a sponge, making sure it gets into the spaces in the stencil.

Instant texture!

Omni-Man from *Invincible*

Using Tools to Create Different Textures

Another way you can save yourself time creating interesting textures is by getting creative and using objects you have available around the house.

Stipple Sponges

Stipple sponges are great when it comes to fake blood. You can get some great textures using them that you can't achieve using just a brush.

Toothbrushes

Toothbrushes can be used to spray paint to get a great splatter effect. This is also great for fake blood but can also be used with more paint.

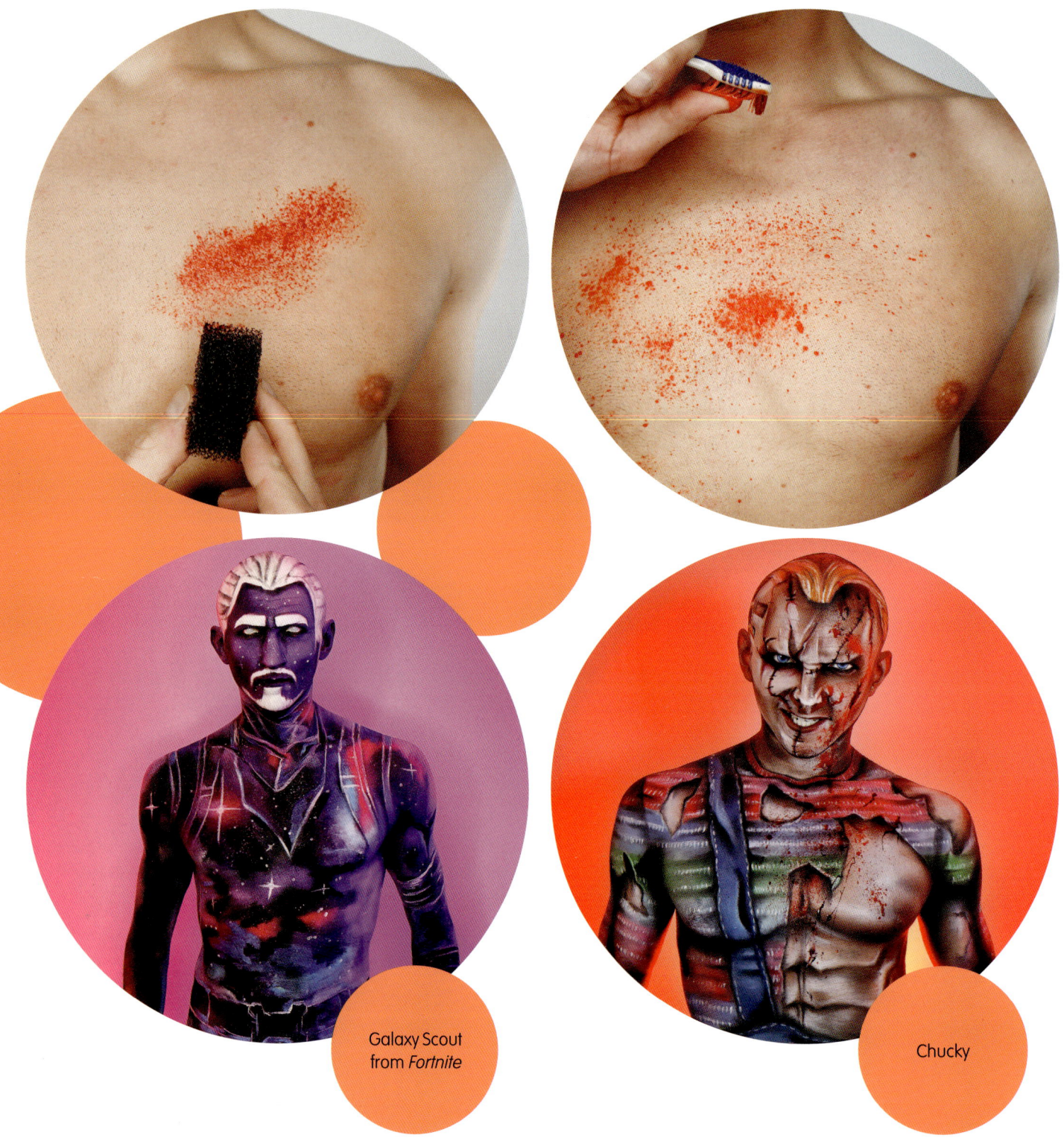

Galaxy Scout from *Fortnite*

Chucky

Cotton Swabs

Cotton swabs are great when it comes to creating dot work. It's much easier to stamp a dot this way than it is to create a circle using brush strokes.

Foil

Scrunch up the foil and dip it in some wet paint. You can get some interesting random patterns.

Plastic Cling Wrap

Mix some wet paint into a pot, dip scrunched-up plastic cling wrap into pot, dab the outside of the plastic cling wrap onto the skin to create some cool effects. I got this idea from Mei Pang (@meicrosoft).

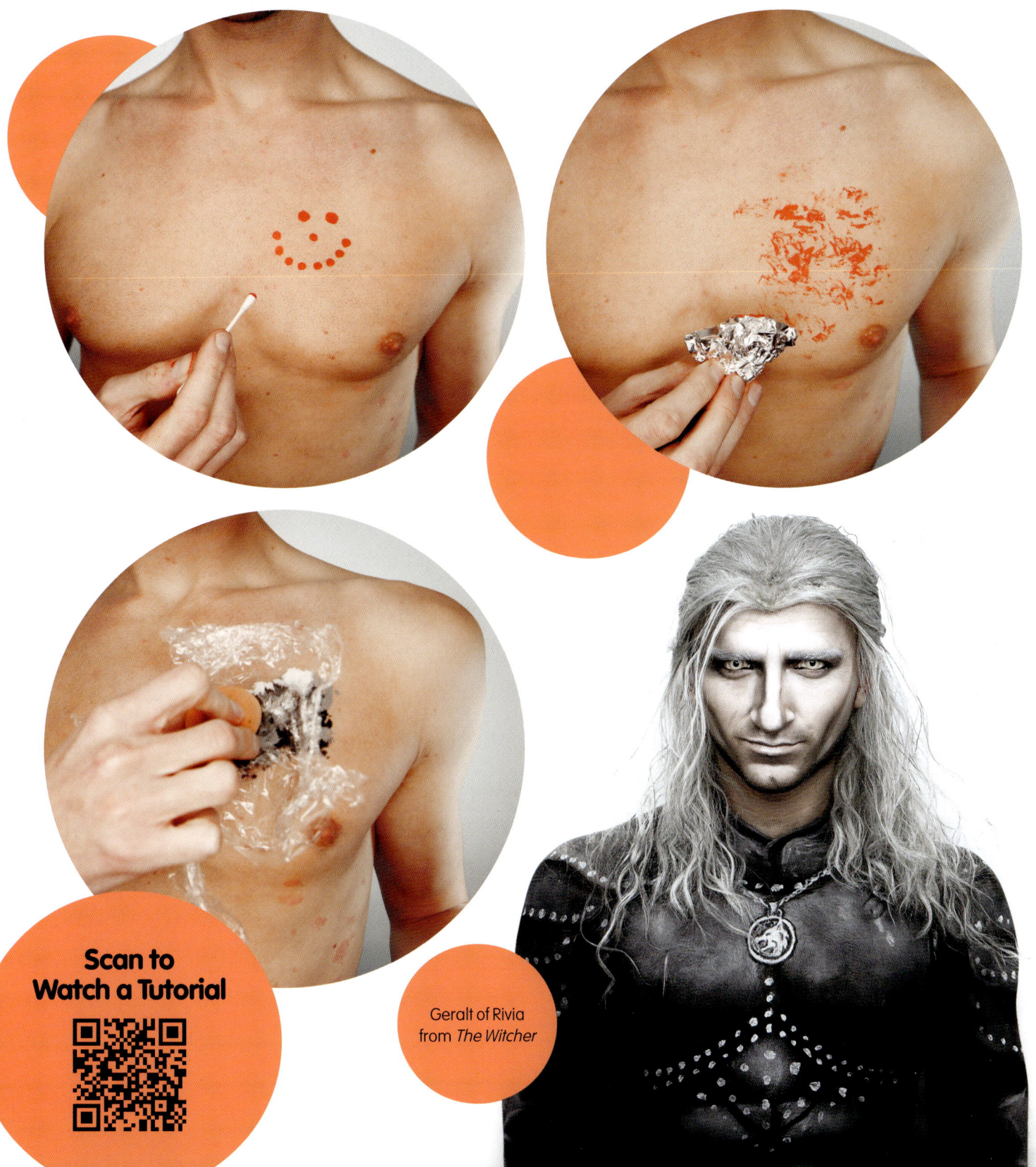

Scan to Watch a Tutorial

Geralt of Rivia from *The Witcher*

HOW TO COVER TATTOOS

To cover tattoos most effectively, you need to understand the color wheel. Certain colors complement one another and therefore cancel each other out. This makes it easier to cover up using a full coverage foundation in your natural skin tone.

If you take green face paint and mix it with red face paint, it will turn a shade of brown. The same works for orange and blue and for purple and yellow.

Adjust your color depending on what color your tattoo is. If your tattoo is primarily in red, you can neutralize with green. If yellow, neutralize with purple and so on.

Once you've color corrected, you can use a thick full coverage concealer or liquid foundation to conceal the tattoo and blend in with your skin.

Canva has a great interactive color wheel online at www.canva.com/colors/color-wheel.

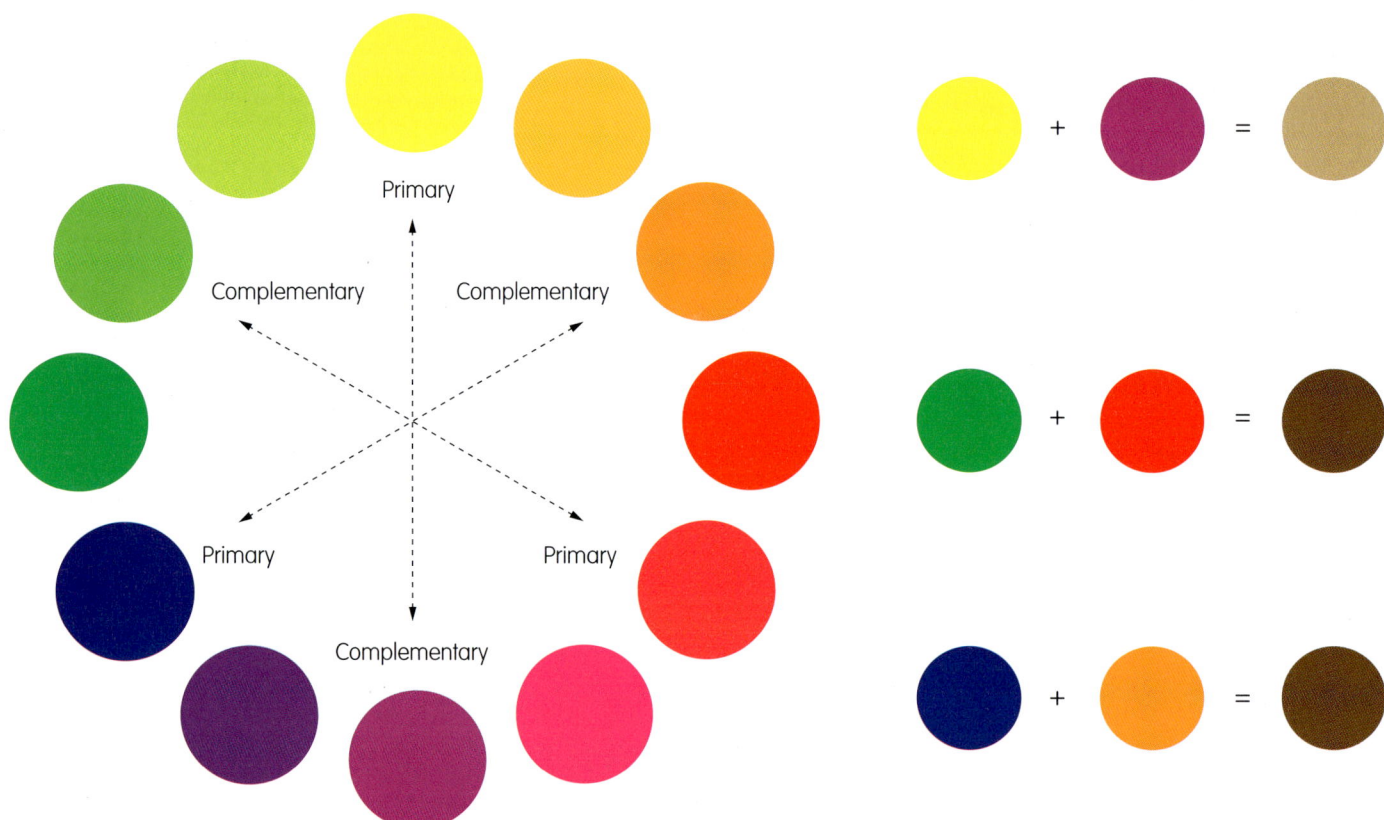

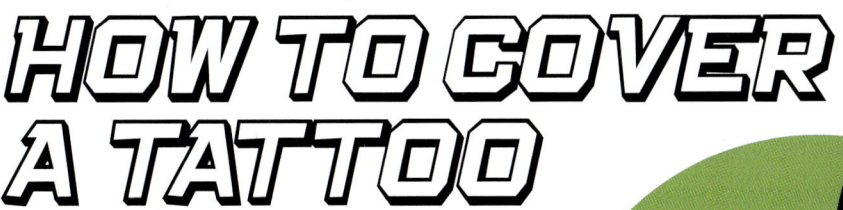

HOW TO COVER A TATTOO
STEP BY STEP

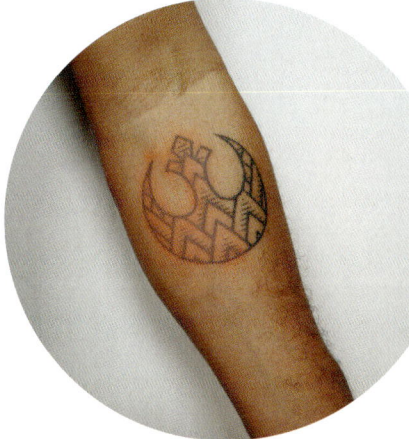

Step 1
Clean and prep skin, then color correct skin using the color wheel as reference.

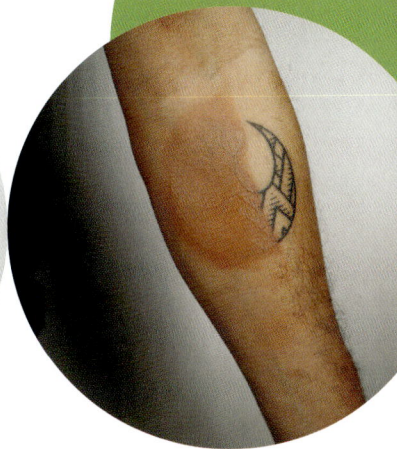

Step 2
Dab on full coverage concealer or liquid foundation covering the entire color-corrected area.

Step 3
Using a fluffy brush or beauty blender sponge, blend the edges out so it blends in smoothly with the skin.

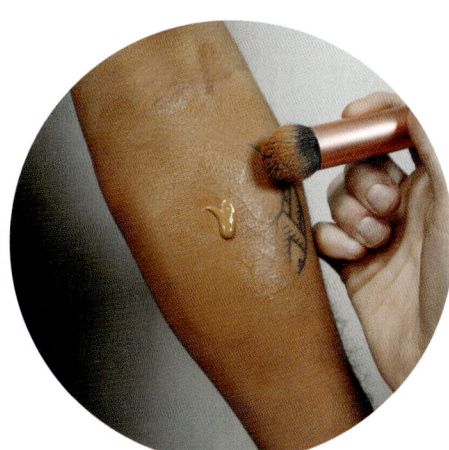

Step 4
Add a second layer.

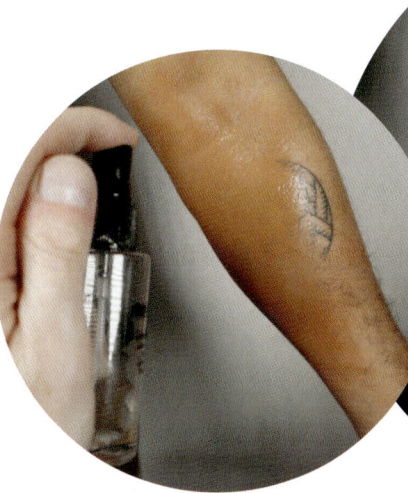

Step 5
Set your makeup with translucent powder and setting spray to ensure it is transfer-proof and smudge-proof throughout the day.

You've successfully covered a tattoo!

PAINTING THE FACE VERSUS THE BODY

Face painting and body painting use the same techniques, but there are a few ways they differ.

For instance, faces are much more expressive than bodies. You need to be aware of how the face moves and be conscious of the amount of paint you put on areas of the face that are likely to crease.

Cream-based makeups tend to last for longer periods of time without cracking, in comparison to water-activated paints. However, this can also be true for areas of the body with high movement, such as hands, elbows, armpits, and necks.

Sweat

Sweat is more common when it comes to painting the body, especially under the armpits or places where skin is likely to crease, for instance the stomach, elbow, and hands. If you're using water-activated paints, sweat will cause these paints to run or smudge. Cream or grease paint are more waterproof. When choosing the type of product you want to use, think about what you want to achieve and how long you need the paint to last, and then select the right product accordingly.

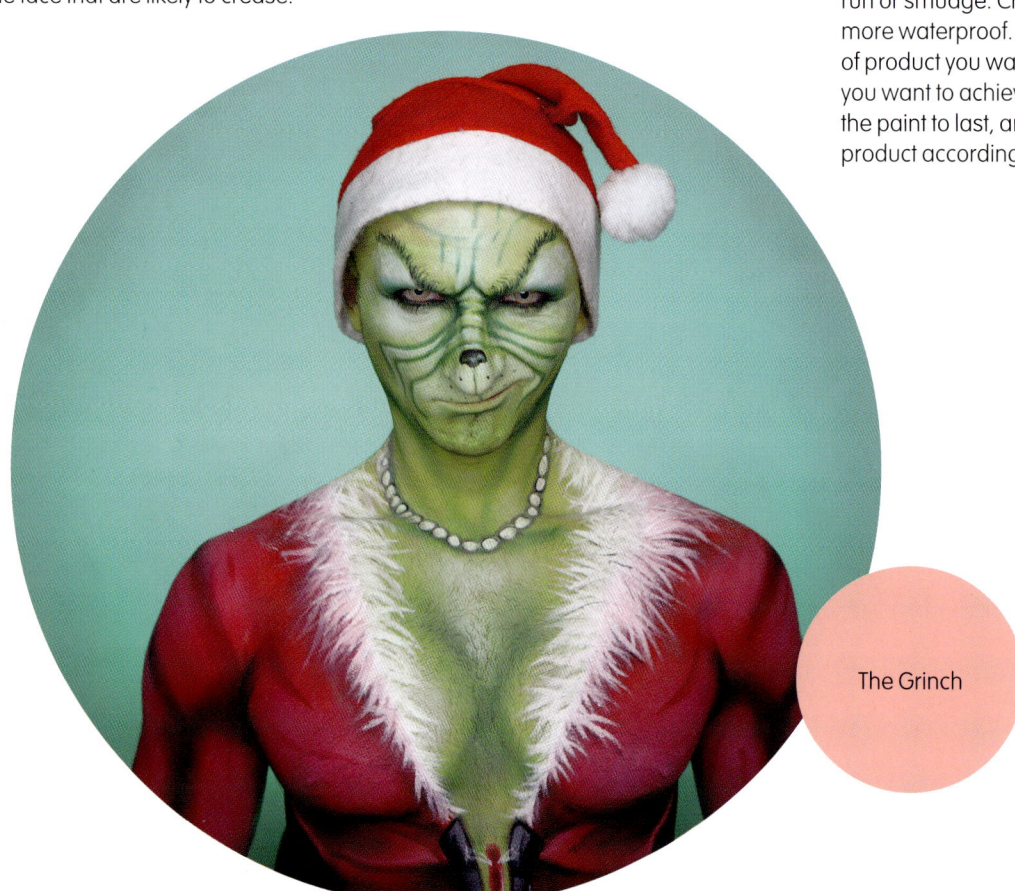

The Grinch

Time

It might sound obvious, but you need more time if you're completing a full body paint because you're working on a much larger surface area. Be mindful of this, and plan your time accordingly, especially if you're painting a model. Tell them how long it is going to take and give them ample breaks.

Skin Tone

Your current makeup kit might be suitable for your skin tone but don't assume it'll be right for everyone you work with. If you're painting someone else, the last thing you want to do is look like you're changing their skin tone. This is especially key when contouring and highlighting. You will need to adjust the different gradients to match your model's skin. One foundation color does **not** match all. If you're going for a more natural look, a sign of a good makeup artist is being unable to detect that person is wearing makeup at all.

Natural Curves of the Face

Where you place a contour differs depending on natural bone structure. Some people have more defined cheek bones, so might need less focus on this than someone with less defined cheekbones. Similarly with the jawline. You can create a jawline with contouring and highlighting but sometimes it's not necessary.

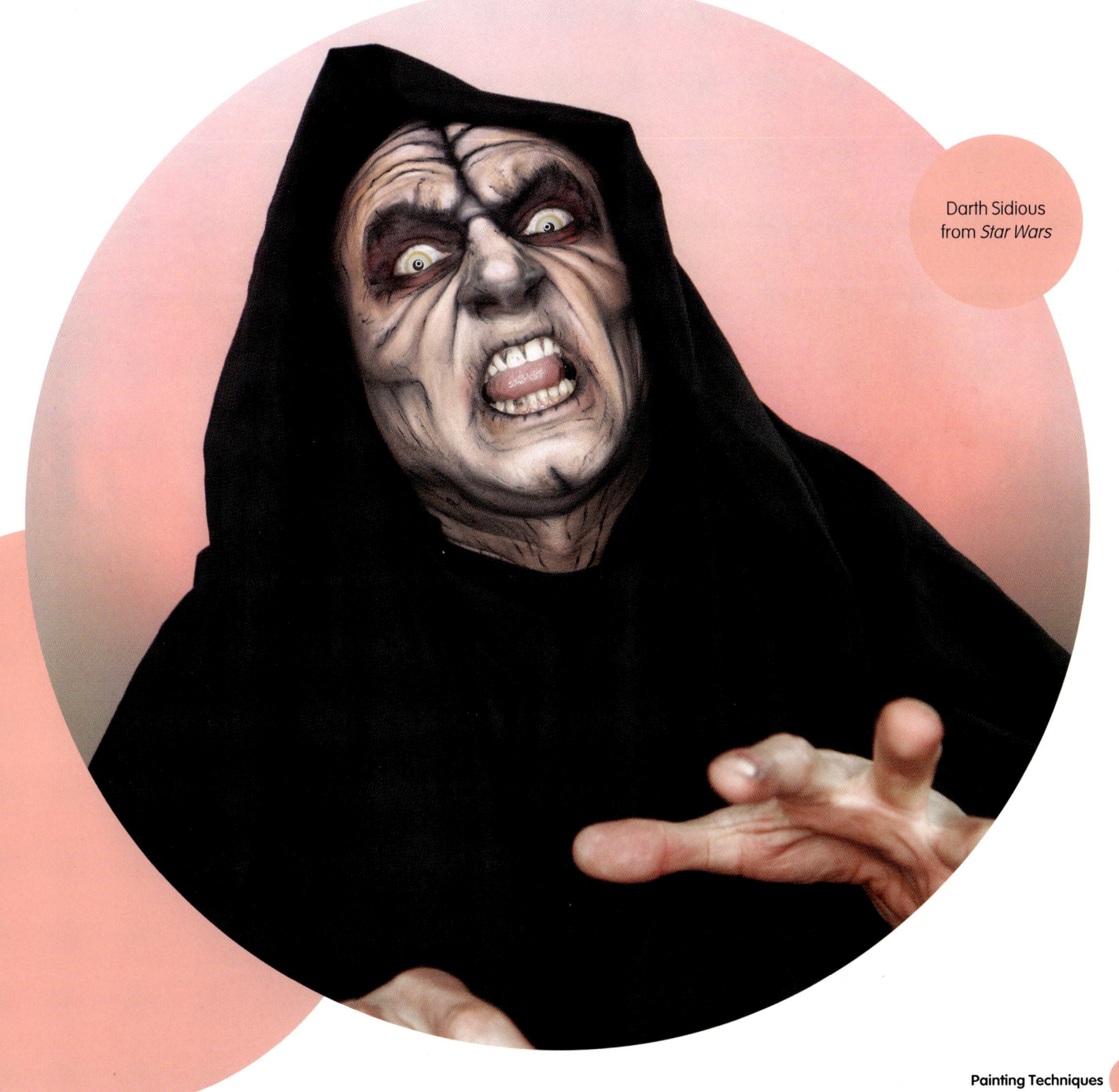

Darth Sidious from *Star Wars*

OTHER THINGS TO THINK ABOUT
WHEN PAINTING

If you are painting yourself there will naturally be areas of your body which are harder to reach than others. For instance, if you're right-handed, you might struggle to paint your right arm, as you'll need to pick up a brush with your left hand. Be patient with yourself. Keep practicing and it will get easier. Body painting is a skill that takes time and effort to master. I've been painting for social media for three years now and I'm still learning new things every day.

It's important to stay hydrated when painting yourself. The paint you're applying to your skin is likely to dry out your skin so drink lots of water.

Take regular breaks! Give your eyes a rest from all the lights shining in your face, stretch your legs, and grab some food! You'll be much more productive with frequent breaks.

If you need the paint to last for a long time, use setting spray. On cream-based makeup it works really well! All it takes is one or two spritzes. This will help lock the paint in place and make it last longer. If you use setting spray on water-activated paints, be careful not to spray too close to your face as this will activate the paint and it will start to run.

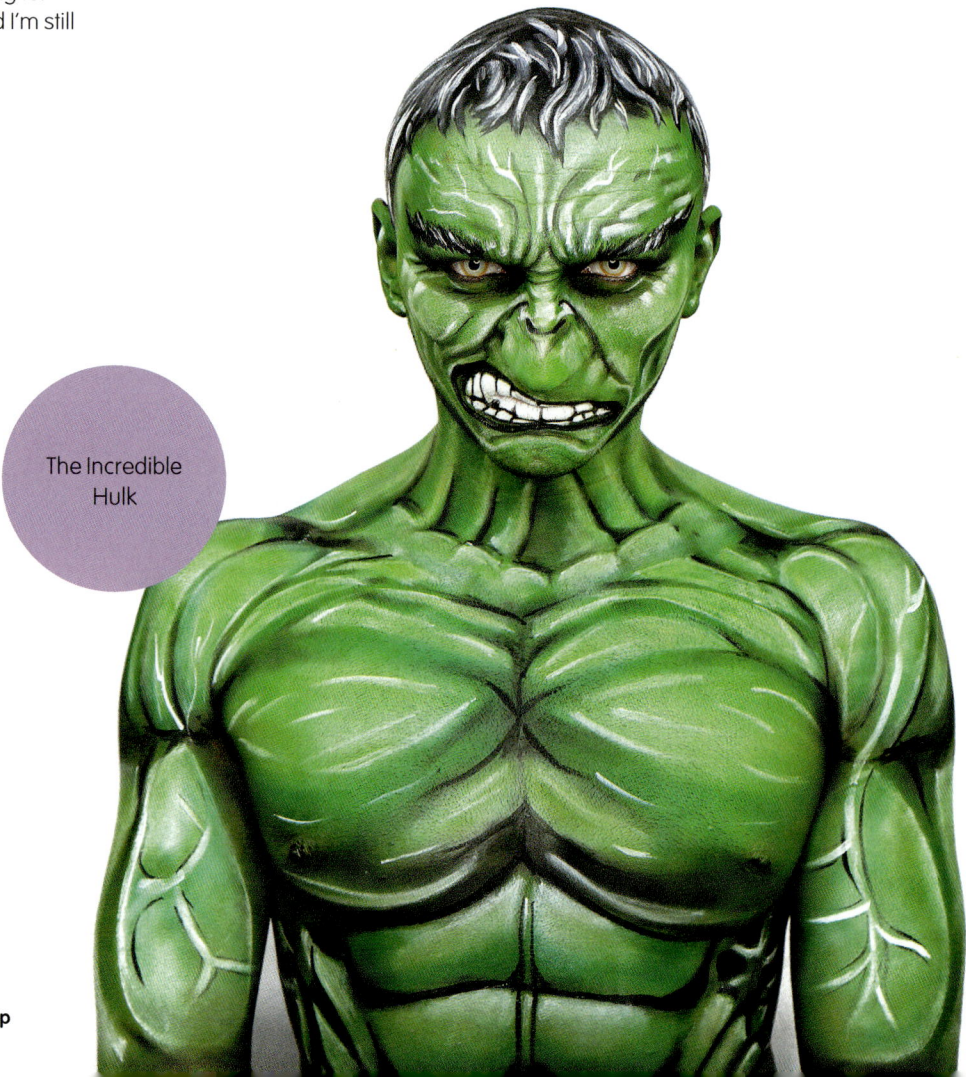

The Incredible Hulk

Use high-quality paints. This helps when it comes to the application and overall effect of the final look. The last thing I'd want to happen is for you to choose the cheapest face paints to experiment with, find them difficult to work with, get frustrated, and give up.

Everyone reacts to paint differently, and while most body painting products on the market are hypoallergenic, make sure that you remove the paint immediately if you or your model experience **any** sort of pain or irritation. It's always a good idea to do a "patch test" on a small piece of skin like your hand first.

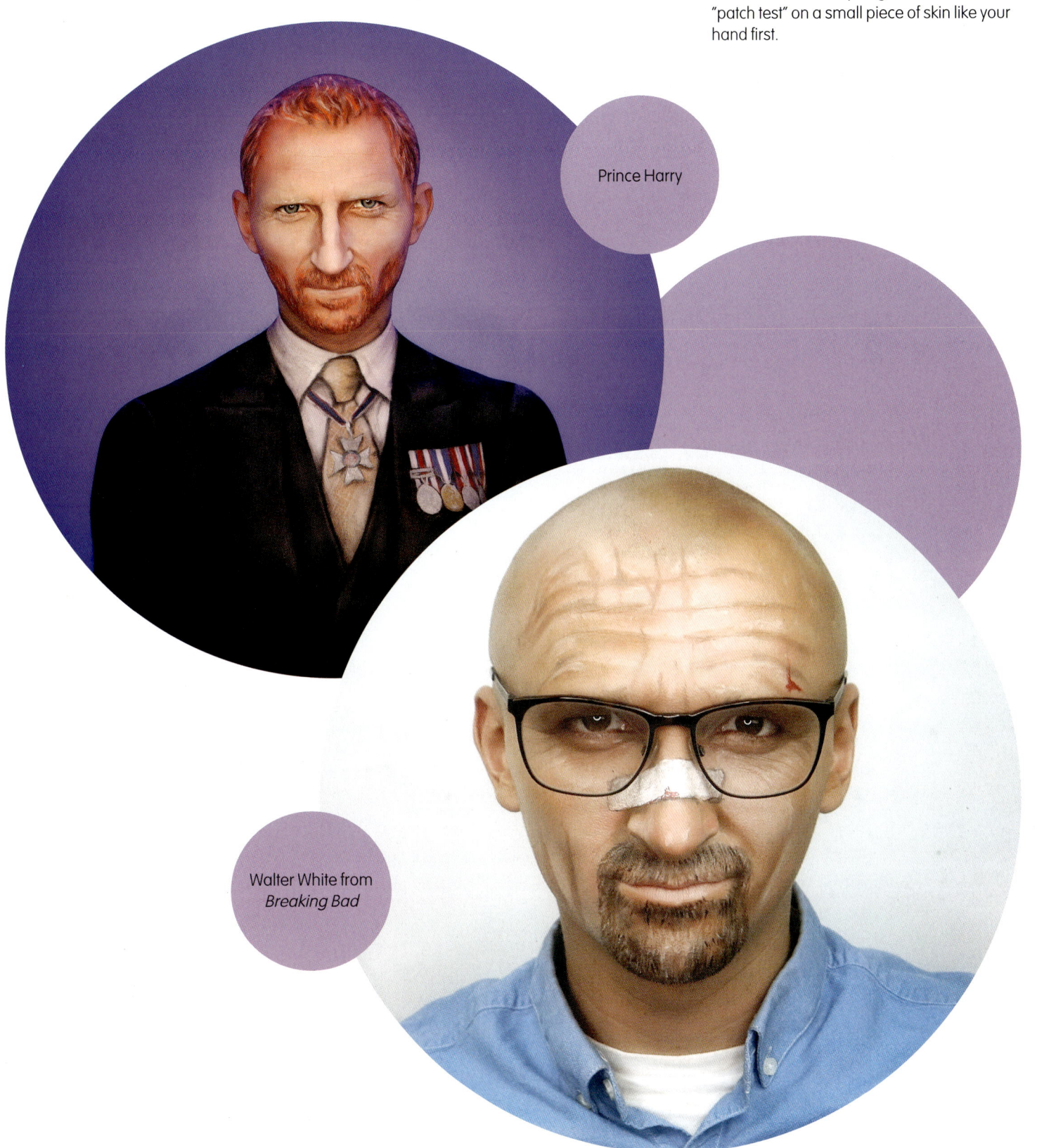

Prince Harry

Walter White from *Breaking Bad*

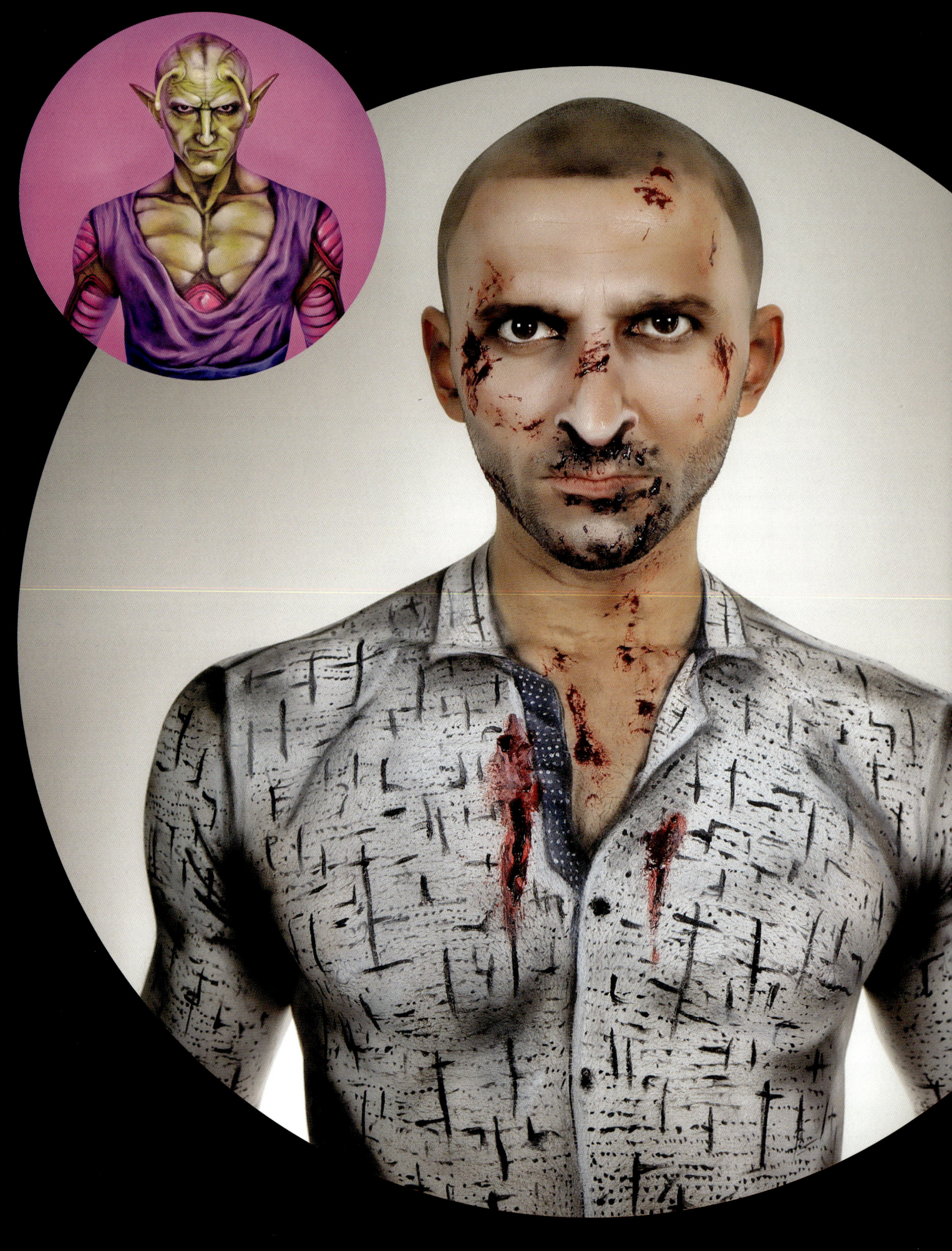

PART 2
BEYOND PAINTING

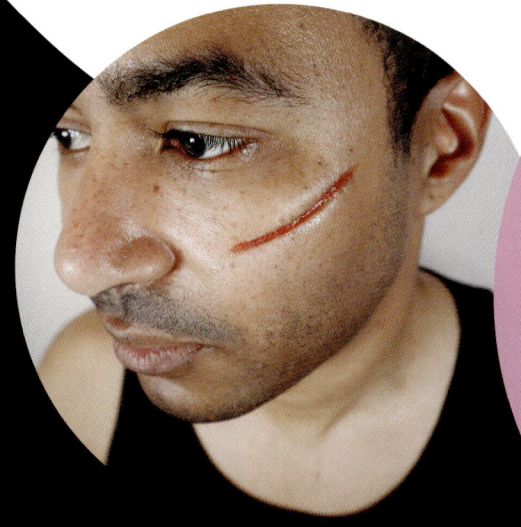

Throughout the next part of the book, we'll be exploring products to help you raise your game when it comes to cosplaying. Some of these are super easy to pick up, others will take a bit of practice and time, but all can elevate your creations if used correctly! While it doesn't sound very sexy, we will be touching on how to use these products safely so you don't hurt yourself or others. I'd say sit back and enjoy but I want you to get involved and try the products along with me!

CONTACT LENSES

Colored contact lenses can really make a huge difference as the eyes are such a key part of the face. But there are some important things you should be aware of before you use contact lenses, as this is your eyesight you're playing with. You don't want to use these incorrectly and damage your vision permanently.

Firstly, you **NEED** to make sure the company or website you're buying your contact lenses from is FDA approved. This means that they have been tested and deemed safe to insert into your eyes. There have been horror stories of companies selling contacts that aren't FDA approved and causing major damage to customers' eyes. I get all my lenses from colouredcontacts.com!

There are a lot of "don'ts" in this section, but don't let that put you off! Wearing contact lenses can really help elevate a look! Give it a try and remember not to get frustrated if you don't get them in first time!

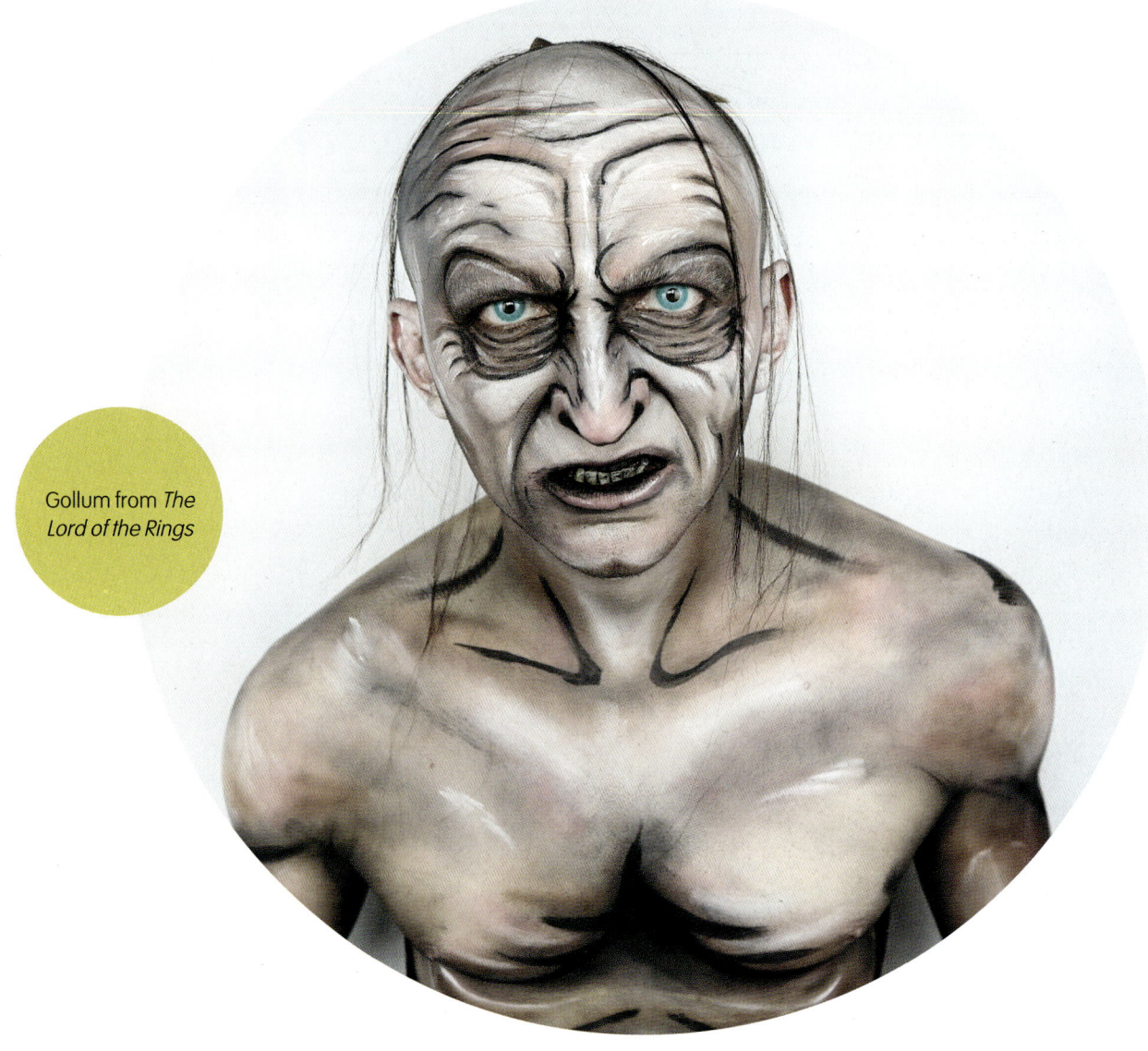

Gollum from *The Lord of the Rings*

How to Prepare Your Contact Lenses for Use

Before touching your contact lenses, thoroughly wash your hands with soap and water. Soak the lenses in contact lens solution for at least two hours before use.

How to Insert Your Contact Lenses

Once they have been soaked in contact lens solution for a couple of hours, they are safe to use in your eyes. Again, make sure your hands are clean before touching the contact lens. I cannot stress this enough! Check the lens is not inside out and place the lens on your index finger. With your other hand, hold your eye open and slowly bring the contact towards your eye, until it takes. You might find you'll need to blink a few times to get it into the right place. The feel of them might take some getting used to, but if they are painful then they are in wrong, so remove them and try again. It might be that you have caught some dust under the lens, or they are inside out.

If this is your first time wearing contact lenses, you're going to struggle. It's unnatural putting something in your eye, but if they're uncomfortable or painful they aren't in correctly.

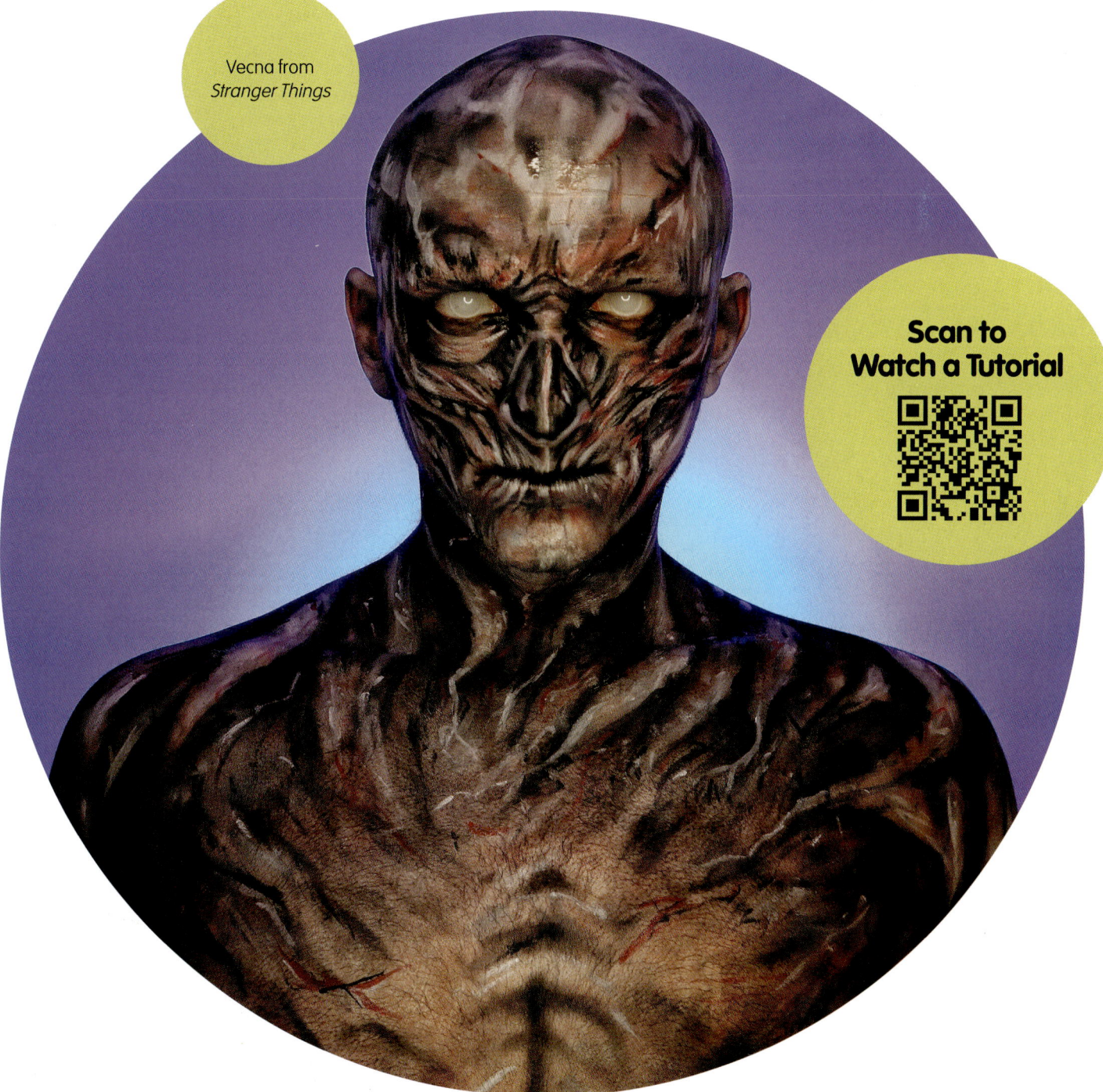

Vecna from *Stranger Things*

Scan to Watch a Tutorial

How to Tell if the Lens Is Inside Out

Depending on the design of the lens, it might be easy to tell if the contact is inside out or not as the design will be more vibrant on the outside of the lens than the other, however the more subtle designs can be difficult to see which is the correct side, so you might assume that both are right, but there is **always** a correct side to the lens.

You want to check the natural curvature of the lens from the side. Stick them on the end of your finger, bring it up to your eye and look at it closely. If it's a perfect smooth semi-circle this is the correct way round. If the edges look like they are curling outwards, like an upside-down bell curve, then it is inside out.

How to Store Your Contacts

Store your lenses in a clean contact lens case, soaked in contact lens solution. Be sure to keep these topped up as the contact solution does evaporate over time. Check your lenses every week to make sure they haven't dried out.

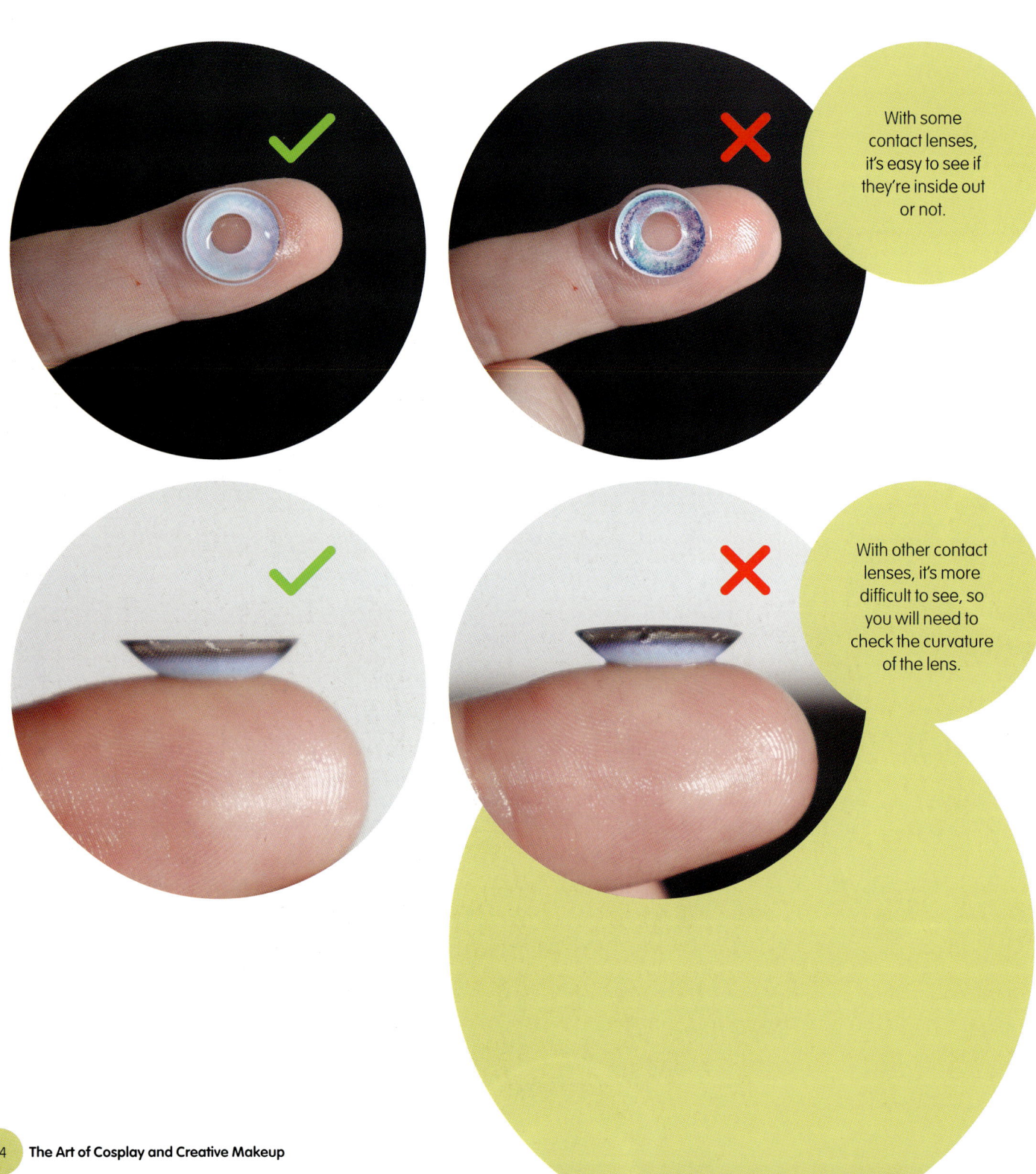

With some contact lenses, it's easy to see if they're inside out or not.

With other contact lenses, it's more difficult to see, so you will need to check the curvature of the lens.

How to Clean Your Lenses If You Drop Them

Clean your lenses thoroughly with contact lens solution **NOT water** before inserting them back into your eye.

How to Remove Contact Lenses

Again, make sure your hands are clean before sticking your finger in your eye! It's easiest to do this in front of a mirror. Hold your eye open with one finger, and then with your other hand, pinch the contact with your thumb and index finger until it comes out.

More Helpful Tips

Pay attention to the duration on the packet. If you opt for single use daily lenses, then its important you **don't** reuse these. They should be disposed of after one use.

The longer the duration, the more durable the contact lens is and is safe to use multiple times so long as they have been cleaned, stored, and prepared properly.

Avoid wearing contact lenses for more than eight hours at a time.

Never stack lenses on top of each other!

Never sleep in your contacts lenses.

Avoid swimming, showering, or bathing with contacts in.

Avoid sharing your contact lenses with anyone else. You don't want to end up with conjunctivitis.

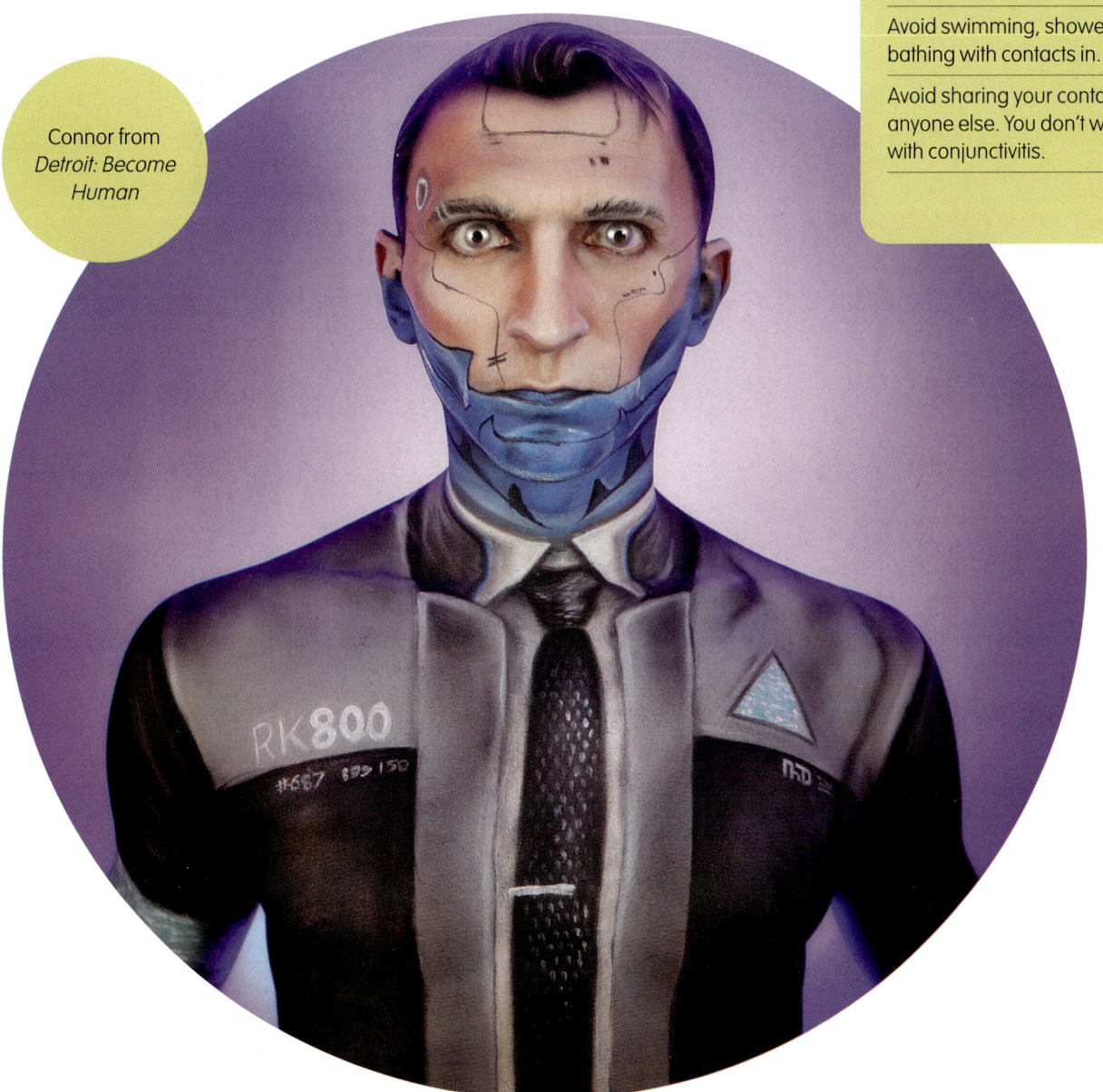

Connor from *Detroit: Become Human*

POLYMORPH PLASTIC

Looking for a pair of fake teeth perfectly molded to your mouth? I've got just the thing for you!

Polymorph plastic is solid at room temperature but when heated in boiling water or blasted with a heat gun it becomes transparent and highly malleable. In other words, easy to shape into whatever your heart desires! While it's in this warm, softened state you have a short period of time where it's not too hot to touch, but also not too cool that it's no longer malleable, to manipulate the plastic into a desired shape. Then once you're happy with it, let it cool down. The plastic will harden and go back to being its original color and solid.

Before we start playing around with this product, we need to be aware of the safety hazards! It is very easy to burn yourself using this product especially if you decide to use a heat gun, so I advise wearing heat protective gloves.

The best thing about polymorph plastic is it's reusable. You can make something and let it cool then melt it back down and craft it into something new.

It comes in small beads to increase the surface areas of the plastic, meaning it will melt quicker. If you want to reuse the same plastic which you have already manipulated into a larger combined object, just be aware this will take longer for you melt it down, and you might need to keep filling your cup up with boiling water. If you can break it down into smaller pieces, it will melt quicker.

Polymorph plastic beads before they're melted.

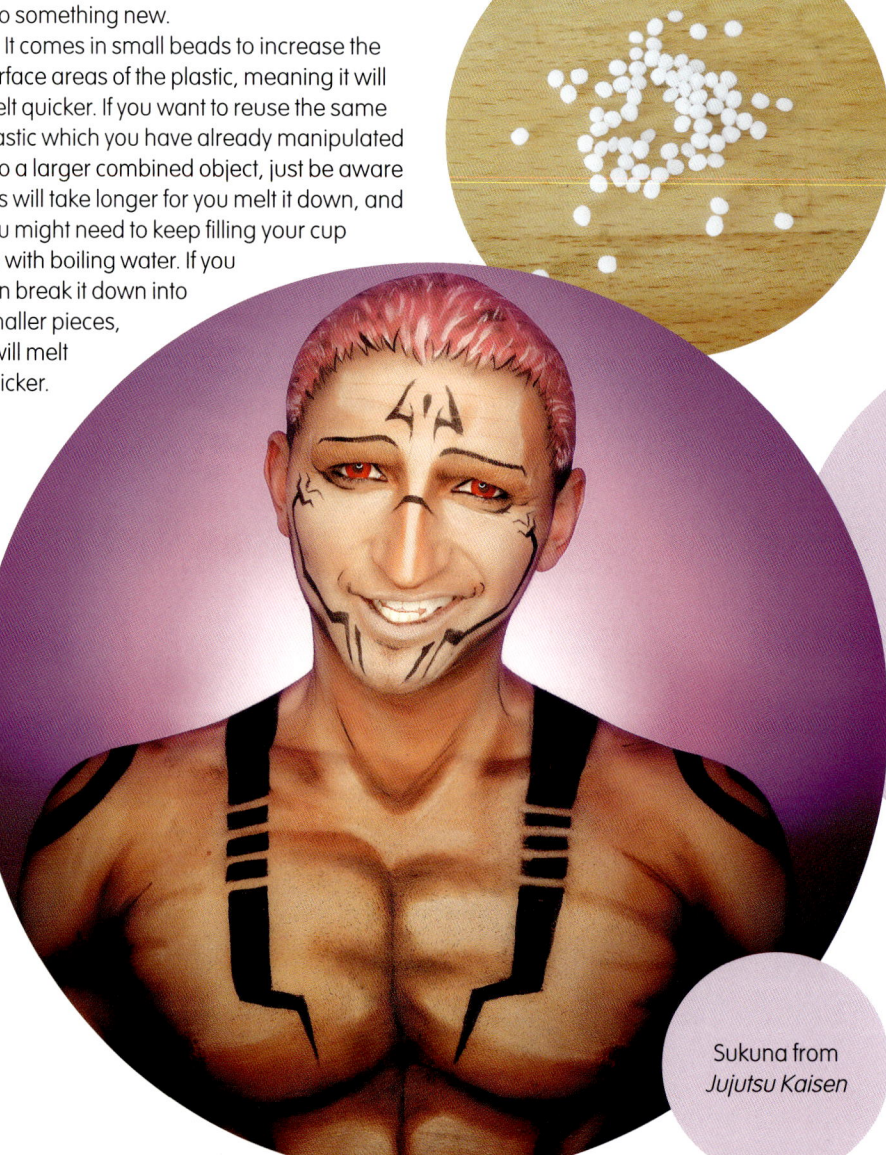

Sukuna from *Jujutsu Kaisen*

Scan to Watch a Tutorial

WORKING WITH POLYMORPH PLASTIC

Here is the basic process for using polymorph plastic for any application.

STEP BY STEP

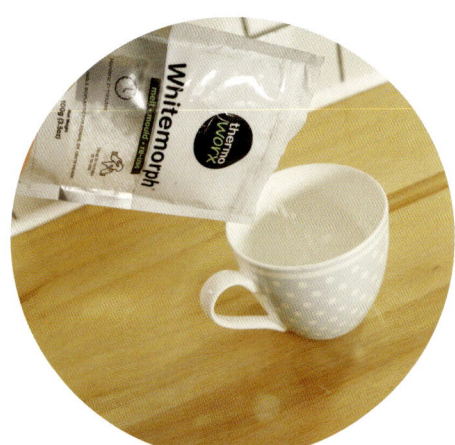

Step 1
Pour a small number of beads into a heat-safe bowl or mug.

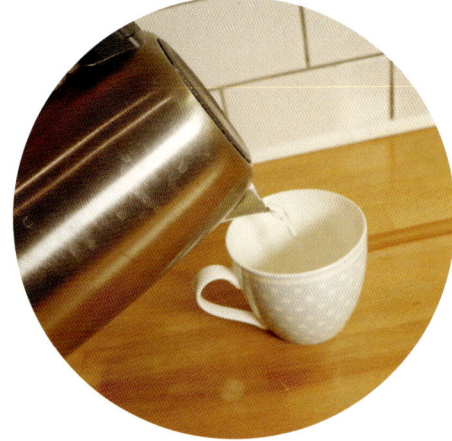

Step 2
Pour boiling water into the bowl.

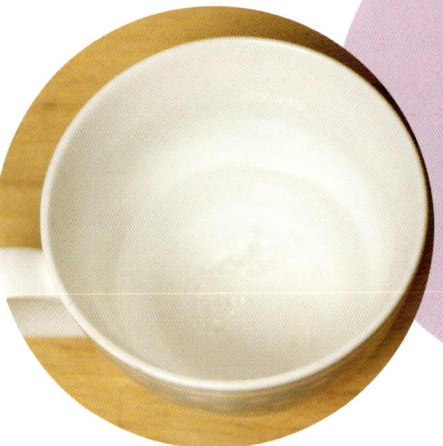

Step 3
Wait until the balls turn transparent and start to stick together, this is an indication they are ready to be used. At this point, the plastic will be too hot to work with and mold straight away, so either leave the balls in the hot water for about five to ten minutes while the water cools or remove the balls with a spoon, and allow them to cool for about a minute before touching them.

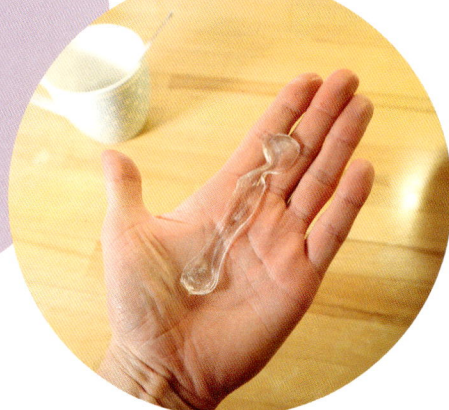

Step 4
Once cooled down enough to stretch and bend, manipulate the plastic into any shape you like.

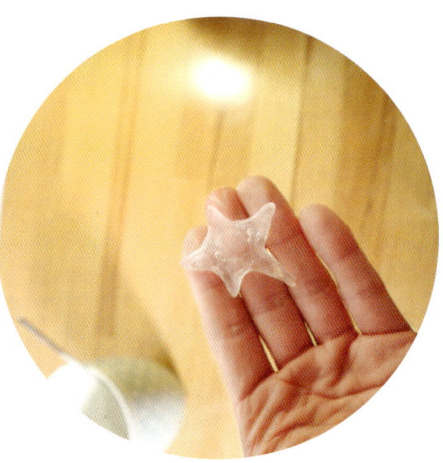

Step 5
You have around thirty seconds to a minute before the product starts to turn less translucent and get harder. You will feel this happening as you work.

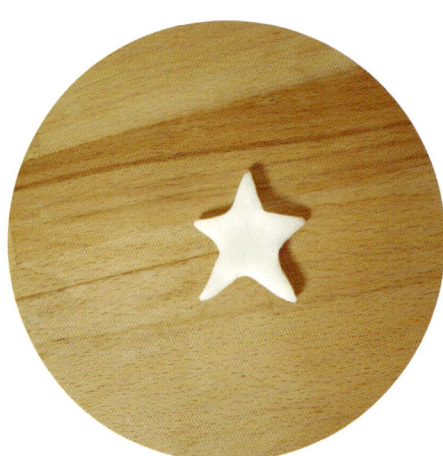

Step 6
Once you're happy with the shape, you can leave the product to set completely for about five to ten minutes and it will turn back into a white solid.

HOW TO
MAKE FANGS
STEP BY STEP

Polymorph plastic is the perfect material for creating really elevated fangs.

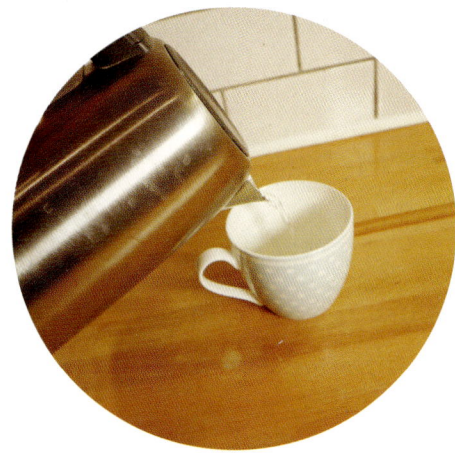

Step 1
Heat the polymorph plastic up in boiling water.

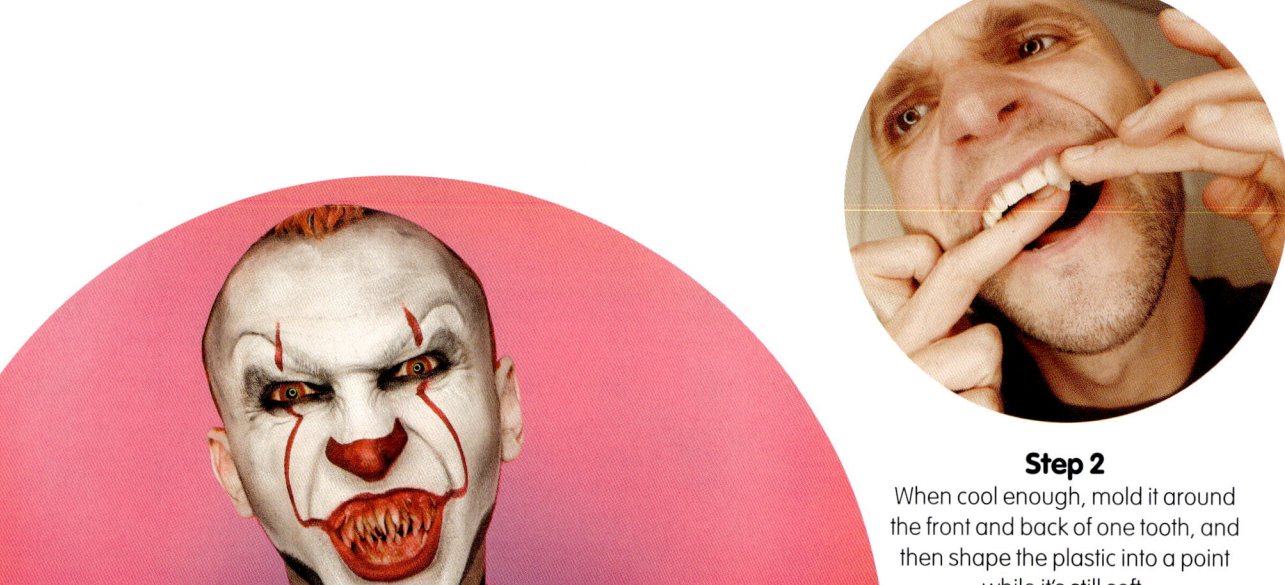

Pennywise from *It*

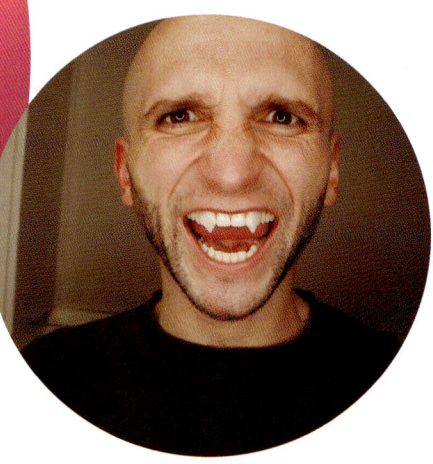

Step 2
When cool enough, mold it around the front and back of one tooth, and then shape the plastic into a point while it's still soft.

Step 3
Do the same for the second tooth. Let them dry and you've got a set of customized fangs!

HOW TO MAKE A FULL SET OF TEETH

STEP BY STEP

Sometimes fangs alone just won't do.

When making a full set of teeth, you want to wiggle the gum guard around slightly while it's drying before taking it off. This will create a bit more space for your teeth as the plastic sometimes expands when it dries which means a tighter more uncomfortable fit for the final product.

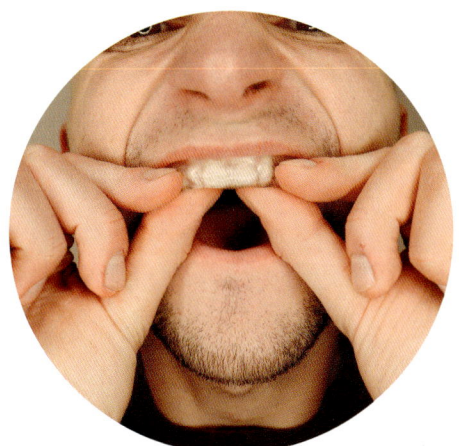

Step 1
Once heated, mold an entire gum guard around your teeth.

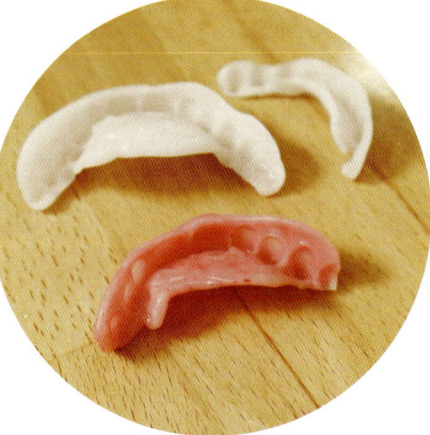

Step 2
Repeat this for your bottom teeth and let these dry. (See page 70 for how to color them.)

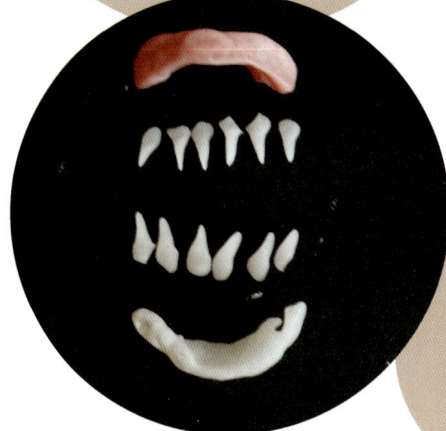

Step 3
Make your individual teeth with softened polymorph plastic, trying to mold them thinly.

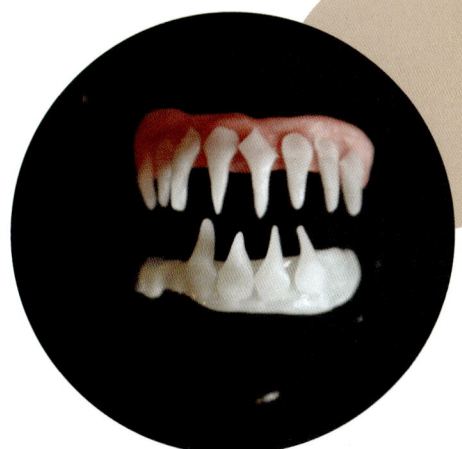

Step 4
Superglue individual teeth to the ready-made gum guard. Use gloves to avoid glue getting on your fingers.

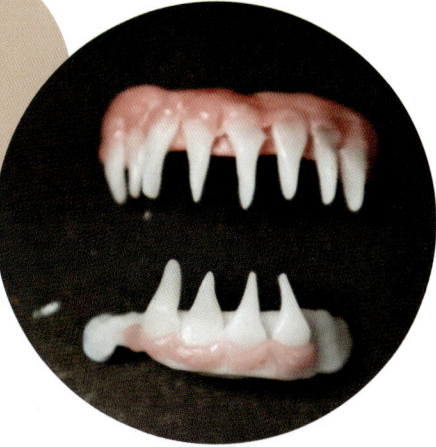

Step 5
Add an additional layer on polymorph plastic along the base of the teeth so it looks like the teeth are inserted into the gum.

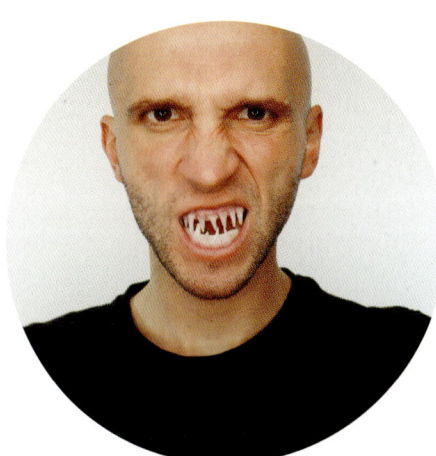

Step 6
Once dried and hardened, you've got a set of teeth perfectly molded to your mouth.

DYEING POLYMORPH PLASTIC
STEP BY STEP

In its dried state, polymorph plastic can be difficult to recolor as many paints don't stick well to plastic. However, I've found while it's in its warmed, malleable form you can use food coloring to change the color of the plastic. This can be helpful if you want to create a set of dentures which look like gums, or you're building up a set of teeth onto a gum base. I find gel food coloring works better than the water-based coloring.

Whether you choose to dye them or not, polymorph plastic teeth are an important tool to have in your cosplay kit.

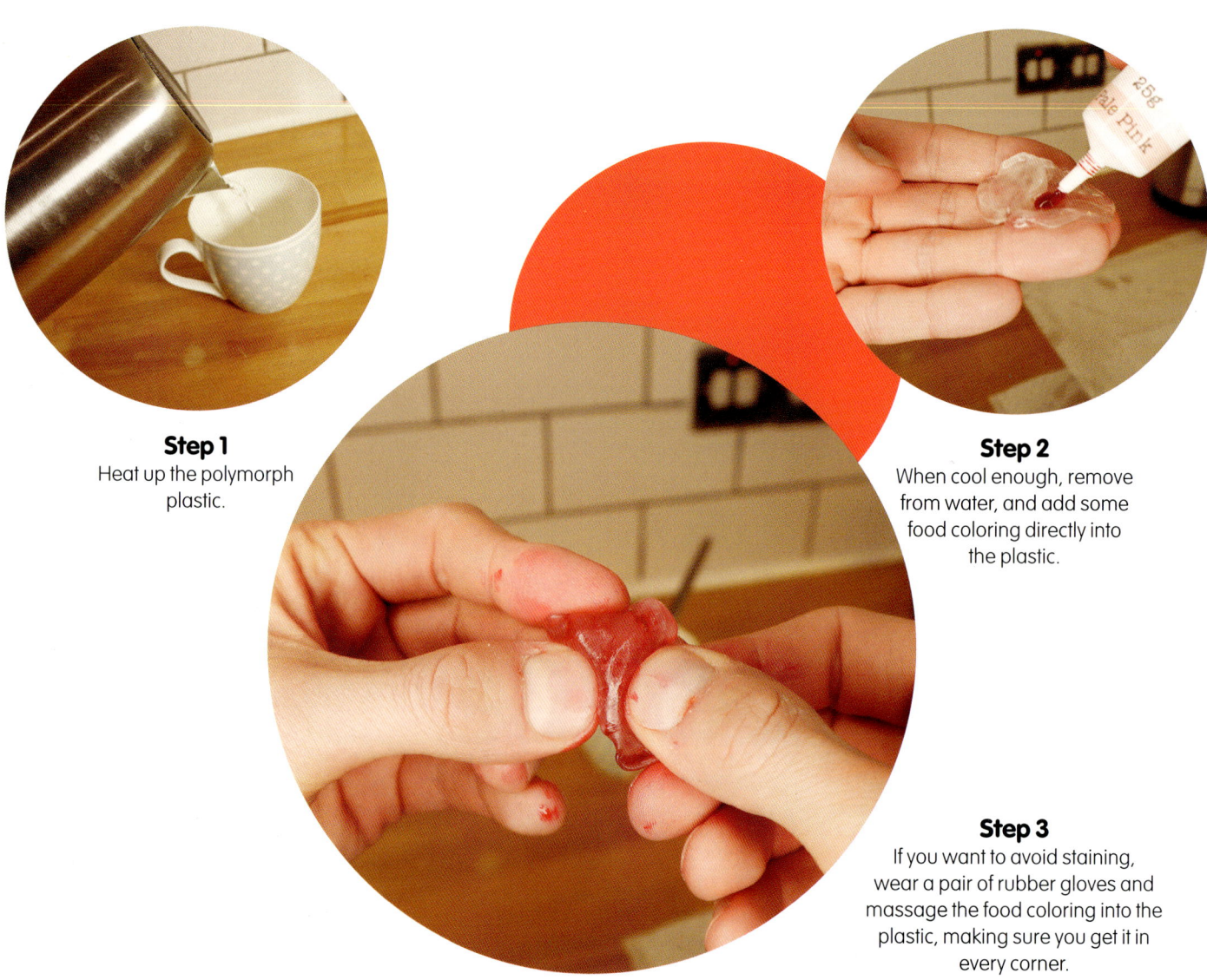

Step 1
Heat up the polymorph plastic.

Step 2
When cool enough, remove from water, and add some food coloring directly into the plastic.

Step 3
If you want to avoid staining, wear a pair of rubber gloves and massage the food coloring into the plastic, making sure you get it in every corner.

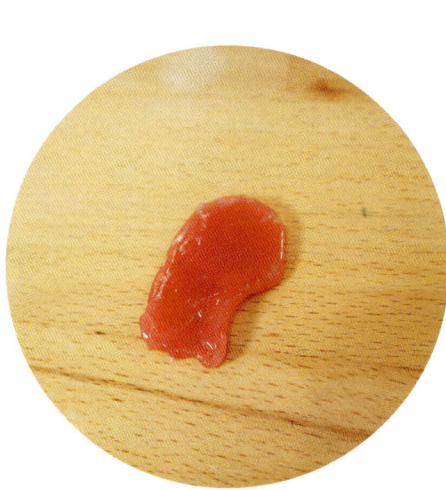

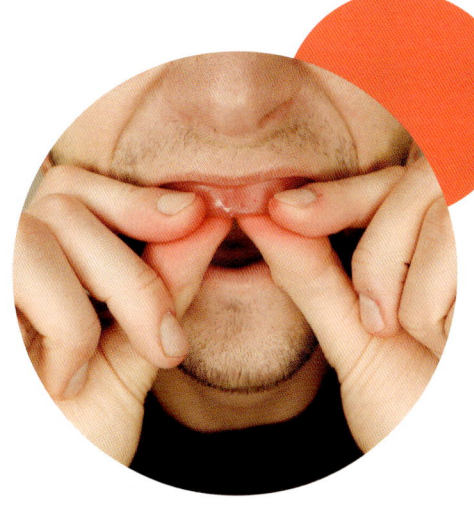

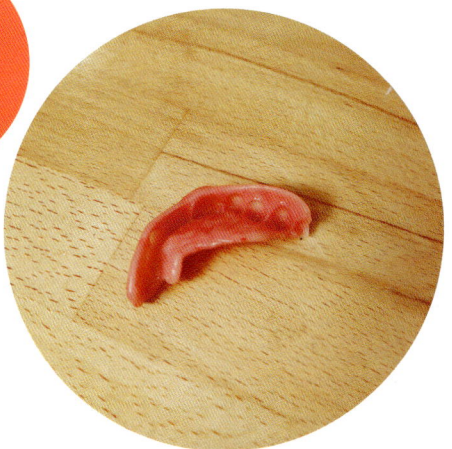

Step 4
Let the product dry. You might need to keep reheating the plastic and adding more food coloring until you are happy with the color.

Step 5
If you're making gums, mold it around your teeth when the product is malleable.

Step 6
Once dyed, these beads will always dry that color. You can now build teeth onto this gum guard for complete set of fake teeth.

Ban from *Seven Deadly Sins*

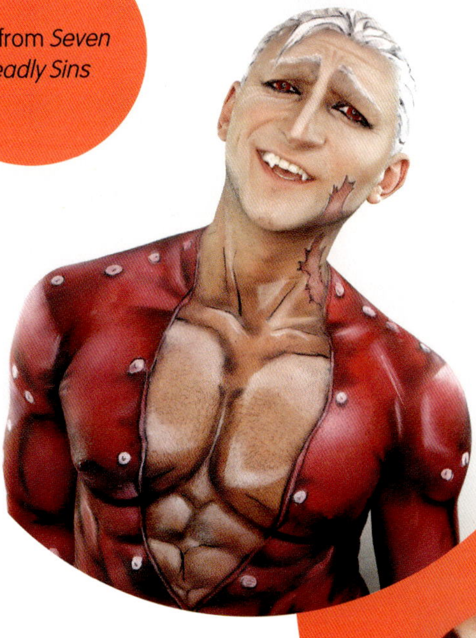

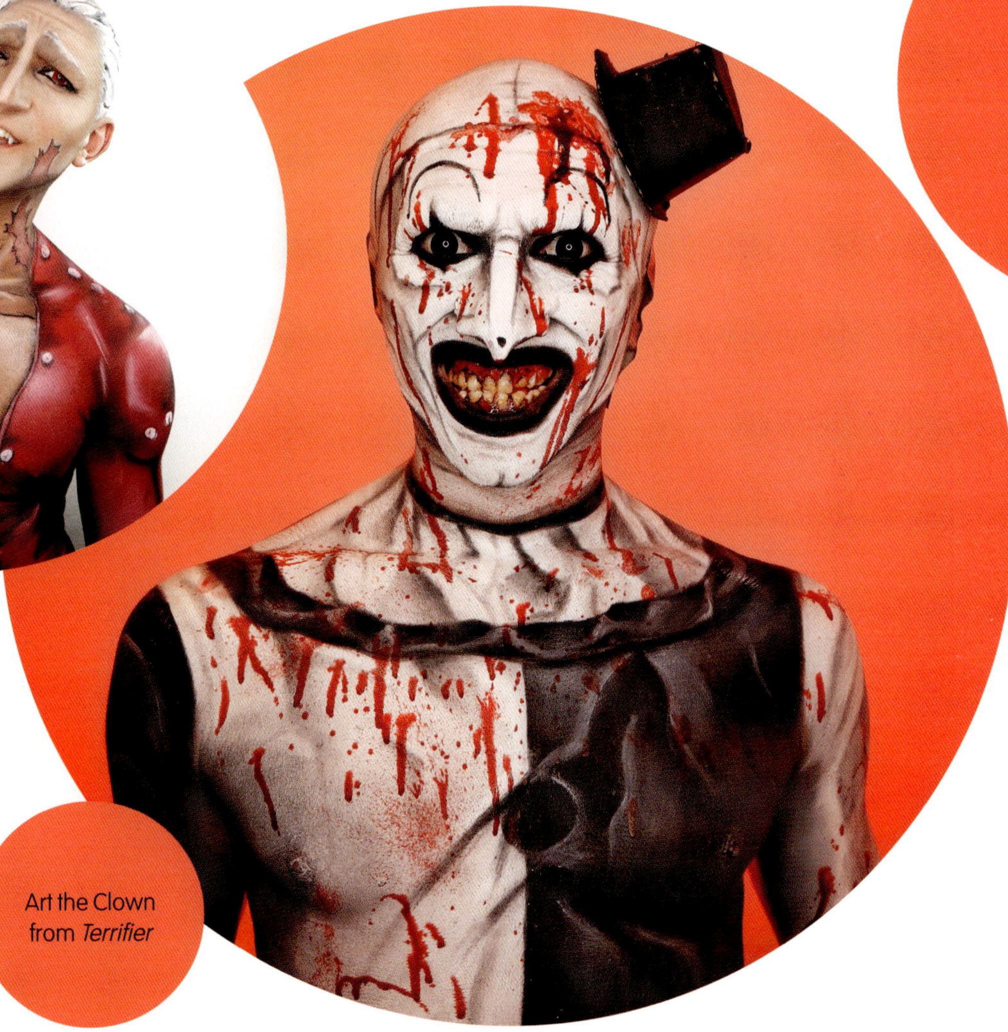

Art the Clown from *Terrifier*

TOOTH ENAMEL DYE

You'd be surprised just how effective something as small as changing your eye color or tooth color can be. Painting tooth enamel is a great makeup skill to learn, as it can really help elevate your look as a final touch. It's used to temporarily change the color of your natural teeth. If used correctly, this should last until the next time you brush your teeth.

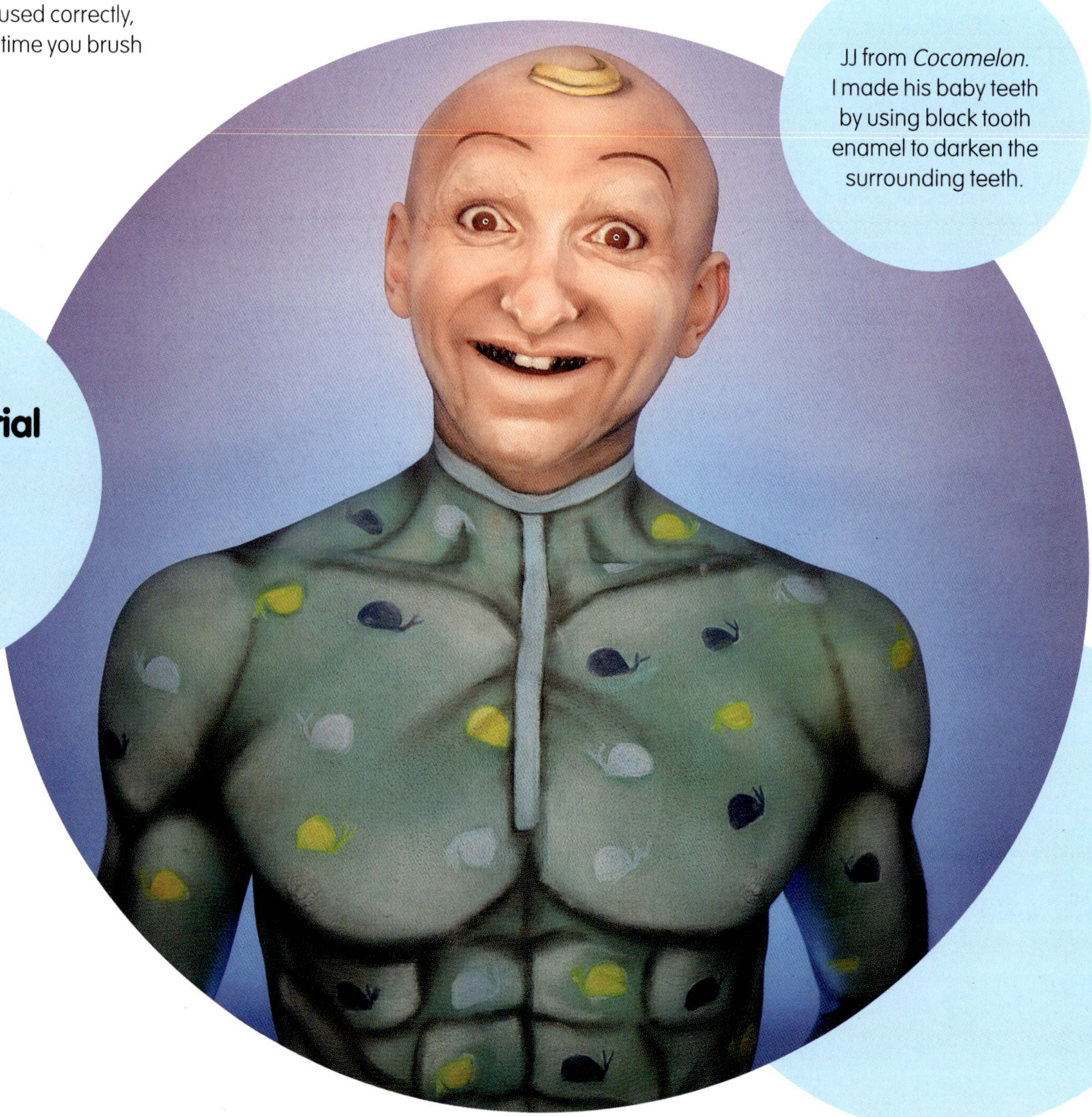

JJ from *Cocomelon*. I made his baby teeth by using black tooth enamel to darken the surrounding teeth.

Scan to Watch a Tutorial

APPLYING TOOTH ENAMEL
STEP BY STEP

To achieve this effect, you'll need just a few things: tooth enamel in your chosen color, some toilet paper or tissues to dry your teeth, and some detail paintbrushes. The enamel product comes with an applicator similar to a nail polish brush but if you want to cover only part of a tooth, a smaller brush will be beneficial.

I'm demonstrating with black tooth enamel, but you can get this product in various colors, depending on the brand. Kryolan and Ben Nye are two of my favorites.

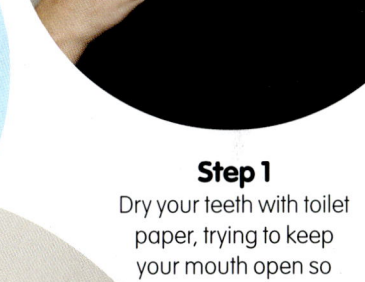

Step 1
Dry your teeth with toilet paper, trying to keep your mouth open so they stay dry.

Step 2
Shake enamel liquid well, then apply a layer of product to your desired teeth. You can apply multiple layers for better coverage.

Step 3
Keep your mouth open and fan your teeth until the enamel dries. This should take around thirty seconds.

Effects You Can Achieve with Tool Enamel

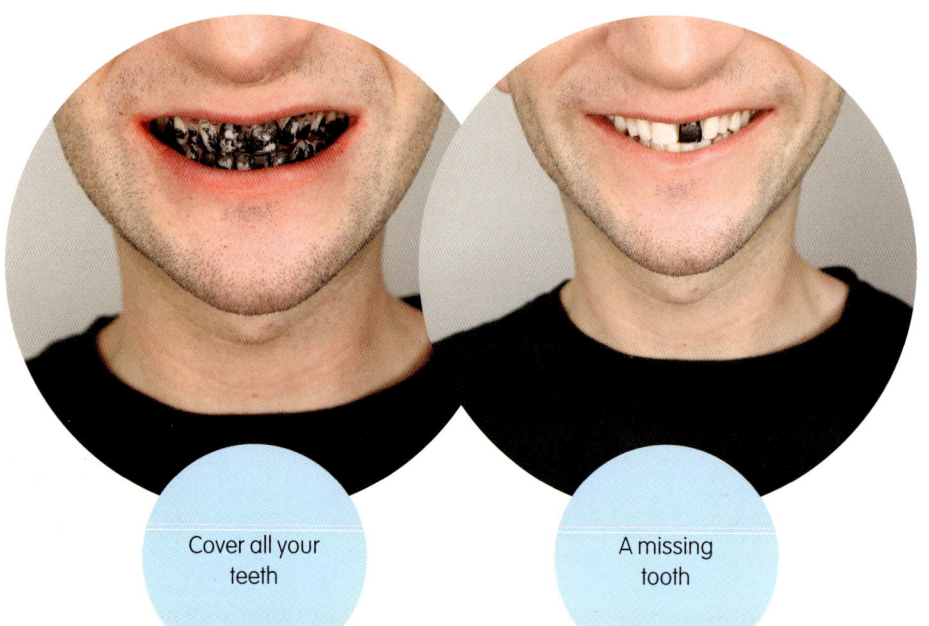

Cover all your teeth

A missing tooth

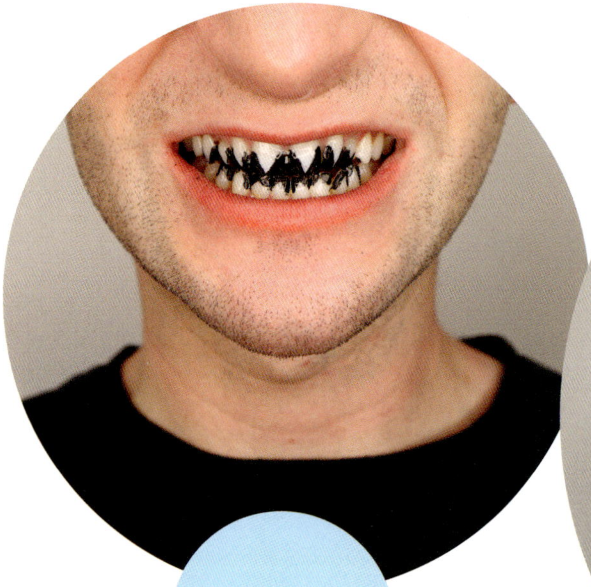

Demon fangs

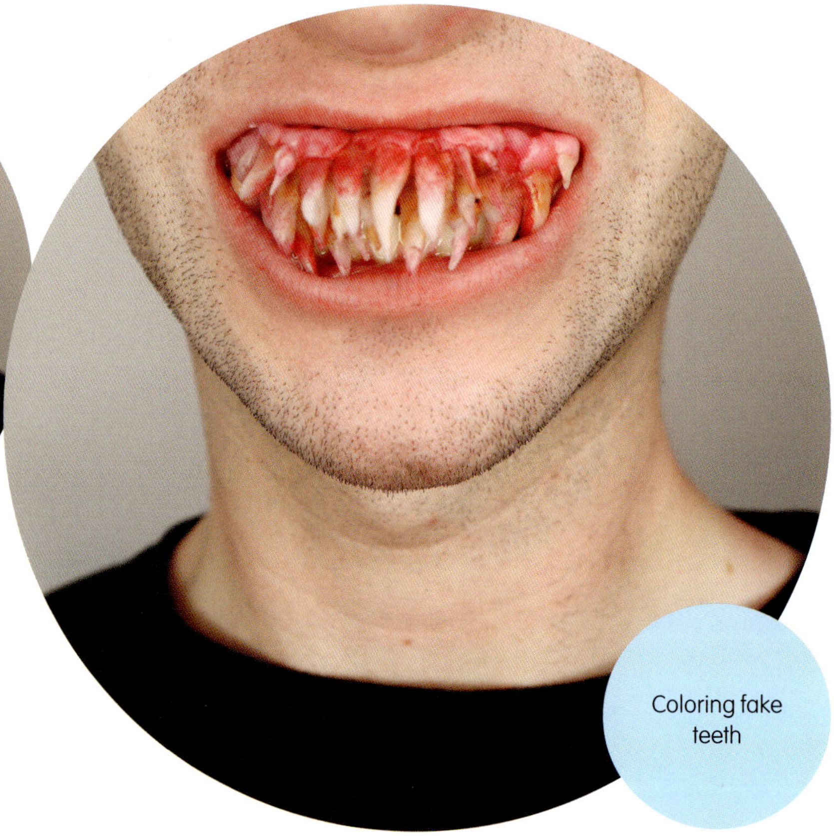

Coloring fake teeth

HOW TO REMOVE TOOTH ENAMEL
STEP BY STEP

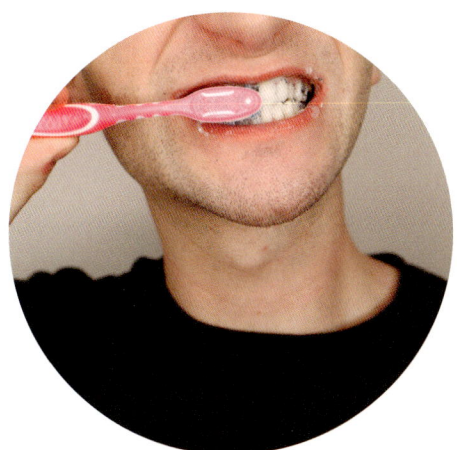

Step 1
Simply brush your teeth, a firm toothbrush will do a better job, and you might need to brush a couple of times.

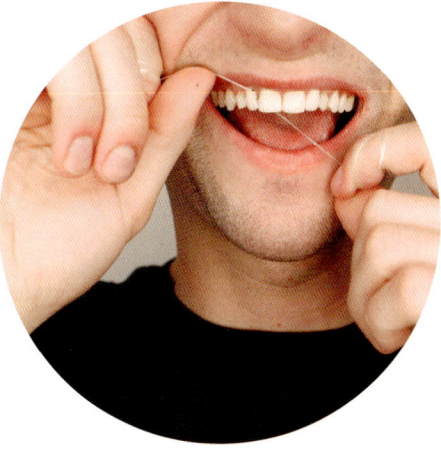

Step 2
You might need to floss as well to get right between the gaps of your teeth.

Safety Tips

Depending on the brand of product you use, the smell can differ, but generally these products have quite a strong alcoholic scent. Ben Nye products have a nice hint of mint.

The product is not designed to be consumed so please be careful not to swallow any of the product.

If you do find that it is irritating you, then remove it straightaway!

If you get the product on your fingers, wash your hands with a nail brush and it will come off just fine.

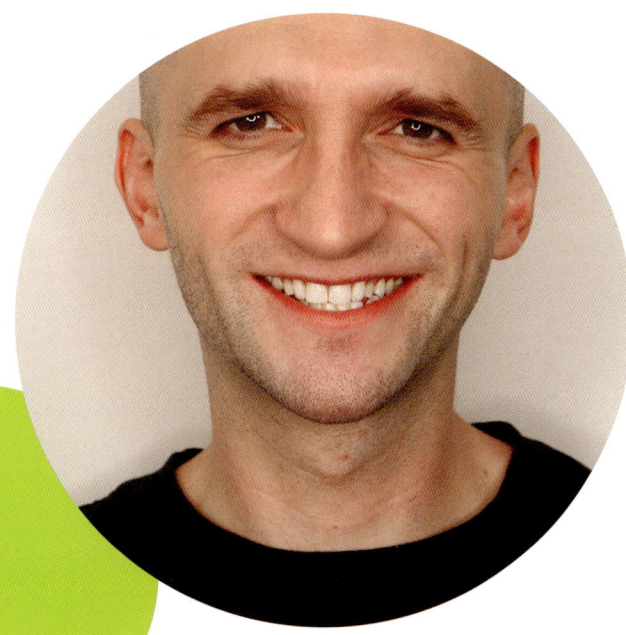

Step 3
You'll see there is absolutely no staining after use.

FAKE BLOOD

Blood is red liquid, what more is there to it? Well, it's a lot more complicated than that! What effect are you going for? Fresh blood? Dried crusted over blood? Blood splatter? The shades will be different, the textures will be different, and it's unlikely you'll be able to use the same product to achieve all of this.

Types of Fake Blood

In this section, we touch on a few different types of blood you can get, how to use them, common mistakes people make when handling fake blood, and how to create your own fake blood if you're working on a tight budget. It's by no means a complete guide as there are hundreds of products on the market, but I can guarantee that by the end of this section, you'll have a better understanding of which products to use and when depending on what you want to achieve.

Please note that a lot of the products in this section **will** stain your clothes. So just be cautious if you use them on clothing.

Scan to Watch a Tutorial

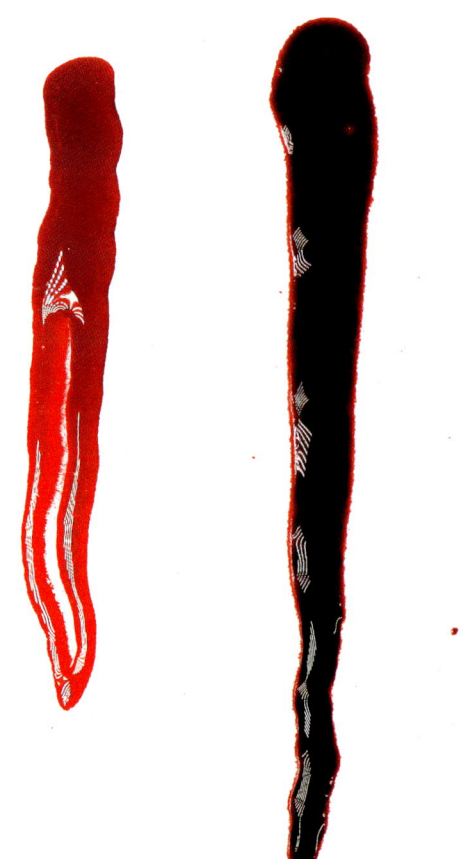
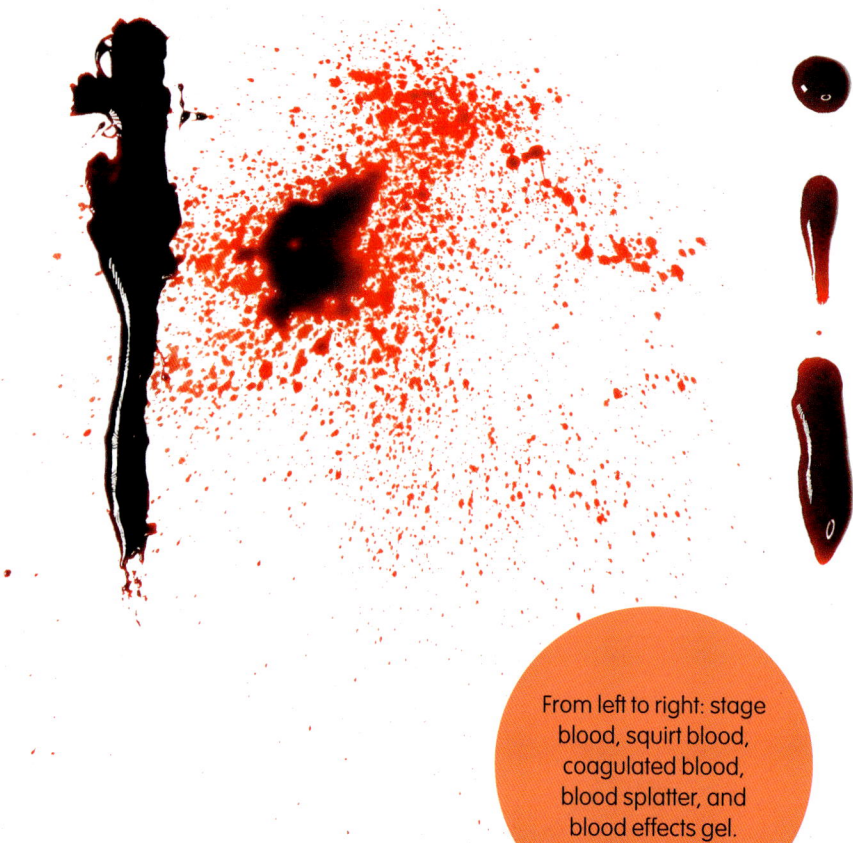

From left to right: stage blood, squirt blood, coagulated blood, blood splatter, and blood effects gel.

Squirt Blood

This blood is a lot runnier than the other fake bloods. It has a thin consistency when wet and creates a splatter effect. You can use this product in an airbrush or spray bottle. When this product dries it crusts like real blood would, and it comes in a brighter shade and a darker shade.

SAFETY TIP: Avoid contact with eyes and mouth.

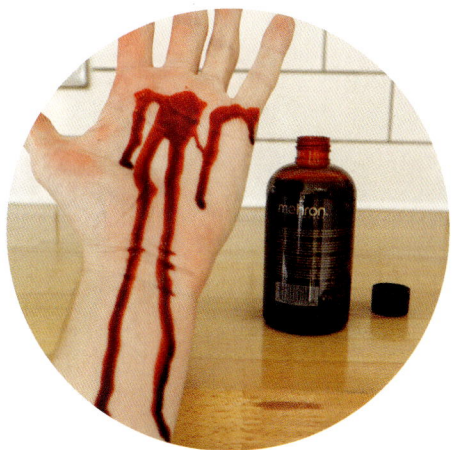

Can be applied directly to skin to let drip.

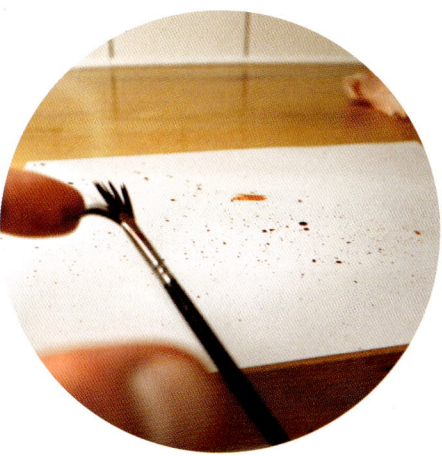

Can be applied with a spray bottle, stipple brush, or stipple sponge.

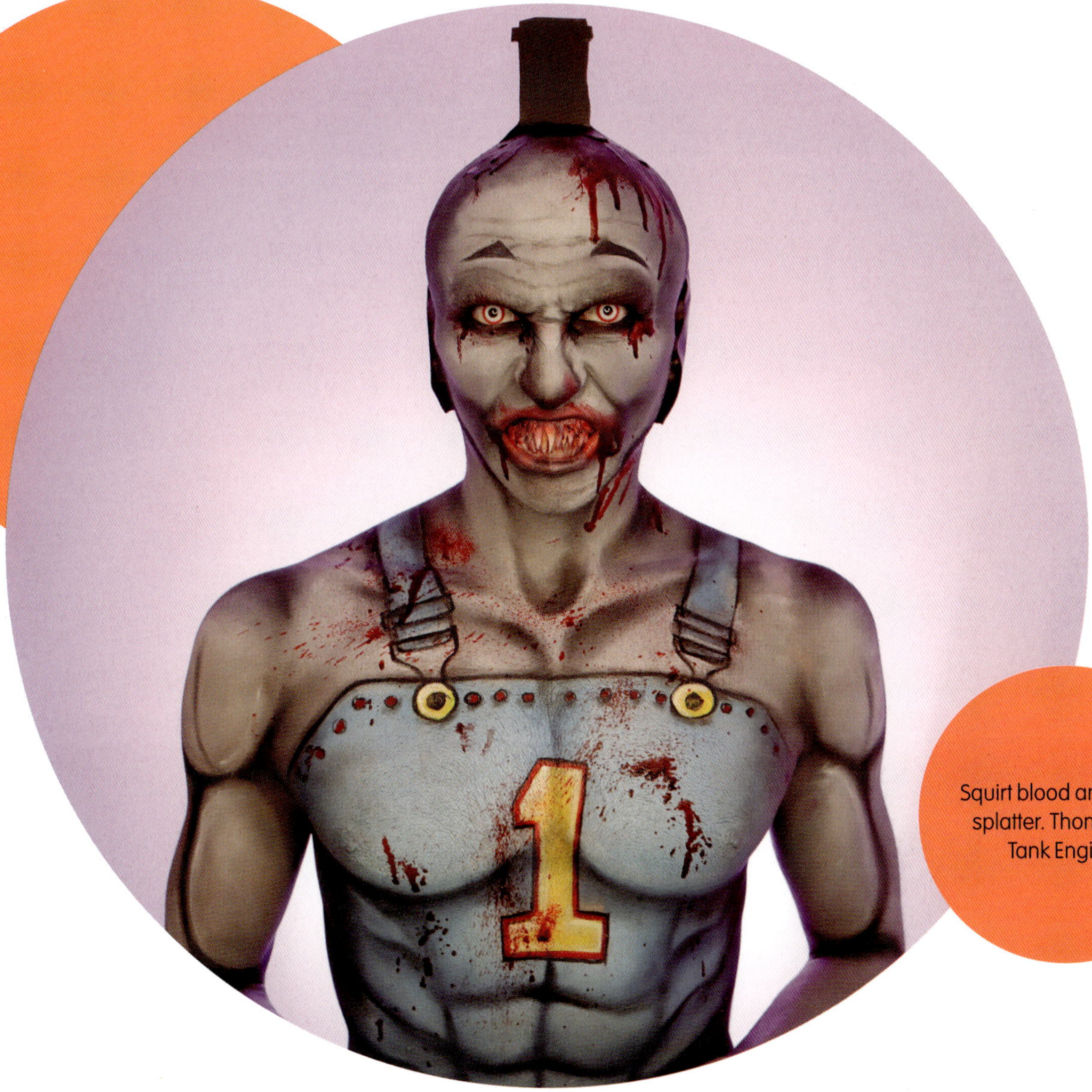

Squirt blood and blood splatter. Thomas the Tank Engine.

Stage Blood

This type of blood has a wet, syrup-like consistency. It will continue to drip as it doesn't dry so bear this in mind if you want to use this for long periods. This product is also edible so it can be used in capsules to achieve the effect of blood dripping from your mouth.

SAFETY TIP: Avoid contact with eyes.

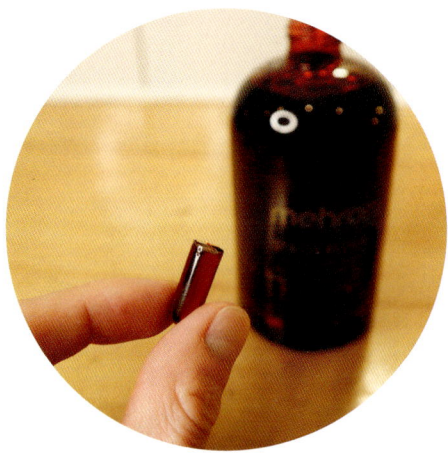

To use stage blood, open an empty digestible capsule, fill it with blood, and close it.

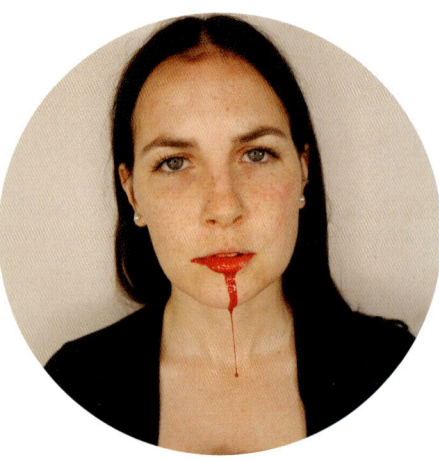

Insert the capsule in your mouth and bite down. The capsule will react with your saliva and dissolve.

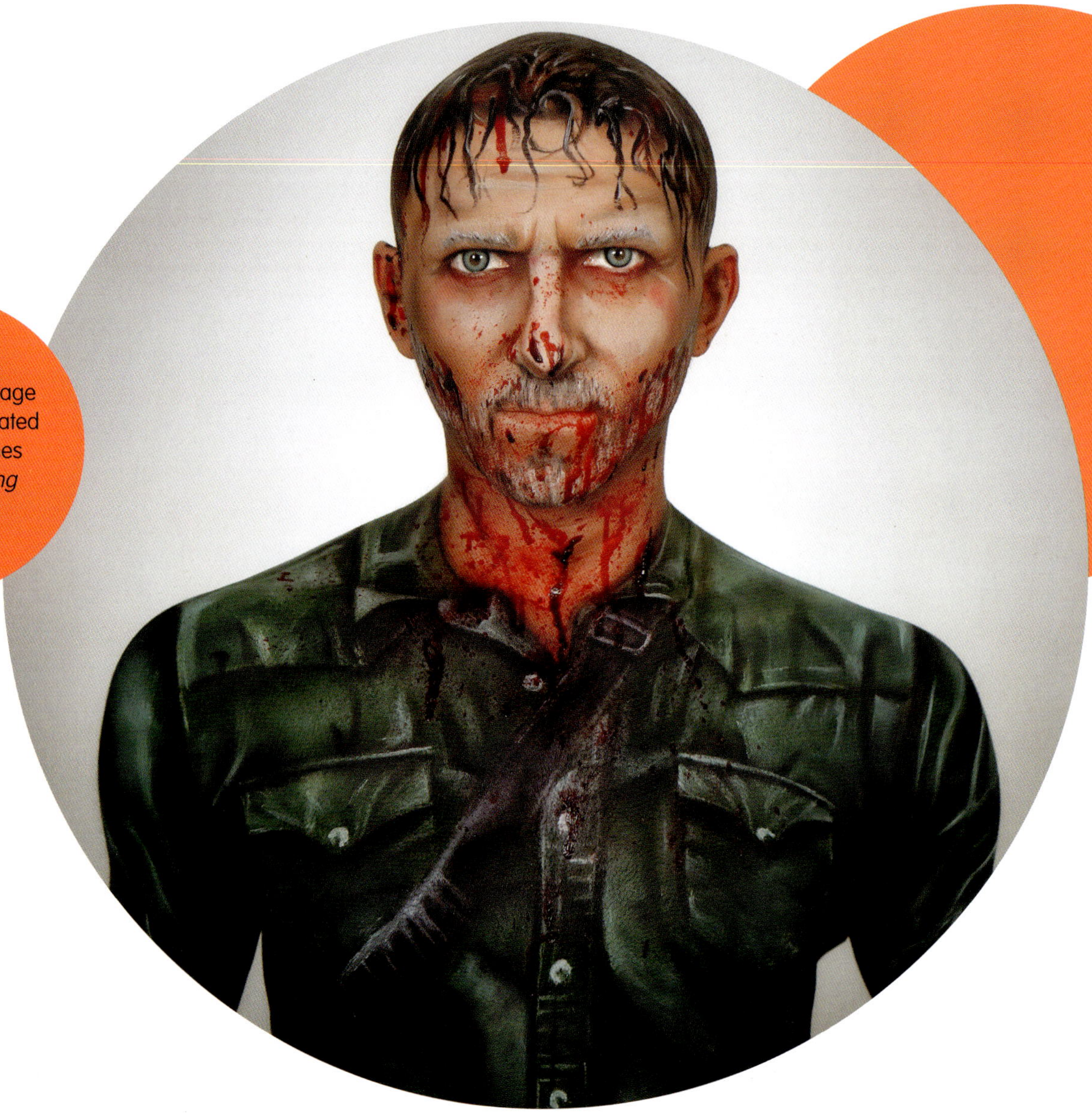

Combination of stage blood and coagulated blood. Rick Grimes from *The Walking Dead*.

Blood Splatter

This is by far the easiest out of all the products to use. It comes ready to spray directly onto any surface in a spray bottle applicator. This product is great to achieve the effect of someone being shot in front of you.

I like to use both methods of application when using this product. I also like to mix this with coagulated blood to create different textures and colors.

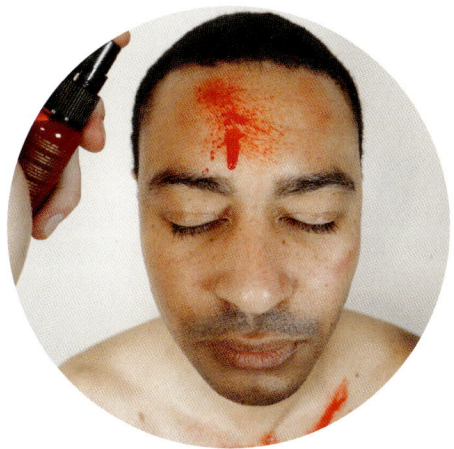

Hold it three to four inches away from targeted area and press down.

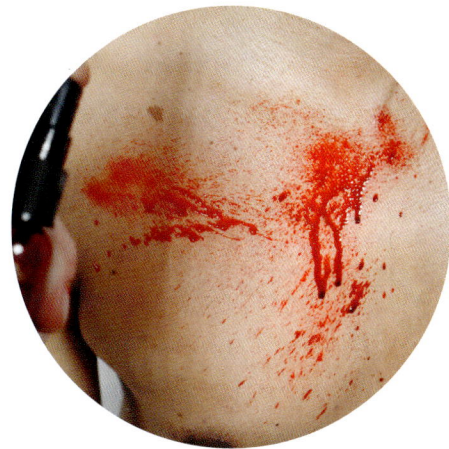

The harder you press the bigger splatter you'll get.

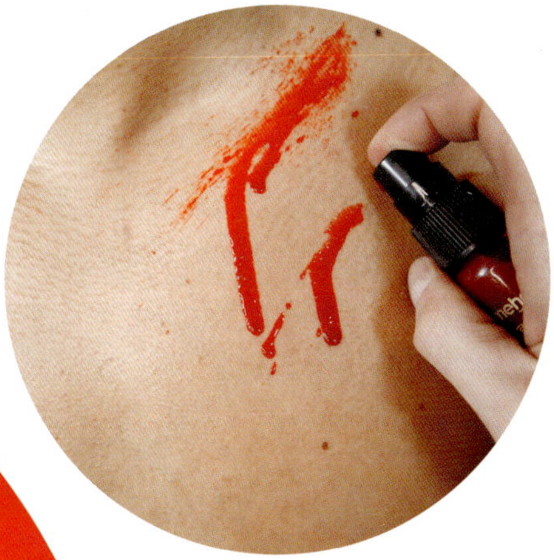

Gently press the applicator to get more of a drip effect.

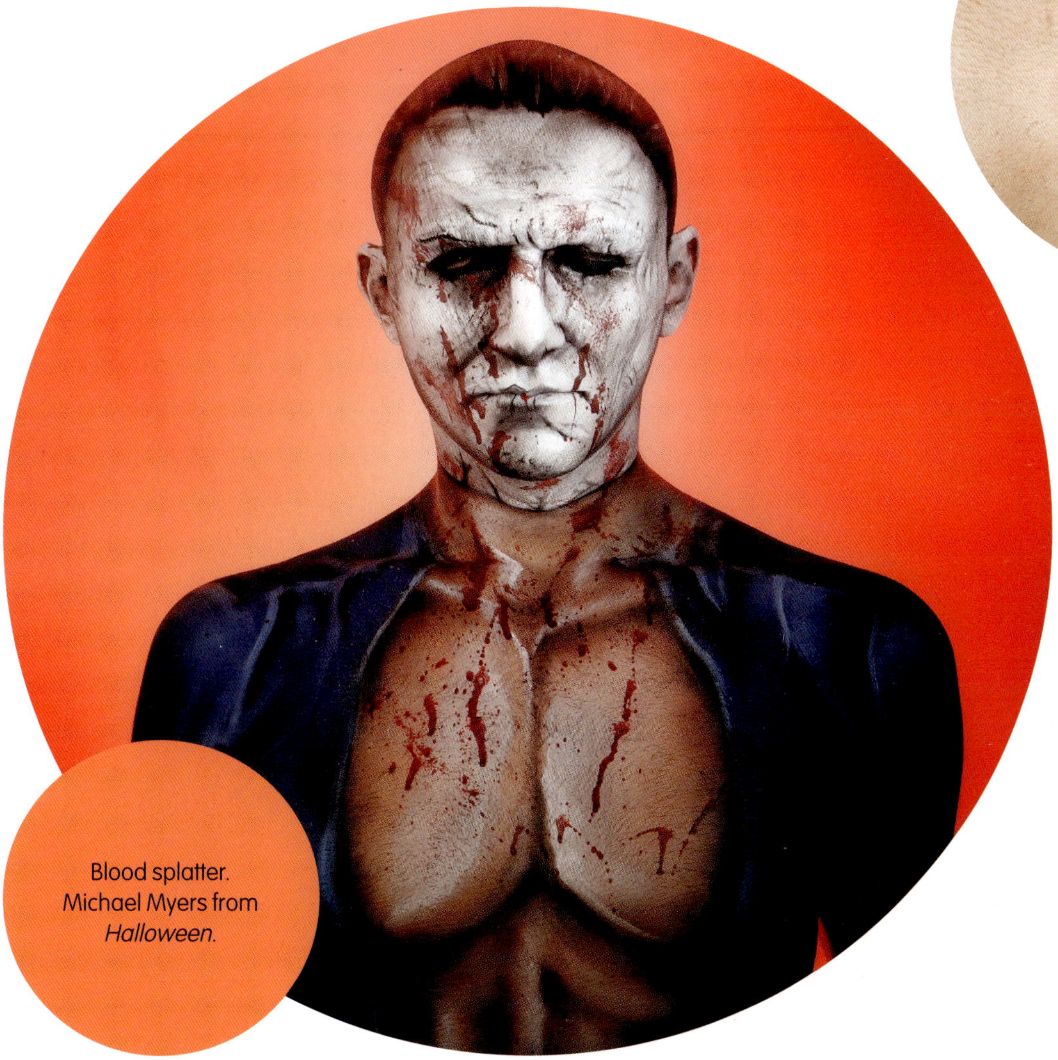

Blood splatter. Michael Myers from *Halloween*.

Coagulated Blood

This product is very thick and very sticky. It stays in place when applied and dries to create a scab-like effect. As this product is so thick, it's great for adding texture to wounds as well.

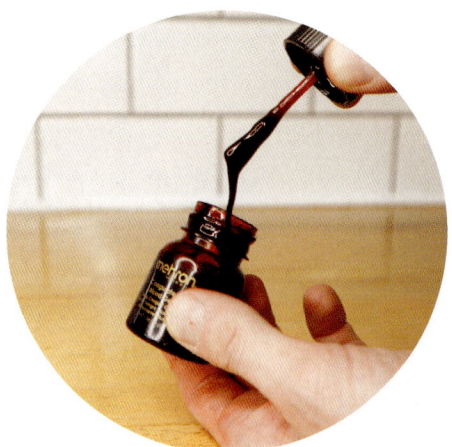

Unscrew cap and use the built-in applicator to apply the product. You can also use a spatula for greater control.

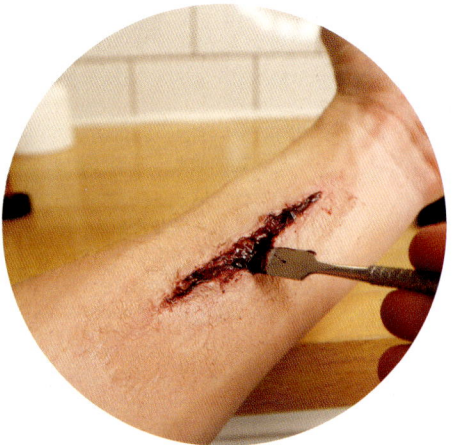

This product is great for creating an open wound effect.

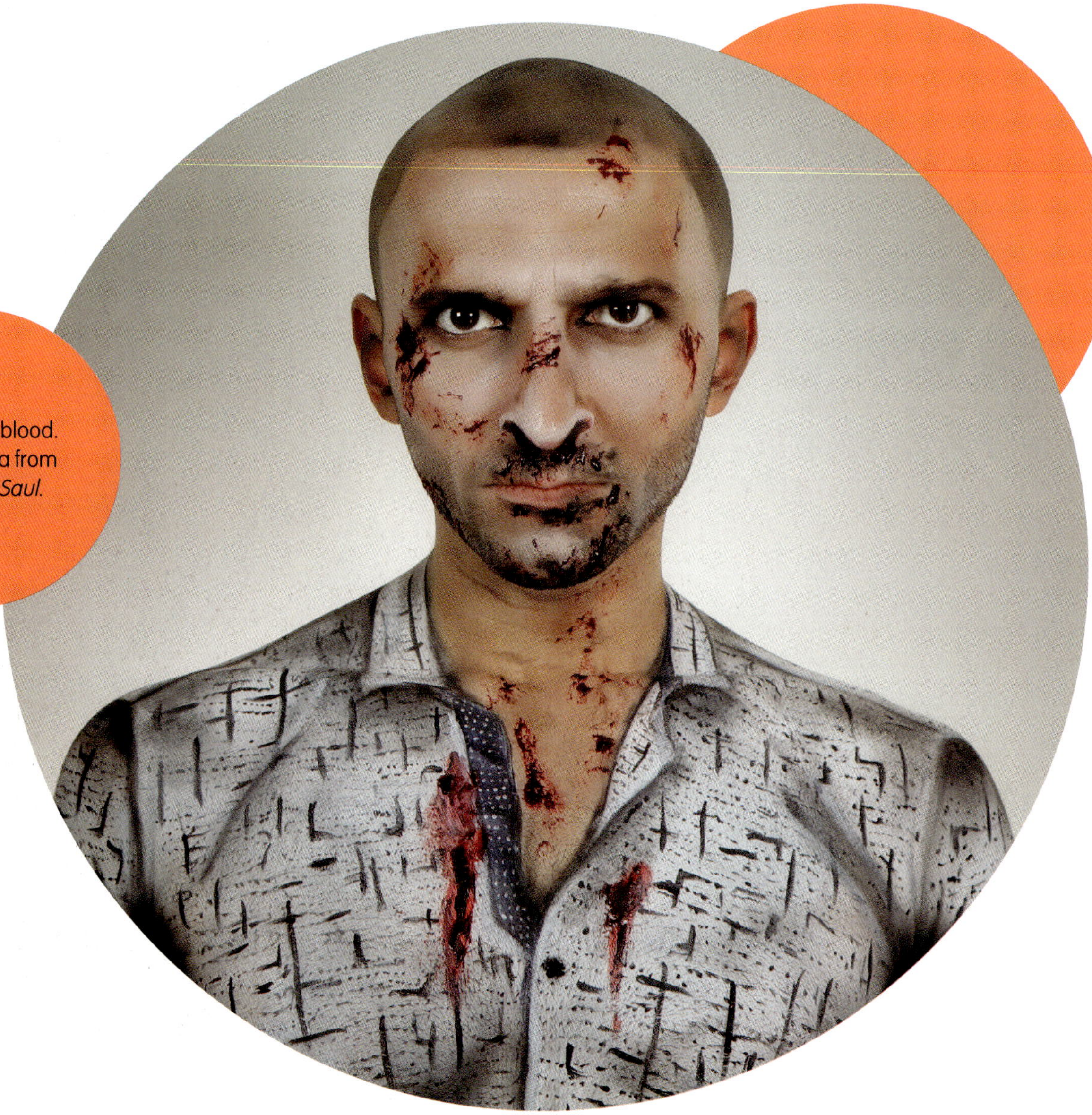

Coagulated blood. Nacho Varga from *Better Call Saul.*

Blood Effects Gel

Unlike the other products we've discussed so far, this product needs to be prepared before using. Warm it in the microwave or in hot water until it liquifies, but be careful not to heat it for too long because the bottle is plastic and could easily melt.

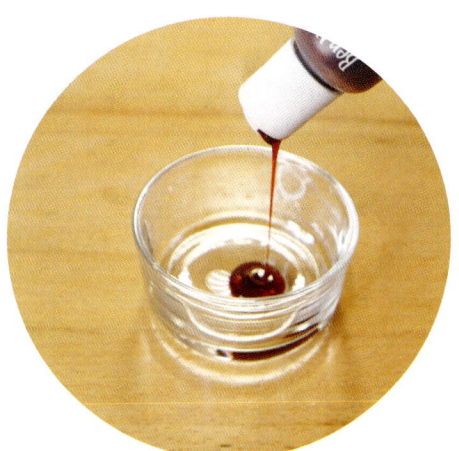

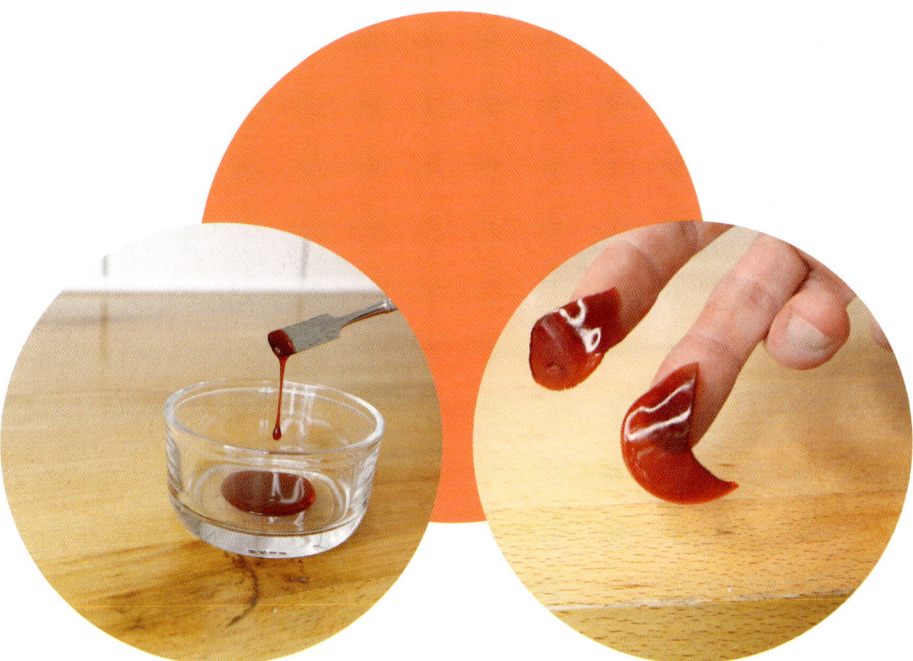

If using a microwave, heat for ten seconds with the lid off and continue with five second increments until fully liquified. Shake the bottle and pour into a small pot. Let it cool before using on skin.

Apply the gel using a spatula. This product dries quickly and is very sticky.

This blood dries as a gel so you can peel it off without any staining. Just be careful to let this product cool before using it directly on your skin. Rather than applying directly onto skin from the bottle, pour it so you can tell how cool the product is before applying.

The Removal Process

All of these products can be removed in the same way. Just wipe off the excess with a wet cloth or makeup wipe.

Fake blood products can be challenging to wash off certain areas of your body. For instance, rougher skin like the palm of your hands will be more difficult to remove than the skin on your wrist. The length of time the blood has been applied for can also affect how likely the product is to stain.

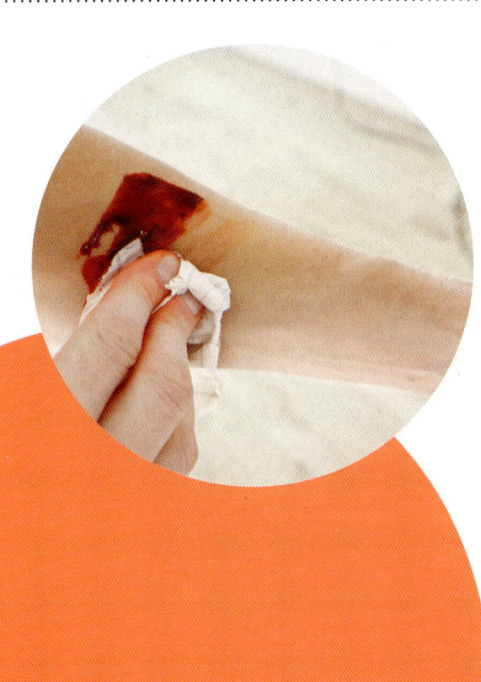

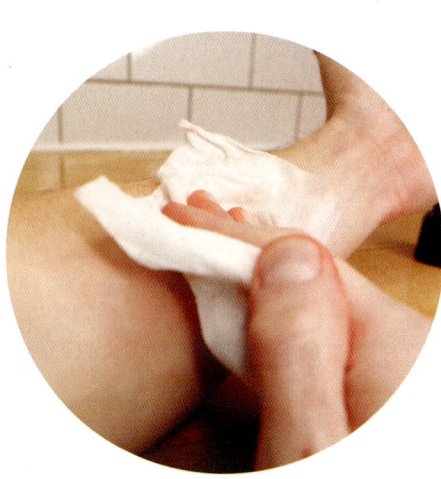

Making Your Own Fake Blood

If you're looking to use fake blood just once, then you might not want to purchase a whole bottle. You can actually create your own fake blood with materials you'll likely already have in your kitchen cupboard. It's also cheaper than buying it. I have to admit it doesn't look quite as effective as the manufactured product, but for occasional use it does the job!

Note that all of these recipes involve food coloring which will stain clothes.

Fresh Blood

This works well for staining clothes with fresh blood stain.

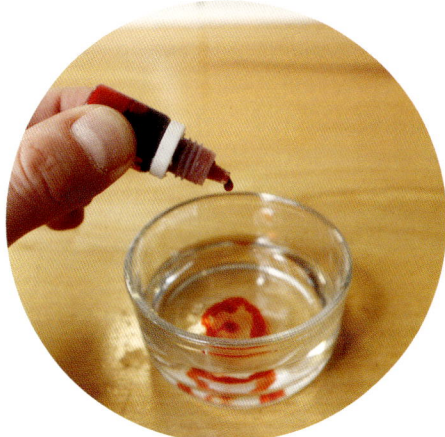

1. Add five drops of red food coloring to ¼ cup water.

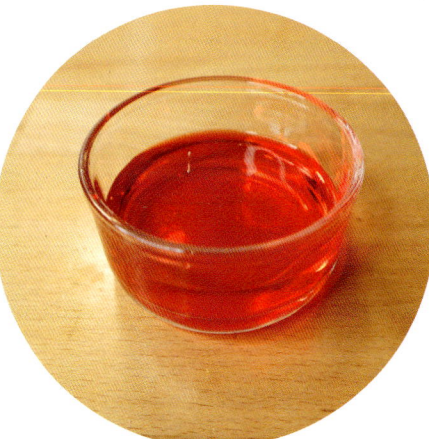

2. The finished product will be very watery and perfect for splattering.

Dripping Blood

This is the most realistic homemade blood visually. It has a very sticky consistency and is most similar to stage blood.

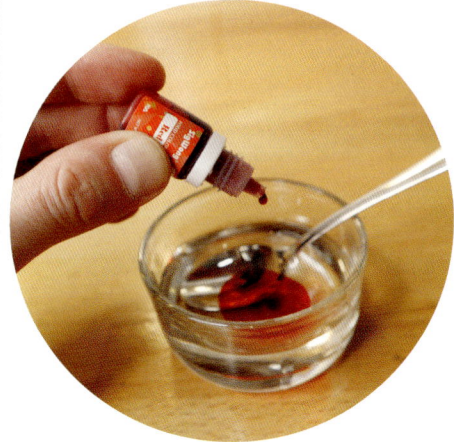

1. Start with two tablespoons of corn syrup and add four drops of red food coloring.

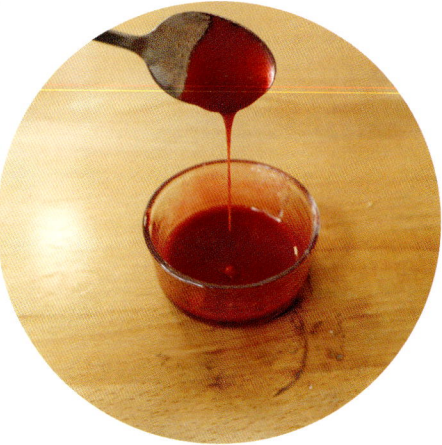

2. Add two teaspoons of powdered hot chocolate or cocoa powder. Add more food coloring or another teaspoon of cocoa powder to darken the color.

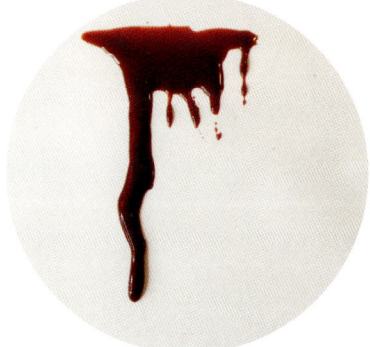

3. The final consistency will be very sticky and great for a dripping blood effect.

Dark Blood

Dark blood spray is good for staining clothes because it's thicker.

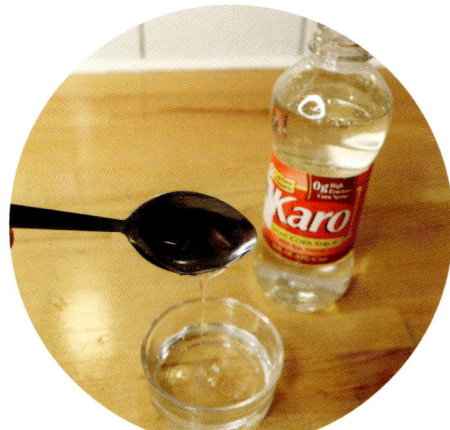

1. Start with ¼ cup water and add ¼ cup corn syrup.

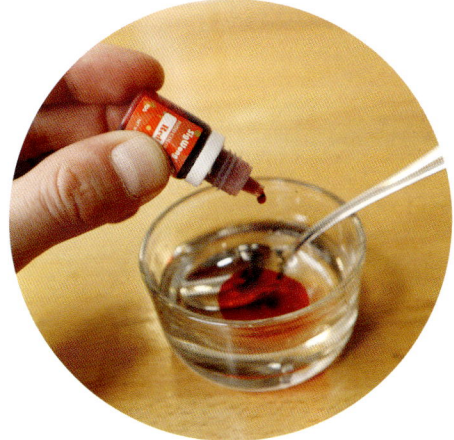

2. Add ten drops of red food coloring.

Tips for Working with Fake Blood

Sometimes less is more. Don't overdo it as it can easily overpower any makeup look you have done underneath.

Try to mix different colors and textures to make it seem more realistic.

Let gravity do its thing. It's unpredictable but it makes it look more realistic rather than perfectly placed blood drips.

If you want your blood to be more gruesome, add onion flakes or dried rolled oats into the mix to add texture.

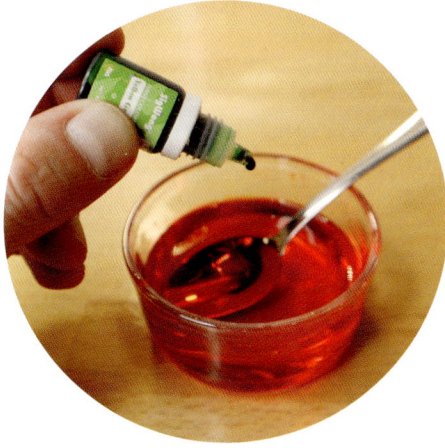

3. To darken the red, play around with adding more food coloring. Experiment with adding one drop of brown food coloring or try mixing in pinks and purples. Add a drop at a time as adding dark colors can quickly overpower the final shade. What works for me might not for you as we might be using different brands and pigments.

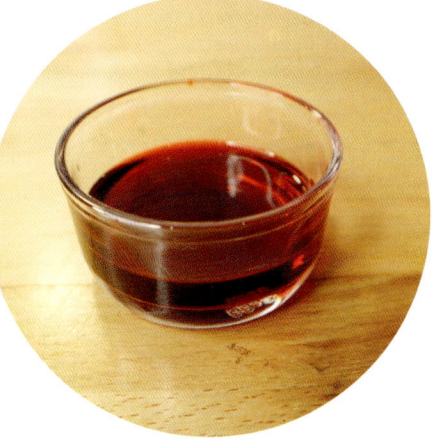

4. The finished product will be much darker and more viscous, but still liquid enough to be sprayed.

RIGID COLLODION

Rigid collodion is this amazing clear liquid that, when applied to the skin and left to dry, puckers your skin, pulling it tighter together and creating a realistic scarring effect.

This product is really popular in the TV and film industry. It creates a realistic finish and is super quick and easy to apply. You can use it to elevate your Halloween costume, cosplay, or any special effects makeup look.

The product I will be demonstrating with is from Mehron however you can also get this product from Kryolan. The product comes with an applicator, similar to nail polish.

Scan to Watch a Tutorial

Tips and Tricks for Applying Rigid Collodion

Think about placement carefully. Avoid areas of skin that are prone to natural movement, for instance around the mouth or palm of your hands. The layer of collodion will likely break and won't last as long an intended.

Avoid placing rigid collodion on top of hair, as this would result in a painful removal.

Don't only apply one thick layer. This will slow the drying process and won't have the same desired effect. Instead, apply multiple thin layers, letting each layer fully dry between applications.

The more layers of collodion you apply, the deeper the scar. The product recommendation states three to five layers, but you can keep applying up to ten layers if you want to achieve a deeper scar.

Be aware of the elasticity of your skin you are applying it to. Applying to looser skin, for instance your cheek, will result in a deeper scar. Areas with tighter skin such as your forehead, nose, and chin won't achieve such a deep scar.

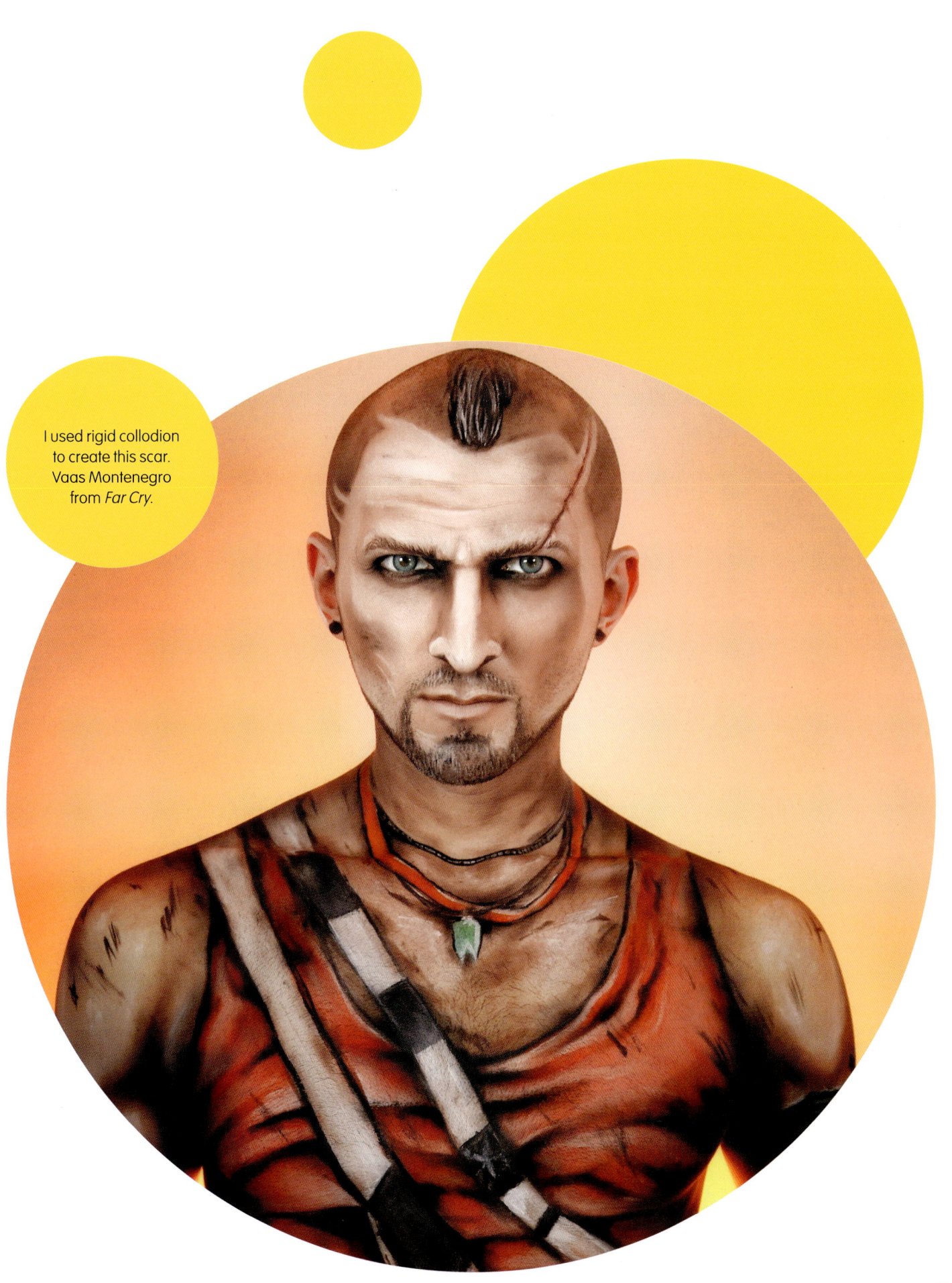

I used rigid collodion to create this scar. Vaas Montenegro from *Far Cry*.

APPLYING RIGID COLLODION
STEP BY STEP

Follow these steps to create a scar that looks scarily realistic.

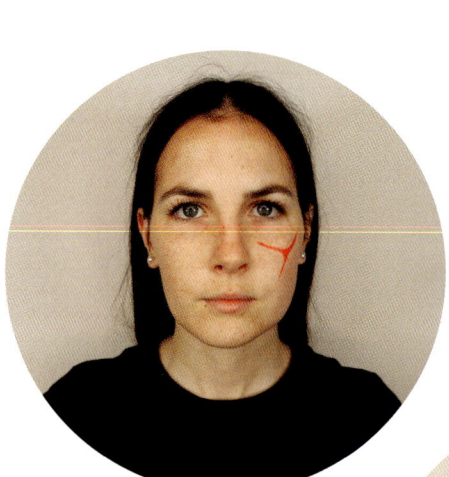

Step 1
Mark with a colored liner where you want the collodion to go.

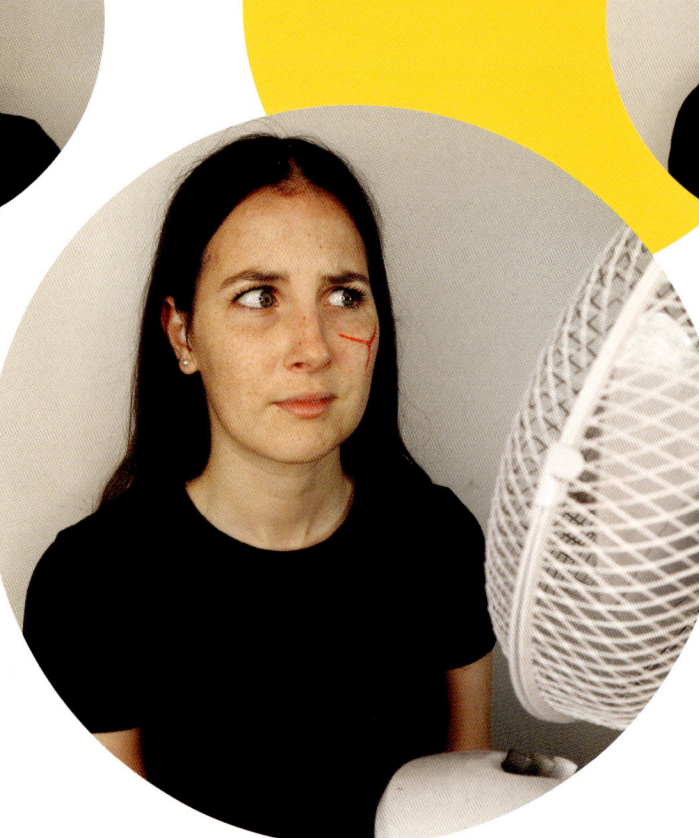

Step 2
Apply the first layer of rigid collodion along the same path as the liner.

Step 3
Allow each layer to dry before applying the next.

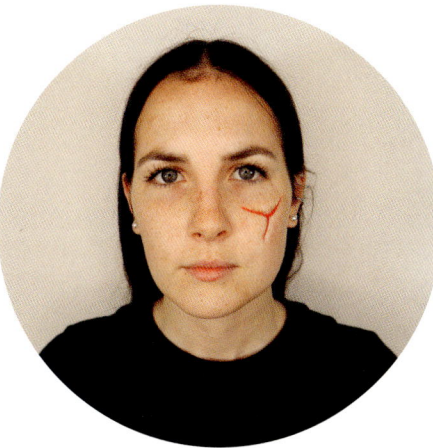

Step 4
Apply three to five layers, depending on how deep you want the scar to be.

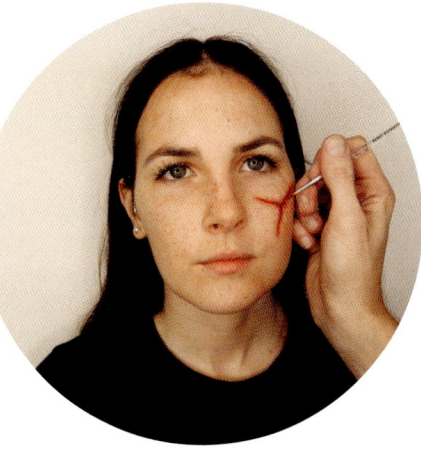

Step 5
Apply additional makeup to really make the scar pop.

Safety Tips

There are a few important safety concerns to keep in mind so you can use this product without harming yourself.

If your skin is particularly sensitive, this product could cause some irritation. Test it on a small patch of thicker skin first, like your forearm or your hands, before applying to your face to ensure you don't have a bad reaction.

Never apply this product around the soft tissue of your eyes, eyelids, or lips. The removal will be very painful.

If you are applying it anywhere near the eyes, get someone to assist you so you can keep your eyes closed. The fumes will irritate your eyes.

This product has a very strong alcoholic smell. Make sure you open a window or work in a well-ventilated room to minimize any inhalation.

To safely remove, use spirit gum remover. Do **not** try to just peel this product off. You will likely peel a top layer of skin off with it. If you're using this product on a regular basis with the same placement, you will eventually cause real scarring, so please be careful!

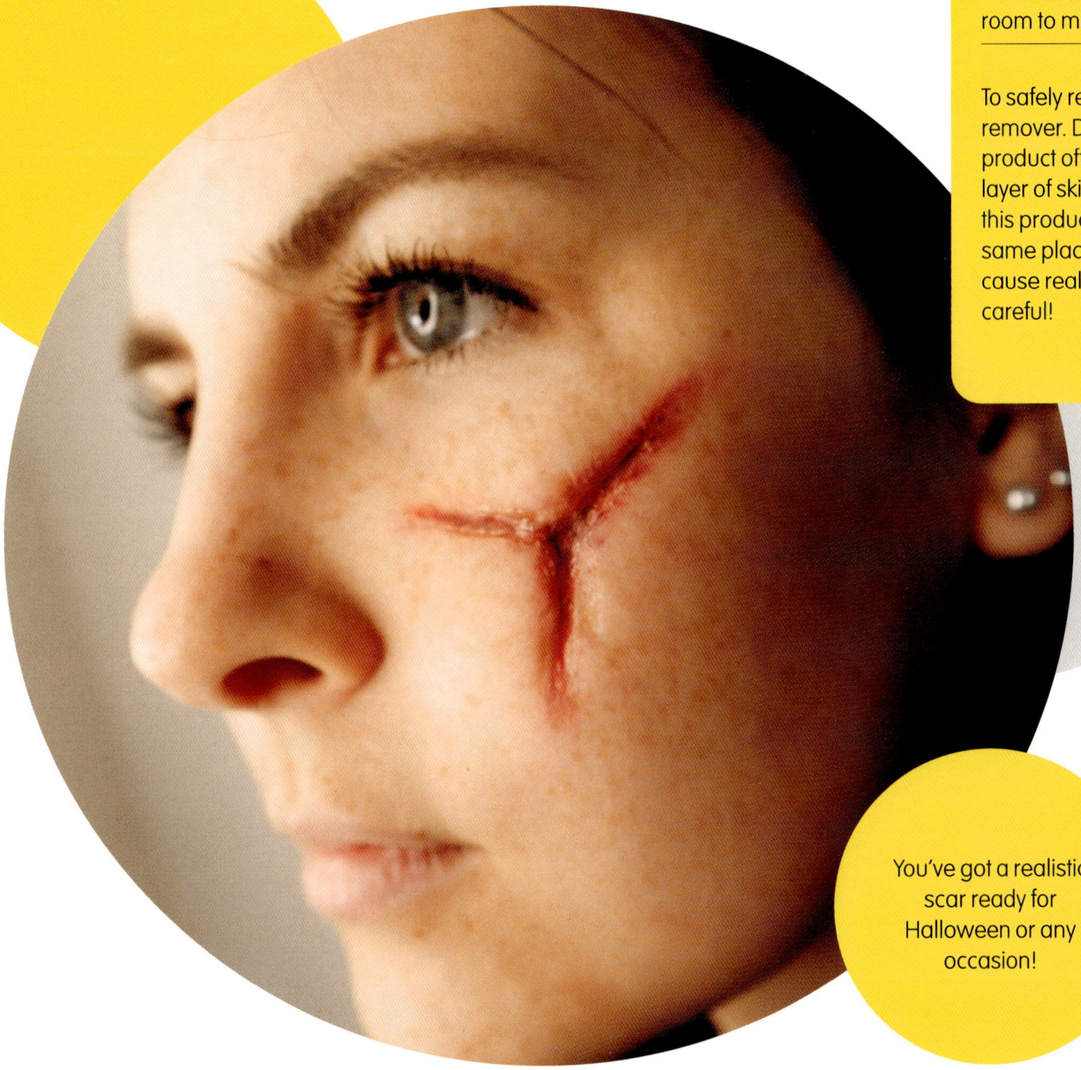

You've got a realistic scar ready for Halloween or any occasion!

HAIR PIN HACK
STEP BY STEP

Here is a trick that speeds up the drying process.

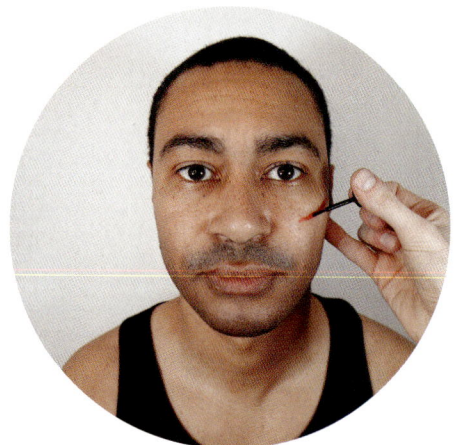

Step 1
Apply your first layer of collodion.

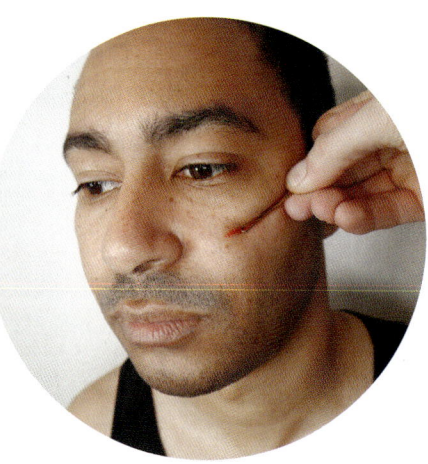

Step 2
While wet, run a hair pin or blunt spatula along the center of the collodion. This helps pinch the skin together and speeds up the drying process.

Coloring the Scar

You can choose to color your scar before applying the collodion or after. You could also do both.

Rigid collodion is a clear product so coloring underneath it will be seen once the product has dried and puckered the skin together leaving a realistic scarring effect. Applying color also allows you to create the desired shape of the scar before applying the product. Use a reddish-purple liner to sketch this out.

Rigid collodion is a very shiny product when dry, so you may choose to apply some additional makeup after application as well. To get rid of the shine, you can use a powdered foundation or setting powder. You may also choose to add fake blood or darker shades of red to indicate dried blood to bring a gore factor to your scar.

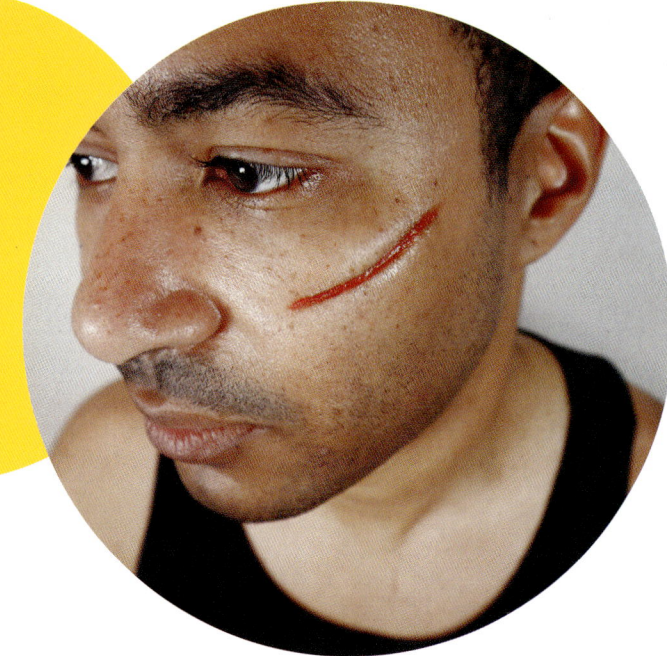

Step 3
Repeat the process for each layer until you end up with a realistic deep scar.

HOW TO SAFELY REMOVE RIGID COLLODION

Please do **NOT** try to just peel this product off. While it will peel off, you will also likely peel a top layer of skin off with it. If you're using this product on a regular basis with the same placement you will eventually cause real scarring.

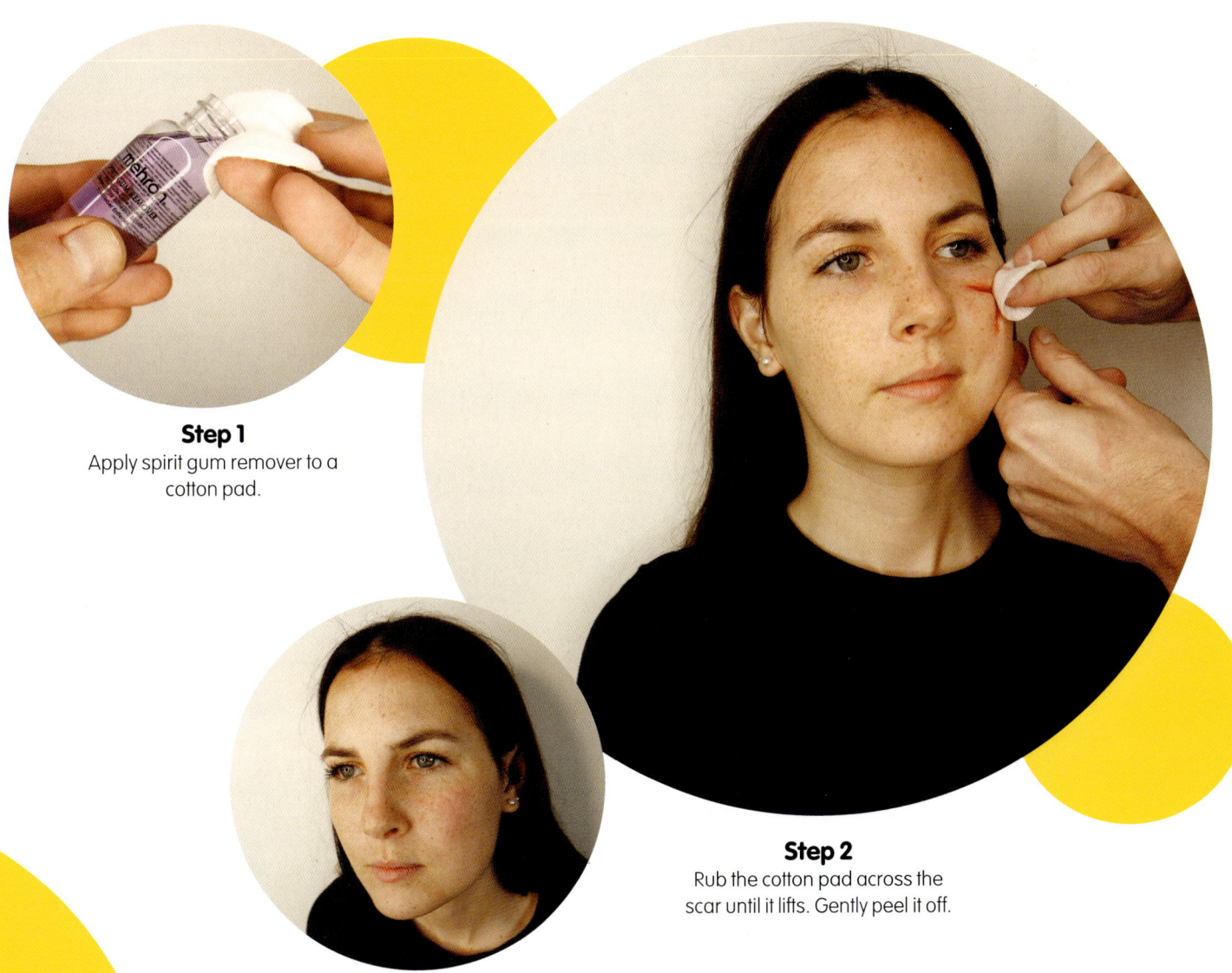

Step 1
Apply spirit gum remover to a cotton pad.

Step 2
Rub the cotton pad across the scar until it lifts. Gently peel it off.

You might find your skin is slightly red due to the liner we applied underneath.

SCAR WAX

Scar wax can be referred to as many different things depending on what manufacturer you get it from. Names include: effect wax, synthetic wax, modelling putty, modeling wax, derma wax, and mortician's wax. The wax brand in this demonstration is Mehron SynWax.

SynWax is a hard wax substance which can be manipulated into a malleable wax to create realistic wounds that move with your skin and body. The first time I used this product I thought I was sent a faulty batch because it was literally rock hard in the pot! Don't panic though. Simply remove it using a metal spatula and warm the product up in your hands then you can manipulate it into any shape you would like.

This product is commonly used in special effects (SFX) makeup to create realistic open wounds, bullet holes, gunshot wounds, vampire bites, warts, and so on. You can also use this product to smooth out the edges when applying prosthetics to the body. Less commonly, it can also be used to cover your eyebrows.

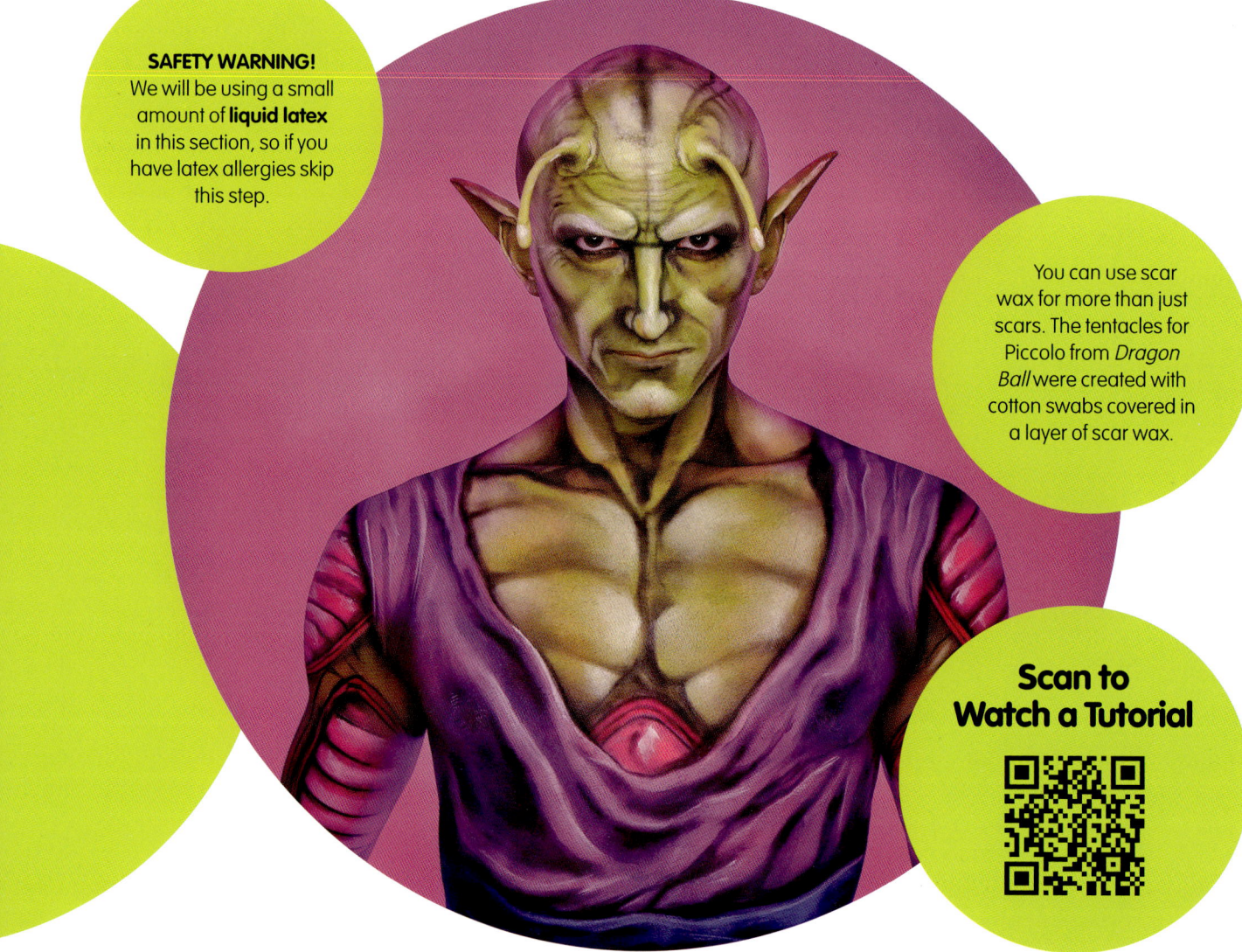

SAFETY WARNING!
We will be using a small amount of **liquid latex** in this section, so if you have latex allergies skip this step.

You can use scar wax for more than just scars. The tentacles for Piccolo from *Dragon Ball* were created with cotton swabs covered in a layer of scar wax.

Scan to Watch a Tutorial

USING SCAR WAX
STEP BY STEP

What You Need

SynWax

Fixative "A"

Liquid latex

Colorset powder

Metal spatula

Petroleum jelly

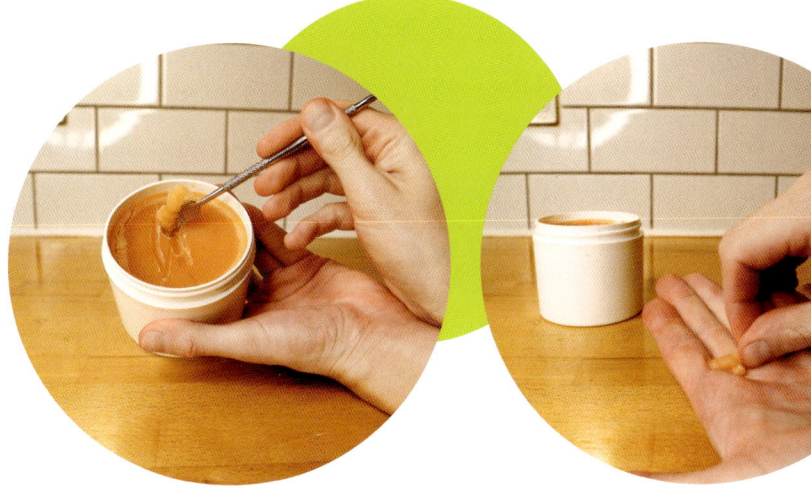

Step 1
Remove product with metal spatula.

Step 2
Roll product between your hands to warm it up until it becomes malleable.

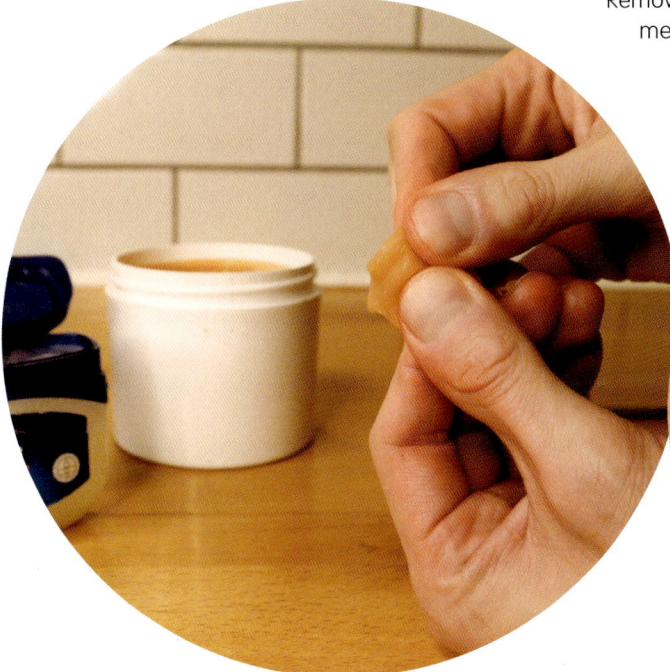

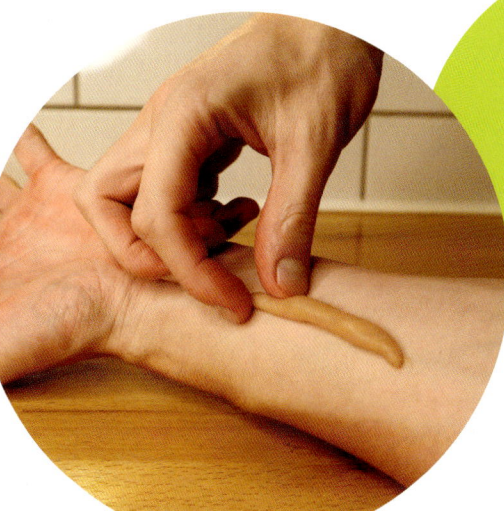

Step 3
Add one part petroleum jelly (like Vaseline) to two parts SynWax to make this product easier to work with.

Step 4
When there are no hard lumps, roll into the desired shape and apply to skin.

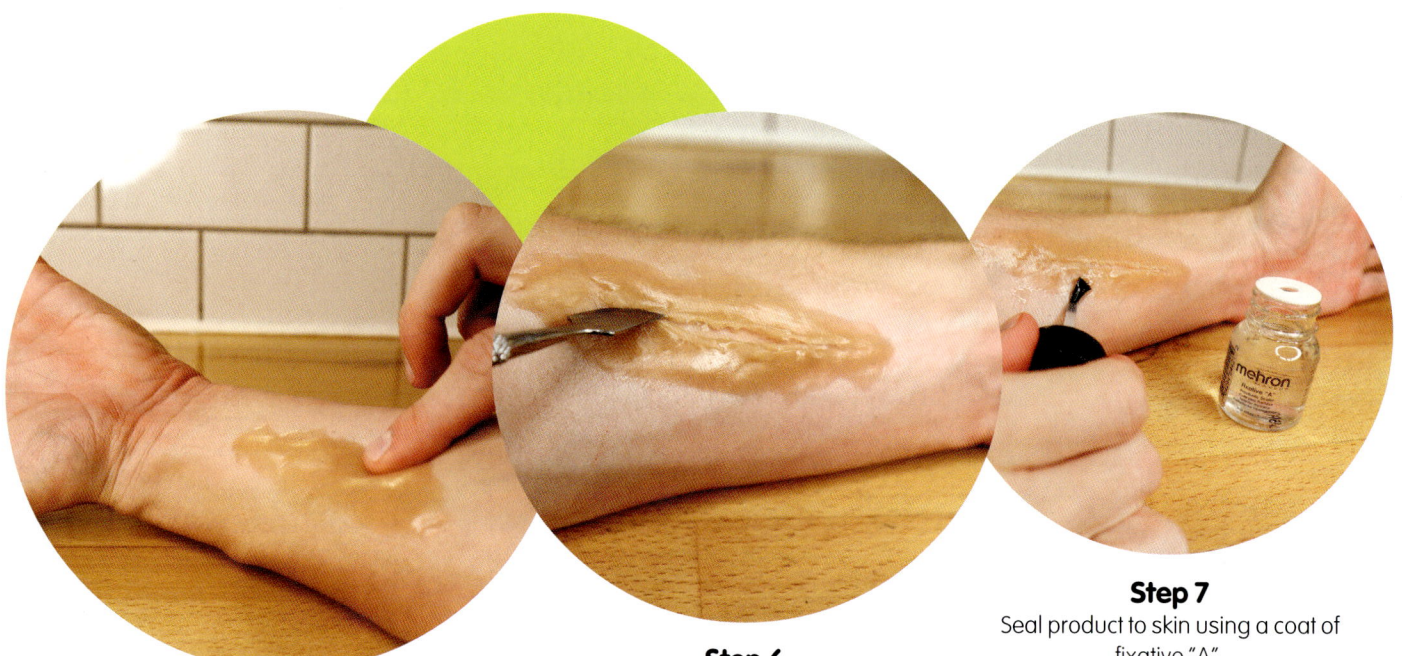

Step 5
Smooth the edges of the product out seamlessly so it looks like it's part of the skin. Covering your finger in the petroleum jelly helps this process.

Step 6
Use a spatula to carve out the shape of the open wound.

Step 7
Seal product to skin using a coat of fixative "A".

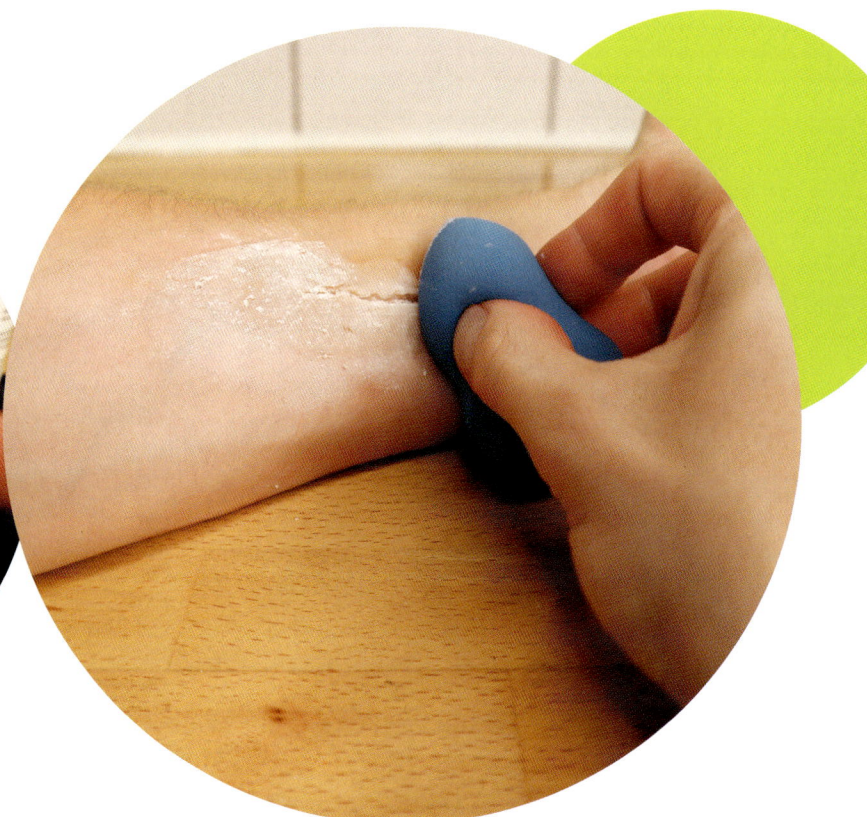

Step 8
Apply a thin layer of liquid latex.

Step 9
Powder the product to remove the shine of the latex.

HOW TO PAINT OVER WAX
STEP BY STEP

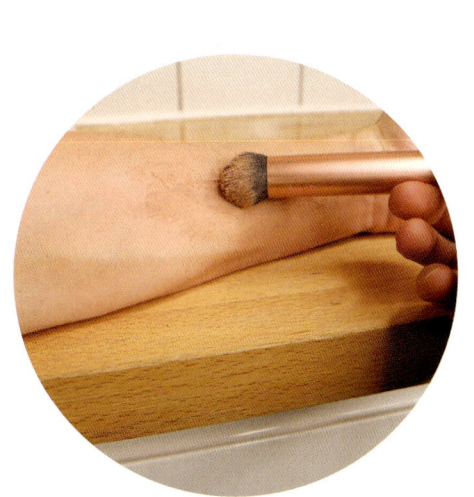

Step 1
Use a layer of foundation to get an even base.

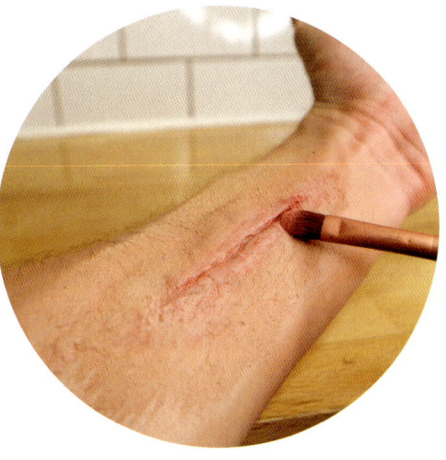

Step 2
Start with a pinkish red base for the inside of the wound.

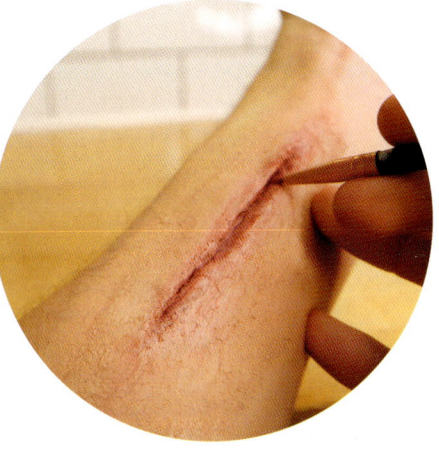

Step 3
Use a darker red to paint deep inside the wound to demonstrate depth.

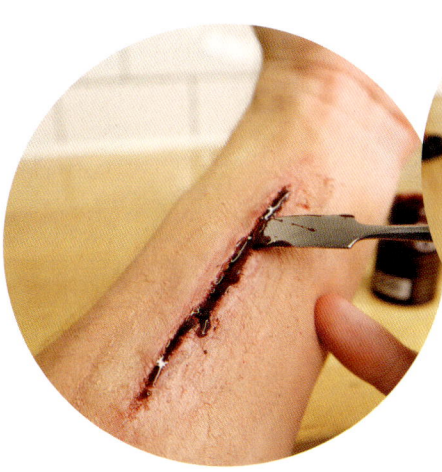

Step 4
Apply some coagulated blood or blood gel to make it look like a fresh wound.

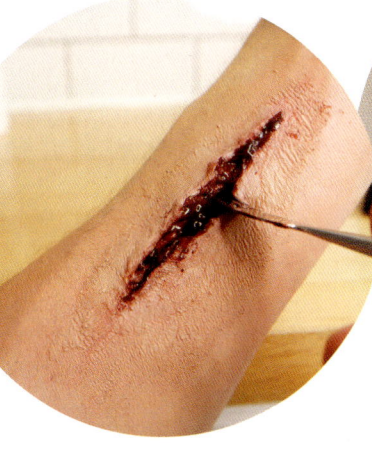

Step 5
Use the spatula to stretch out the wound.

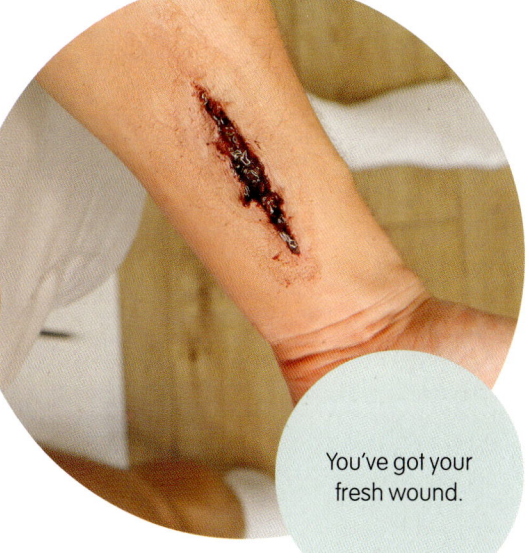

You've got your fresh wound.

Removing Scar Wax
First, wipe off the excess fake blood using toilet paper. Scrape off the wax using a non-sharp metal spatula. Any remaining wax can be removed with makeup remover liquid or wet wipes.

LIQUID LATEX

When liquid latex reacts with the air and dries, it solidifies and turns into a stretchy rubber-like material. This product is predominantly used in the SFX makeup world and prosthetics creation and application.

A few **safety warnings** before we get into the nitty gritty. First, use it in a well-ventilated room. This product has a very pungent smell, and it's not pleasant. Second, people with latex allergies can have an allergic reaction from inhaling latex particles alone so please, please, *please*, be careful if you are working with this product around someone who is allergic to latex. Symptoms of an allergic reaction include skin irritation, rash, hives, runny nose, and difficulty breathing.

Make sure you are using liquid latex which has been modified for cosmetic purposes. I prefer Mehron. Non-cosmetic liquid latex contains **twice** the amount of ammonia, which will burn your skin if applied directly to it.

A practical tip before we get into it. Expect to throw away your brushes and sponges after using them because when liquid latex dries, it's virtually impossible to remove from a brush or sponge. So, use ones you don't mind getting rid of when you're done.

Let's get cracking!

Scan to Watch a Tutorial

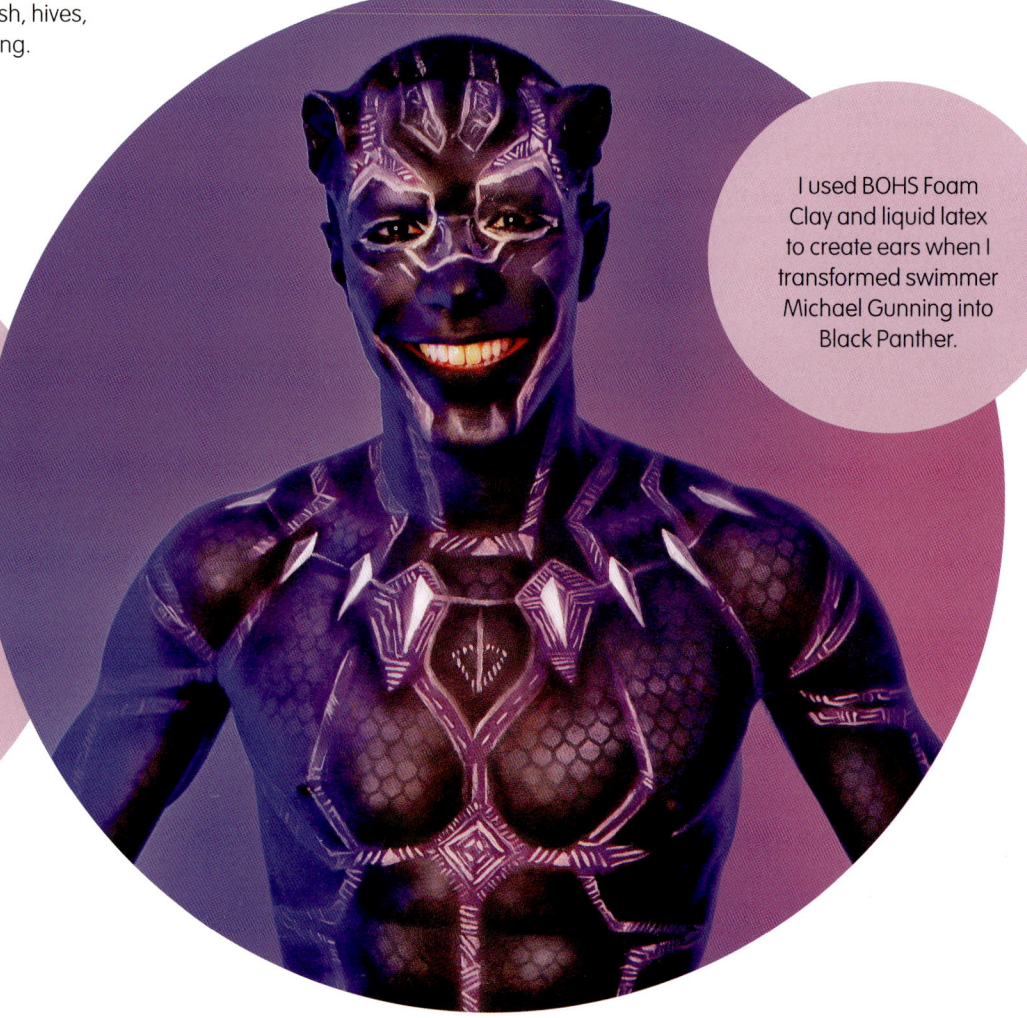

I used BOHS Foam Clay and liquid latex to create ears when I transformed swimmer Michael Gunning into Black Panther.

LATEX AND TOILET PAPER
STEP BY STEP

You can build cuts and scars directly onto your face by mixing liquid latex with toilet paper.

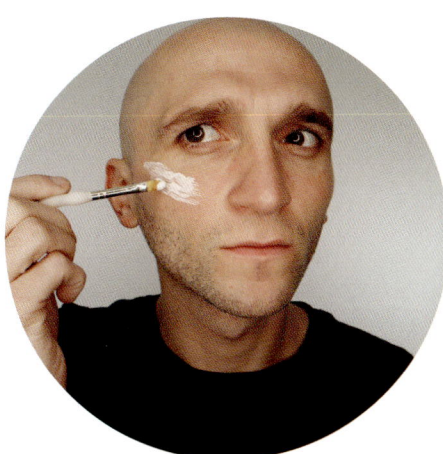

Step 1
Separate toilet paper into single-ply sheets and rip them into small pieces. Apply a layer of liquid latex onto your face where you want the scar to be.

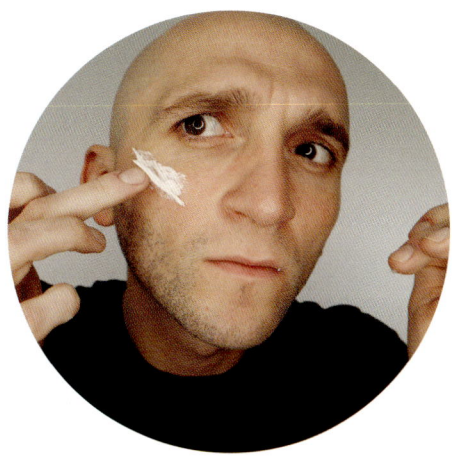

Step 2
While your cheek is still wet, build up the toilet paper onto this area.

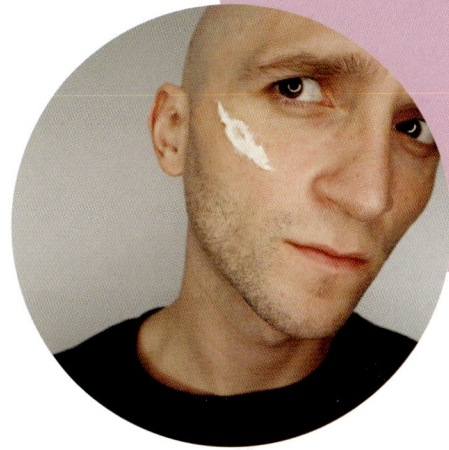

Step 3
Keep building this up until you have the desired shape.

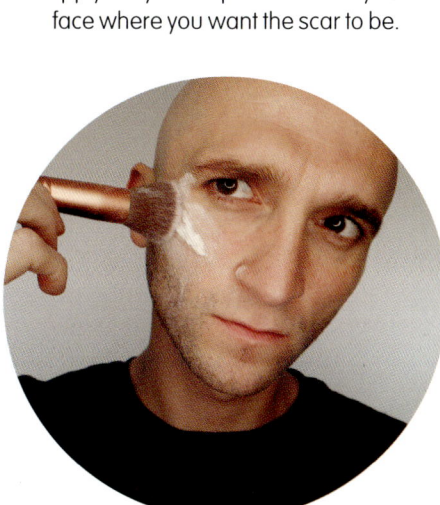

Step 4
Let this dry and cover in setting powder.

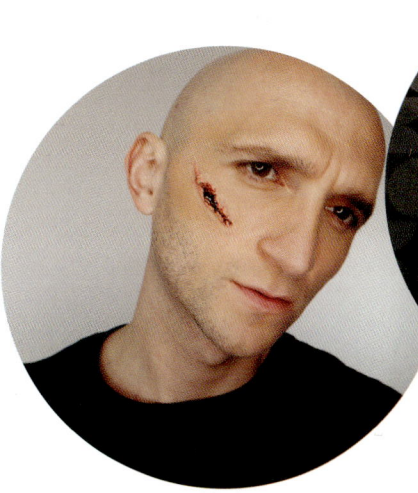

Step 5
You can then decorate this to make it look more like a realistic scar.

If you need to create many scars for different people, you can do this process on a plastic tray and then peel them off once fully dried, then glue them to your skin as prosthetics.

SLIT METHOD
STEP BY STEP

The slit method is also applied directly onto your skin, but please take care not to cut yourself, as you will be using scissors to slit the paper with this method.

While this method can look effective, it is more difficult to seamlessly blend in with your natural skin.

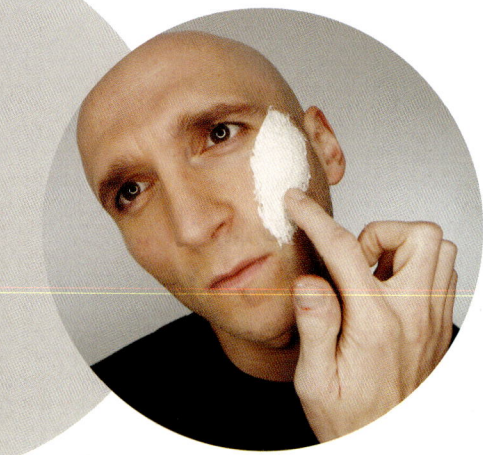

Step 1
Layer up liquid latex and toilet paper, three or four times. Let dry and set it with setting powder.

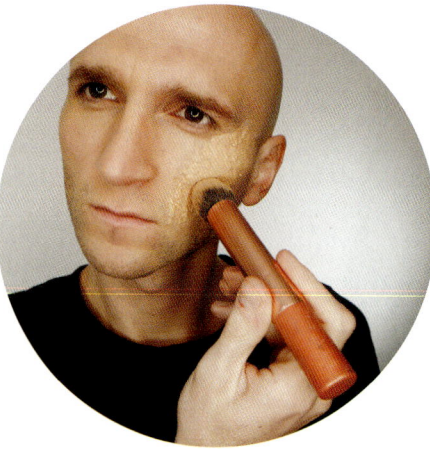

Step 2
Cover with a layer of foundation to blend in with your skin.

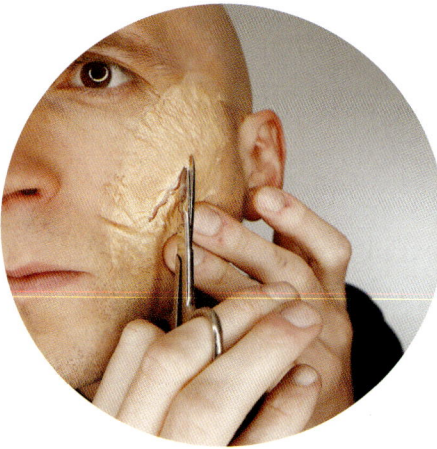

Step 3
Carefully cut a slit into this with scissors without cutting your cheek.

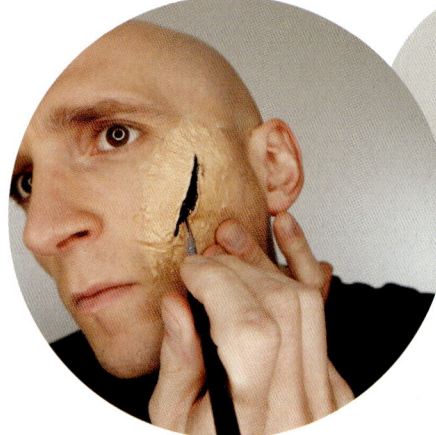

Step 4
Add black paint inside the cut and shade the outside to make it look irritated.

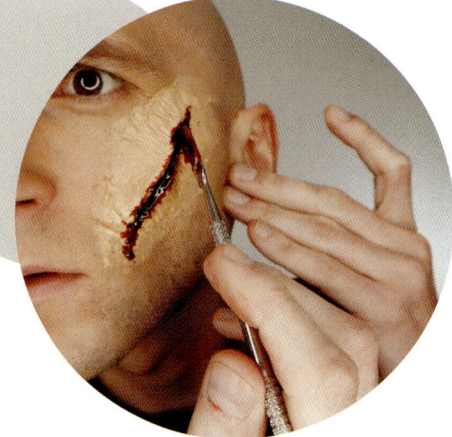

Step 5
Add some coagulated blood inside the wound, and stage blood for some drip.

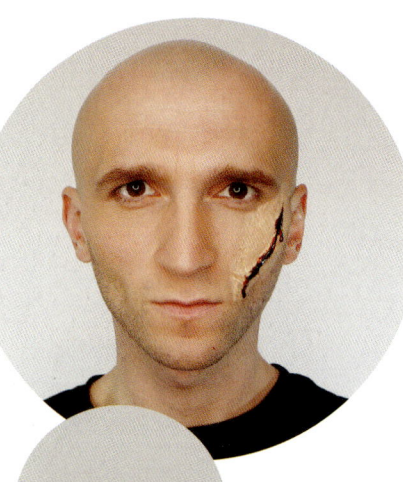

The finished result.

LATEX AND COTTON BALLS
STEP BY STEP

Follow the same process as the slit method on page 96 but with cotton balls for slightly different texture.

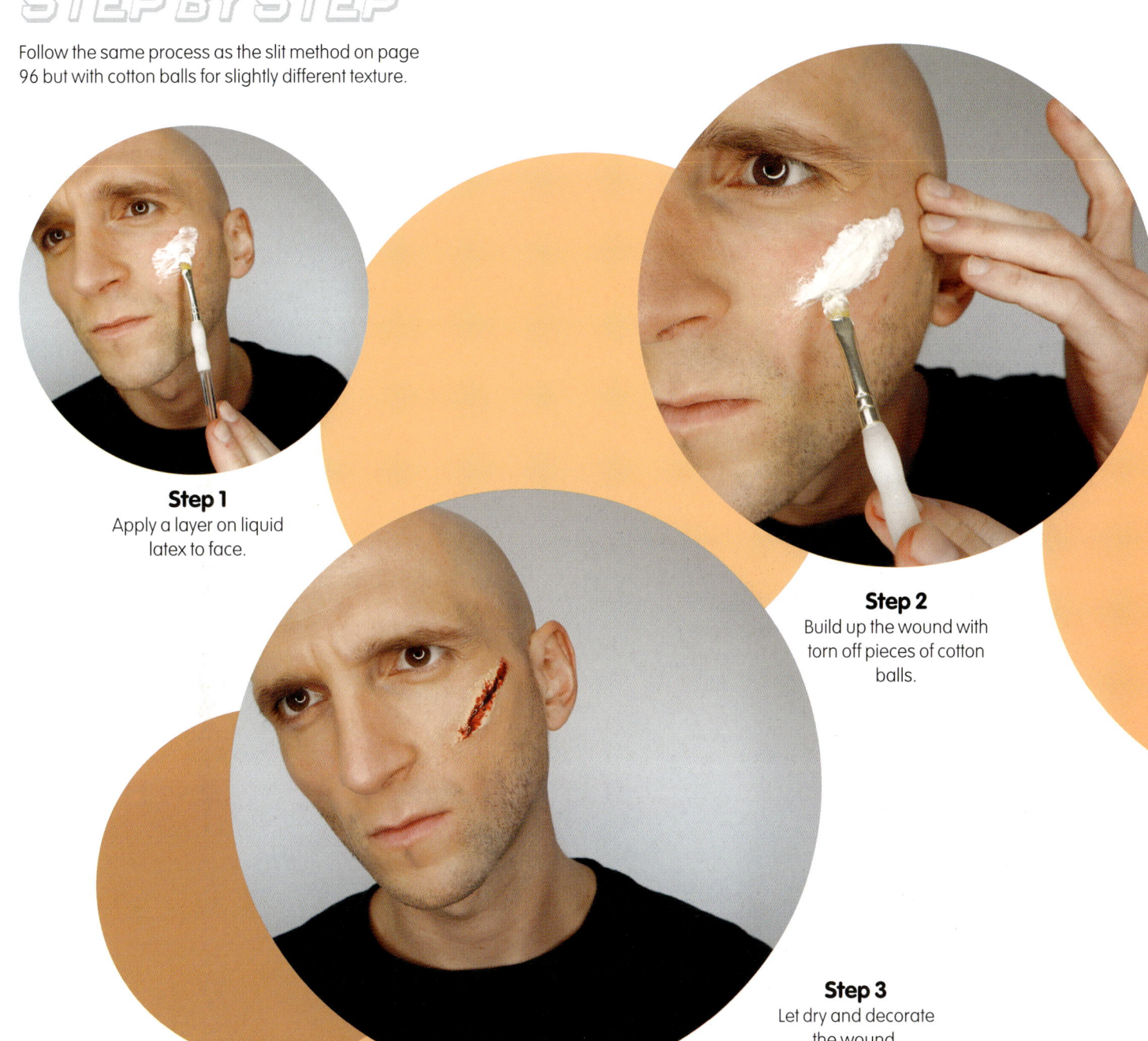

Step 1
Apply a layer on liquid latex to face.

Step 2
Build up the wound with torn off pieces of cotton balls.

Step 3
Let dry and decorate the wound.

PROSTHETIC APPLICATION
STEP BY STEP

Liquid latex can help with a smooth prosthetic application.

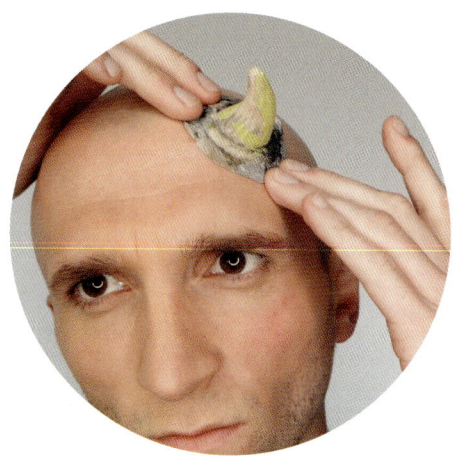

Step 1
Apply the prosthetic using spirit gum.

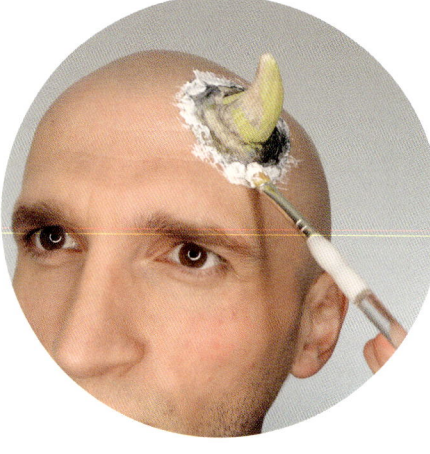

Step 2
Use liquid latex to apply a thin layer along the edges of the prosthetic.

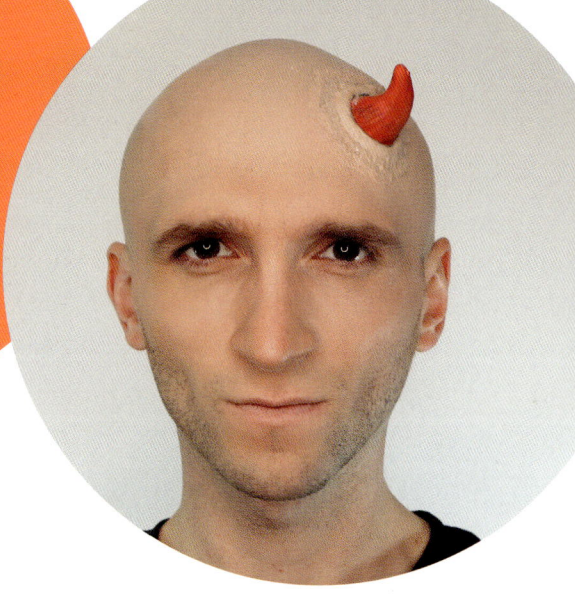

Step 3
If need be, decorate this to blend in with the rest of the look.

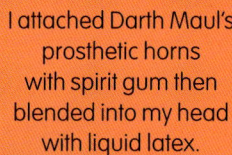

I attached Darth Maul's prosthetic horns with spirit gum then blended into my head with liquid latex.

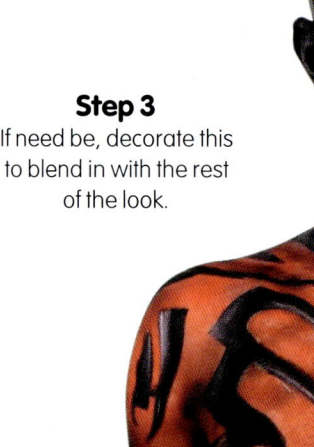

LIQUID LATEX AND SYNWAX

STEP BY STEP

Applying liquid latex over the top of SynWax can help keep it from moving.

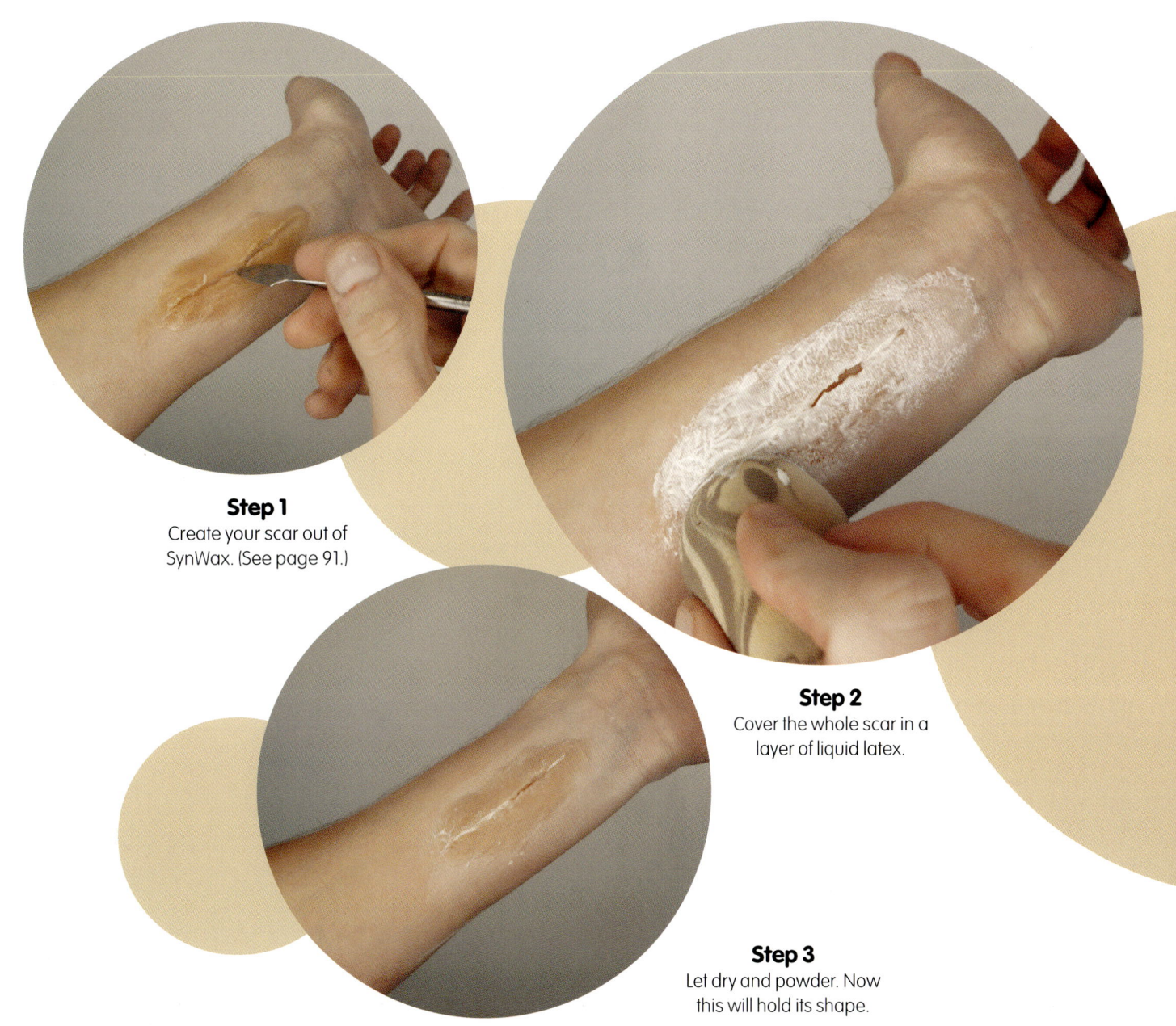

Step 1
Create your scar out of SynWax. (See page 91.)

Step 2
Cover the whole scar in a layer of liquid latex.

Step 3
Let dry and powder. Now this will hold its shape.

LATEX PASTES
STEP BY STEP

You can make latex pastes by mixing liquid latex and flour. These pastes can be used to create raised cuts and open wounds you can stick to your face once fully dried. Different types of flours will result in different textures when the paste dries. White wheat-based flour is easy to work with, just remember to sift it into the liquid latex to avoid lumps. Rice flour creates a great skin-like texture and is also easy to work with.

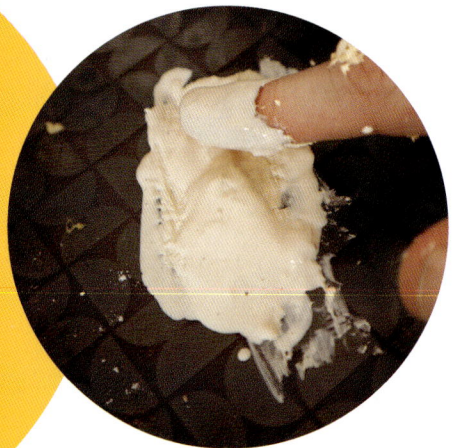

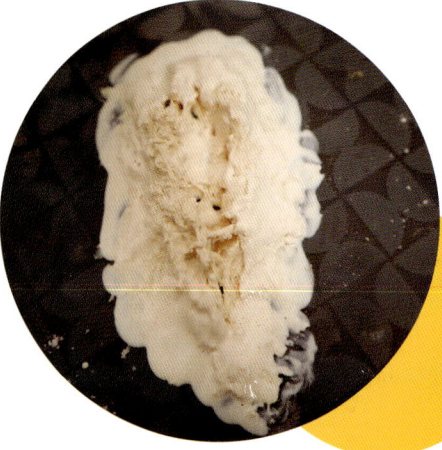

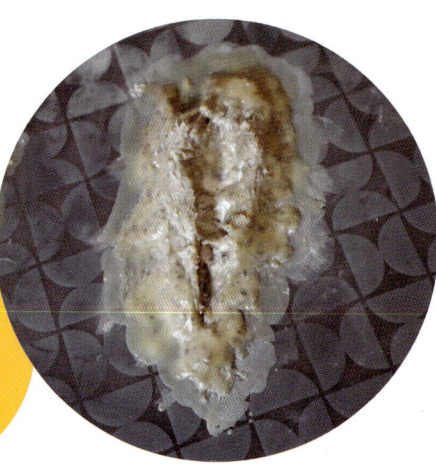

Step 1
Add two parts liquid latex to one part flour. Mix the flour in with the latex slowly until the paste is thick enough to hold its own shape. Place this onto a plastic tray or face mold and smooth out the paste.

Step 2
Carve out the shape of the wound with a metal spatula or knife.

Step 3
Let dry for twenty-four hours, then powder it so the latex doesn't stick to itself when you peel it off.

Tips

When working to manipulate these pastes on the tray, cover your finger in liquid latex so your finger doesn't stick to the paste.

Experiment with food coloring to dye your prosthetic different colors. Add this to the liquid latex before you add the flour.

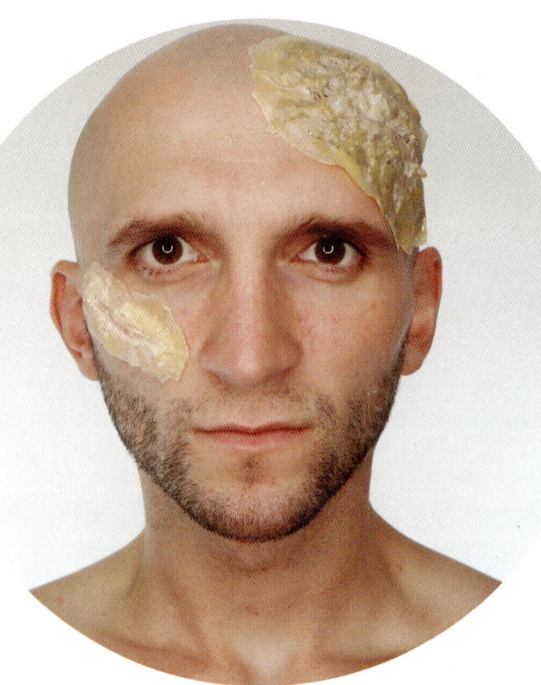

Now you have a wound you can peel off and stick to your own face with spirit gum.

LIQUID LATEX REMOVAL
STEP BY STEP

When it comes to removing liquid latex, your immediate urge is to just peel it off, and we've all seen those online videos where they just rip 100 layers off their face. Heck I've even partaken in them. It was instant regret for me because it was super painful! My face was red raw afterward, because just peeling liquid latex off **also** peels off the top layer of skin, which can cause irritation. You need to remove it slowly. It takes longer but it's much better for your skin.

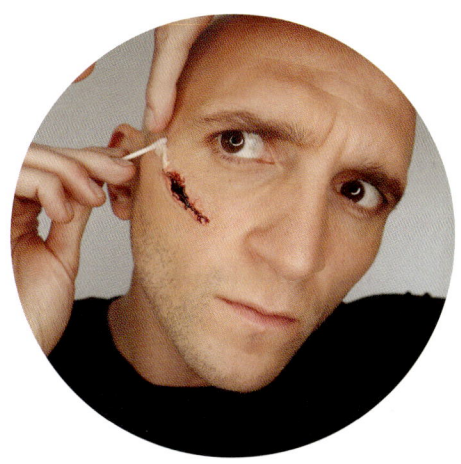

Step 1
Peel off a corner and rub spirit gum remover under the latex with a cotton swab.

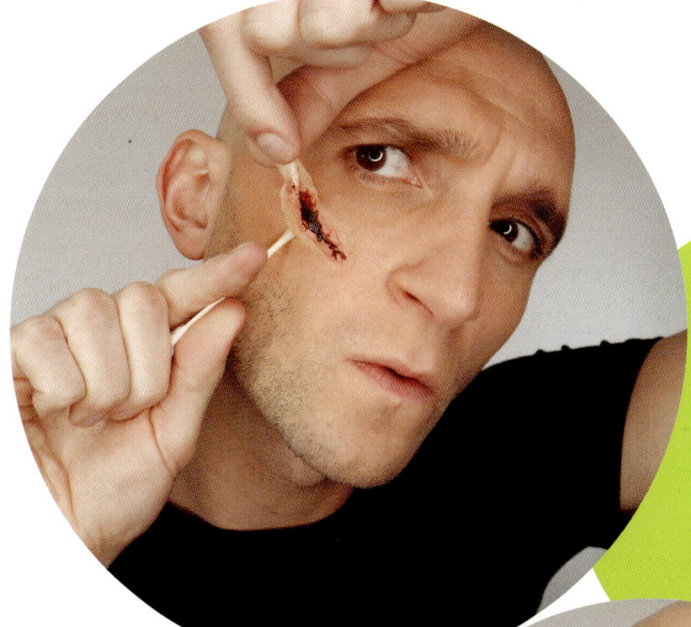

Step 2
Slowly peel while using a cotton swab to reach small areas.

This is a much safer way to remove than just pulling and will result in less irritation.

CREATING A DIY FACE CAST

Creating a face cast is a great way to start practicing with prosthetics. It creates a perfect replica of your own face so you can start building prosthetics directly onto the cast itself knowing that the prosthetics will fit your face perfectly when you apply them.

If you're claustrophobic then this might not be for you, as you do need to cover your face in plaster cast. It's possible to make a face cast by yourself, but you might want someone to help make sure you get all the right areas. Also, you WILL make a mess doing this, so make sure you prepare your workspace in advance: either lay a sheet down or work on a hard surface for easy clean up.

To create this mask of Winnie the Pooh, I made a cast of my face as shown in this tutorial, then used it as a base to create a mask out of BOHS Foam Clay. I was then able to paint it and take it on and off.

What you'll need to make this at home:

Plaster cast rolls

Petroleum jelly

Sandpaper

Metal files

Plaster mixture

Hair dryer

Wood glue

Plastic cling wrap

Cooking oil (e.g. vegetable oil)

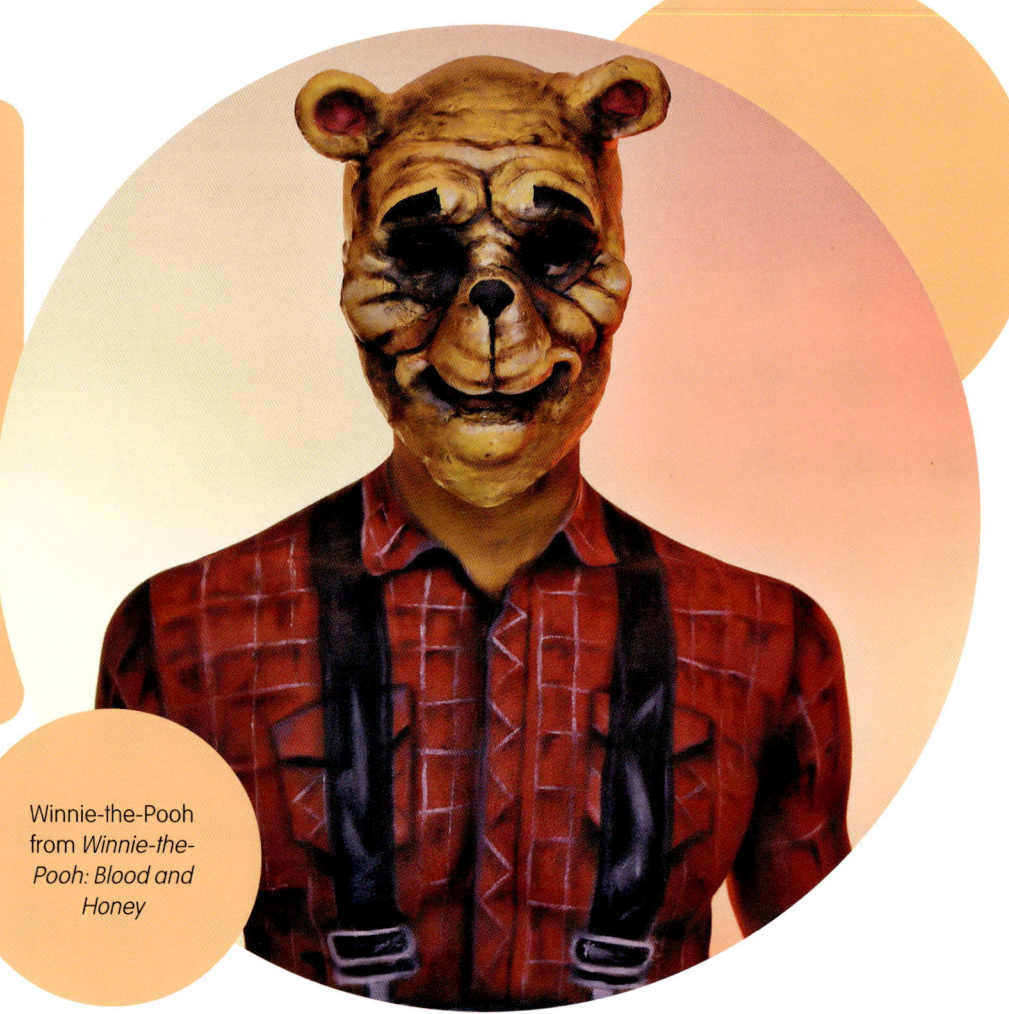

Winnie-the-Pooh from *Winnie-the-Pooh: Blood and Honey*

MAKING A FACE CAST
STEP BY STEP

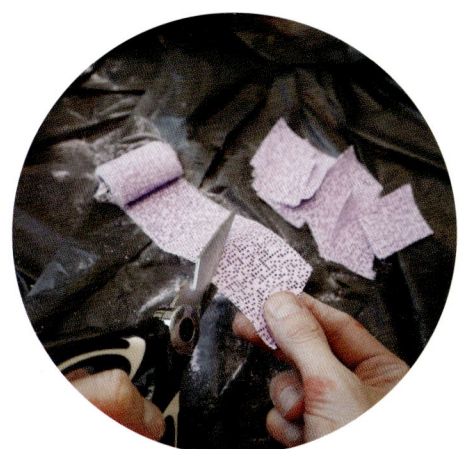

Step 1
Cut plaster cast rolls into small chunks.

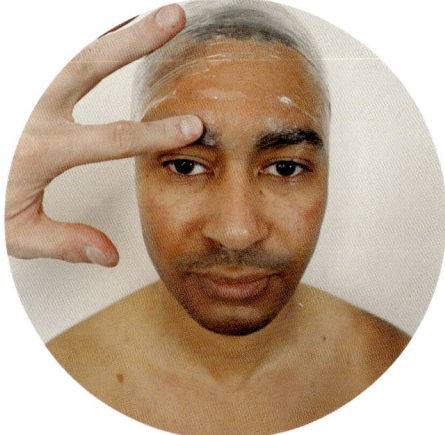

Step 2
Wrap your hair up in plastic cling wrap and cover your eyebrows in petroleum jelly.

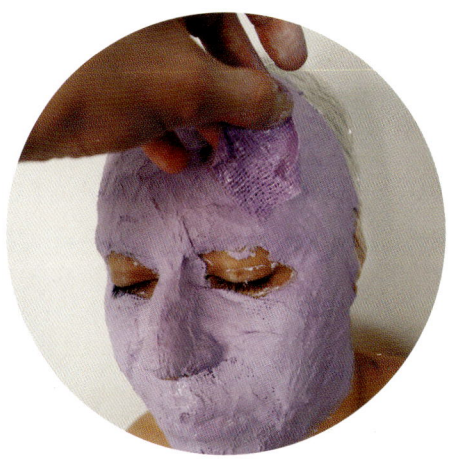

Step 3
Dip the plaster cast in water and start applying it to your face.

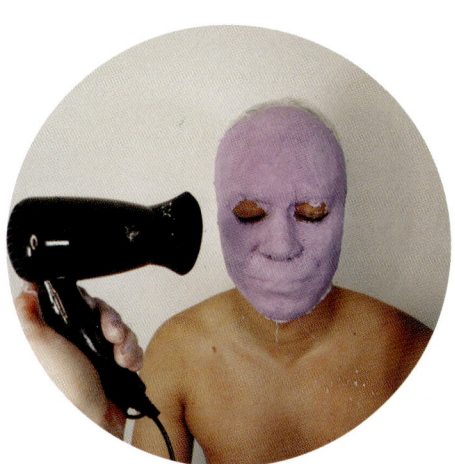

Step 4
Leave nostril holes to breathe and don't cover your eyes. Dry using a hair dryer.

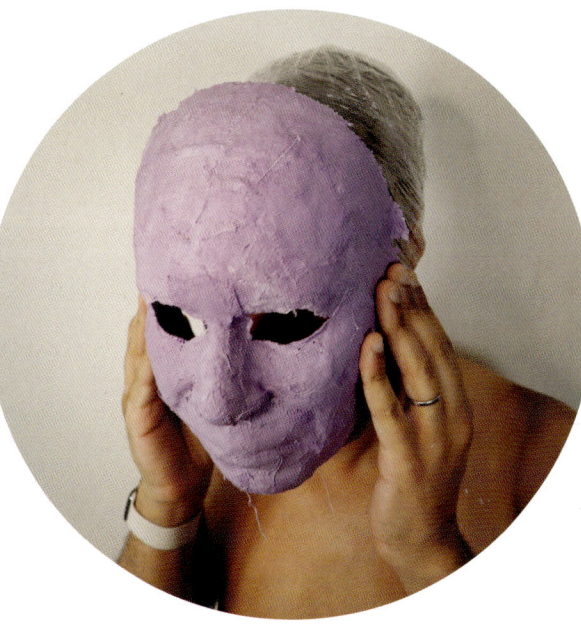

Step 5
Wiggle face and peel this off.

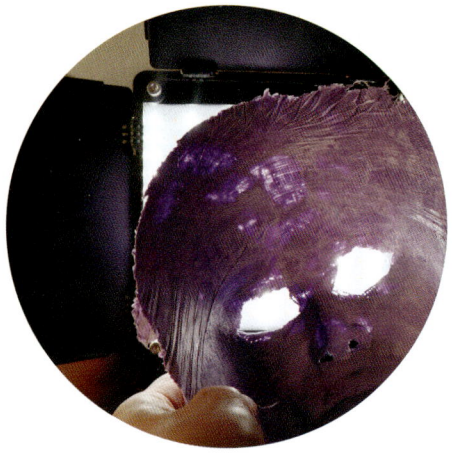

Step 6

Shine it up to the light and see where the thinner areas are to cover them again.

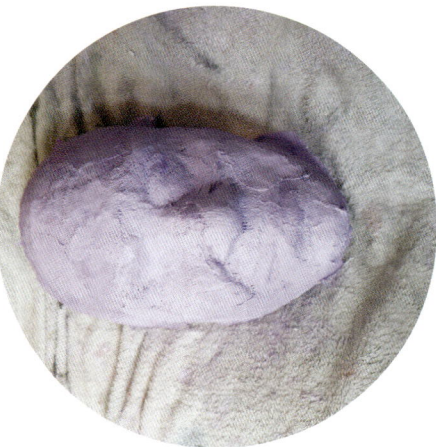

Step 7

Cover up the nostril and eye holes from the outside of the cast.

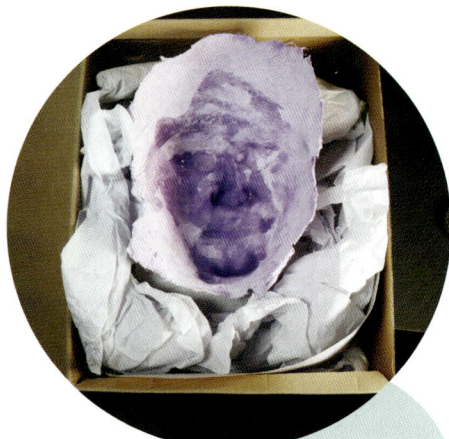

Step 8

Once fully dried, cover the inside in oil so the plaster cast is easier to remove. Create the plaster mix following the instructions of packet. Usually, it's two parts plaster to one part water. Stir until the mixture is creamy and bubble-free. Create a sturdy base for your face cast to lay still facing downwards while the plaster cast dries.

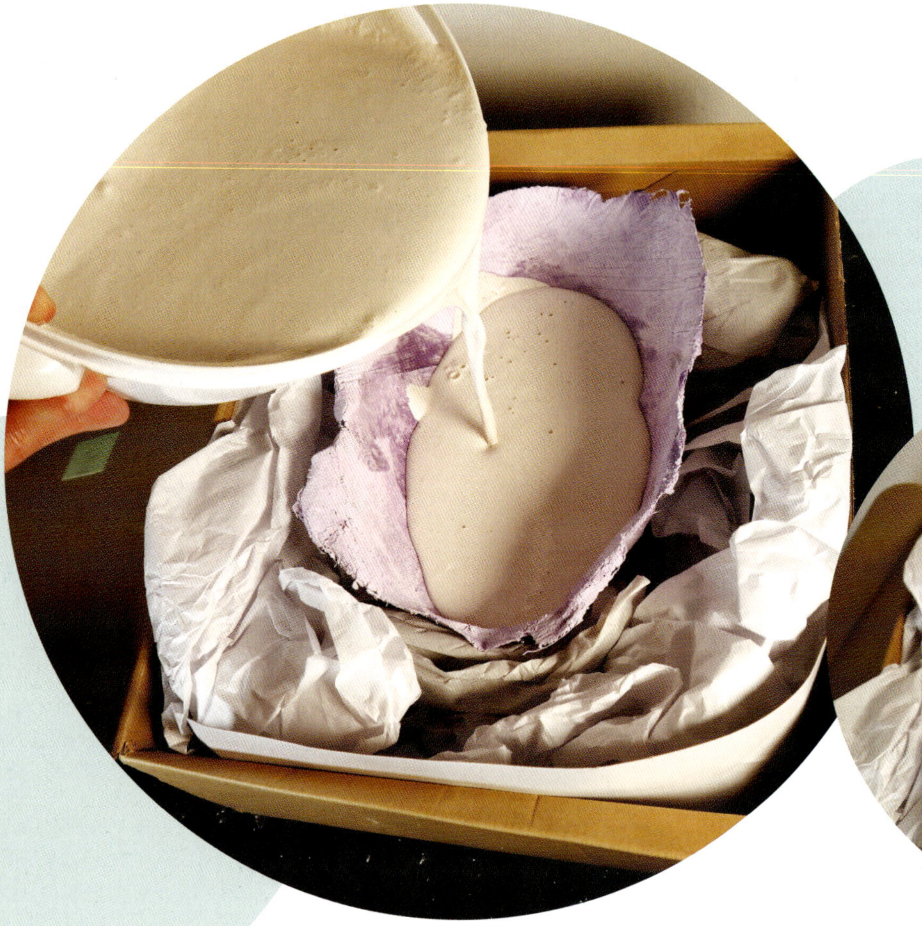

Step 9

Pour the plaster mixture into the face mold.

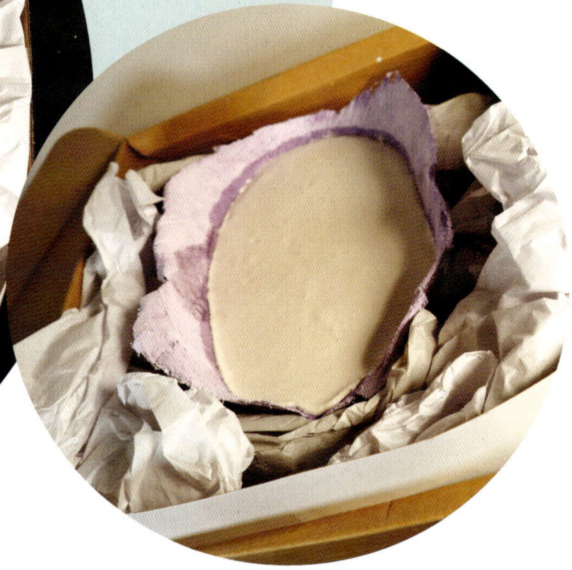

Step 10

Give it a gentle shake to remove any bubbles and let dry overnight.

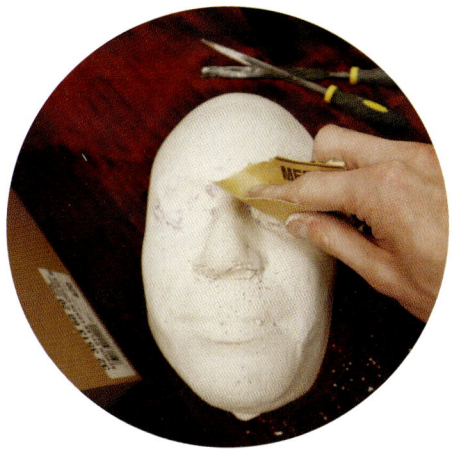

Step 11

When fully dried, remove the plaster cast from the dried plaster mixture. Smooth the edges with sandpaper or file.

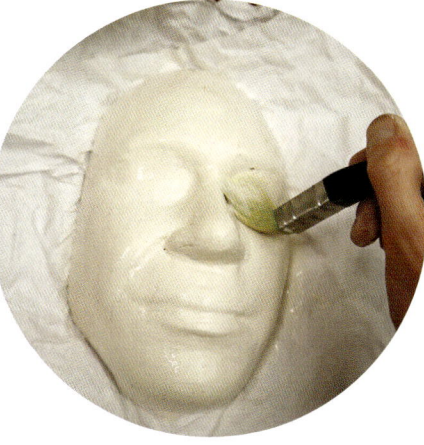

Step 12

Once smoothed out, coat your entire face cast in wood glue, and cover in about five layers of glue.

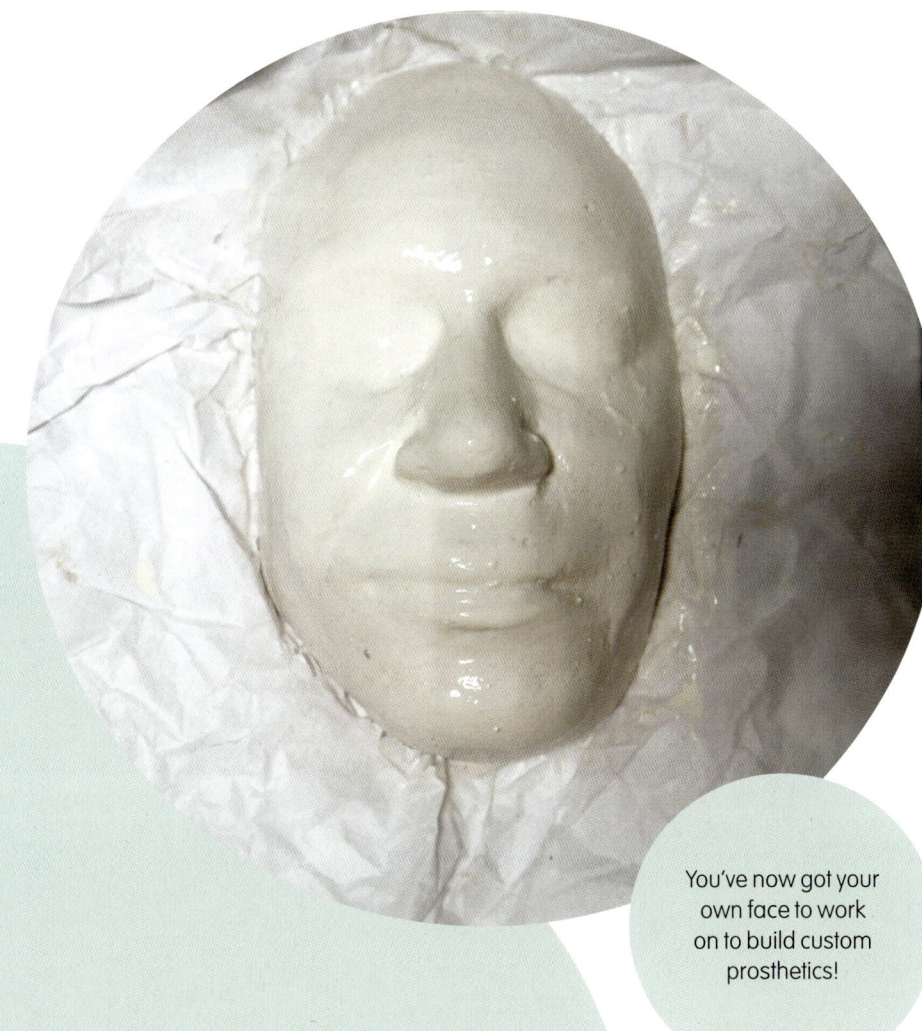

You've now got your own face to work on to build custom prosthetics!

Tips to Remember

Be careful and keep the plaster cast out of your eyelashes or hair as it's difficult to remove.

You don't need to cover your hair in plastic cling wrap if you don't want to, but you will have a larger surface area to work with when creating your prosthetics.

If you decide against using cling film then be careful not to get any plaster cast in your hair.

Make sure when you are applying the plaster cast that you get all the nooks and crannies of your face so you can get the most realistic representation.

Use the skills you picked up from the previous chapter to create prosthetics with liquid latex and latex pastes.

If the face cast starts to lose its shine, cover it in a couple more layers of wood glue again until it gets its shine back.

Cooking oil helps when it comes to removing the plaster cast from the face cast itself. You only need a thin layer covering the inside of the cast. If you have a puddle of oil, that's too much, and could effect the plaster getting into all the nooks and crannies!

Alternative Method

A more professional way to create a face cast involves covering your head to shoulders with a product called Alginate underneath the plaster cast. With this method you get the most realistic and smoothest representation of your face. You need at least one other person to help you with this process as it involves working quickly before the Alginate dries and requires you to cover your eyes completely, leaving only two nostril holes. You then pour the plaster cast into the Alginate and let dry.

DIY PROSTHETICS

Cosplay doesn't always have to be SFX makeup and a bunch of expensive products. We've already covered a lot of how to create your own prosthetics in the liquid latex section, but I wanted to also include a few other materials you might find easy to work with and even find around your house. If you're resourceful, you can create some really impactful looks with cheap products!

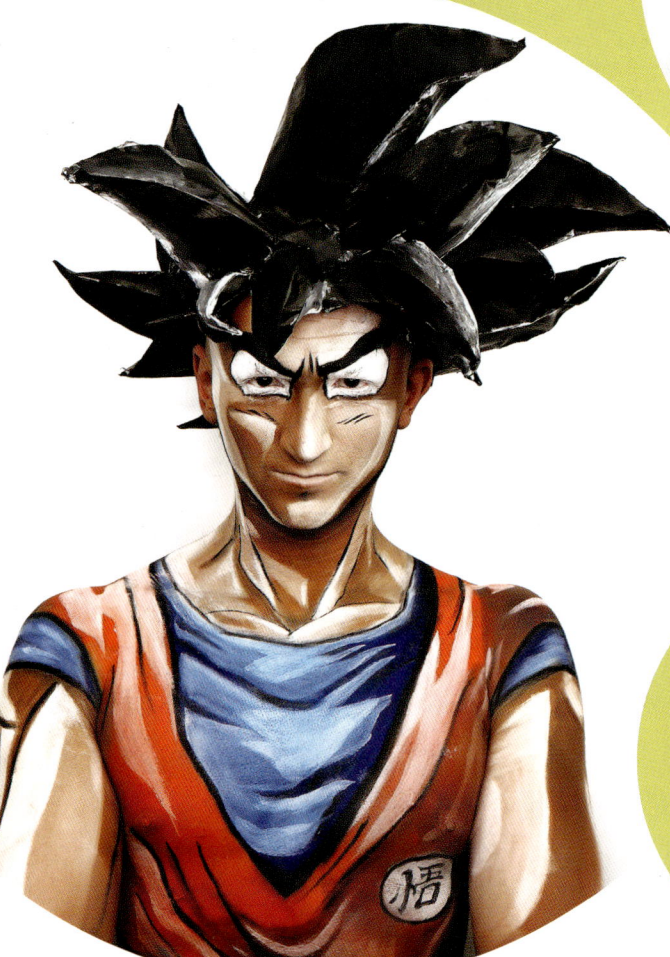

I made Shrek's ears out of paper.

I actually made Goku's hair from *Dragon Ball* out of paper. It took me about 3 months, and I needed to download special 3D printing software to figure out how to piece it all together! I recommend starting with something simpler!

HOW TO CREATE EARS WITH PAPER

STEP BY STEP

Using paper or cardstock is a fairly easy and cheap way to add elements that protrude from your body. This could be anything from a hat, to a collar, or even shoulder pads. In this section I'll demonstrate how you can use paper to create a set of ears.

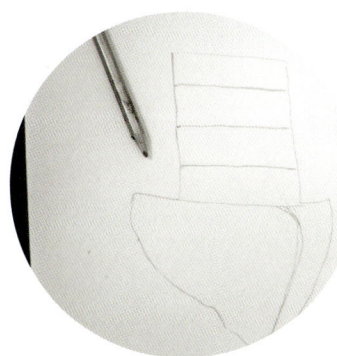

Step 1
Sketch out the shape of ears onto a piece of cardstock.

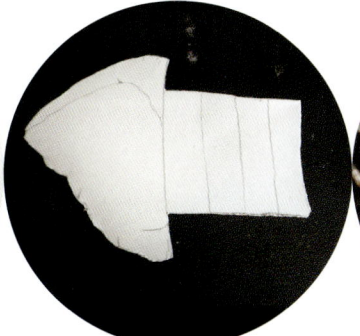

Step 2
Cut out the ear shapes leaving an extra margin or lip where the ears would meet the head as that is where you will stick them on.

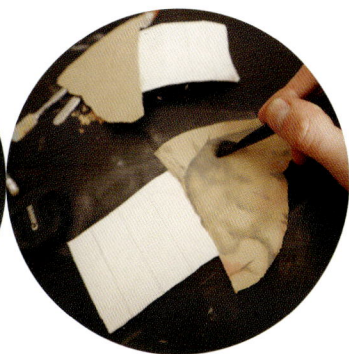

Step 3
Decorate the cardstock using cream paints and eyeshadows.

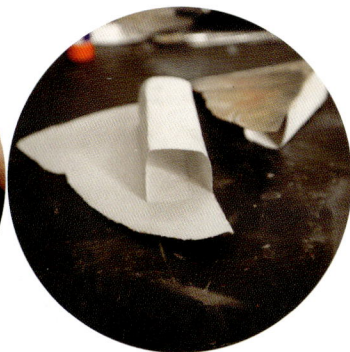

Step 4
Fold the lip into a 3D cube to provide the ears with extra stability when stuck to your head.

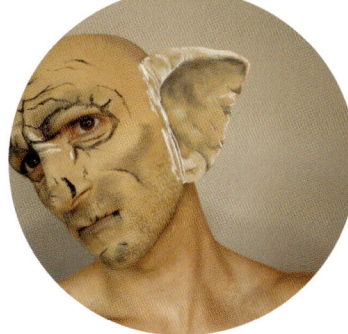

Step 5
Glue one side of the cube to your head. (You can add a thin layer of liquid latex where the card meets your head for seamless transition.)

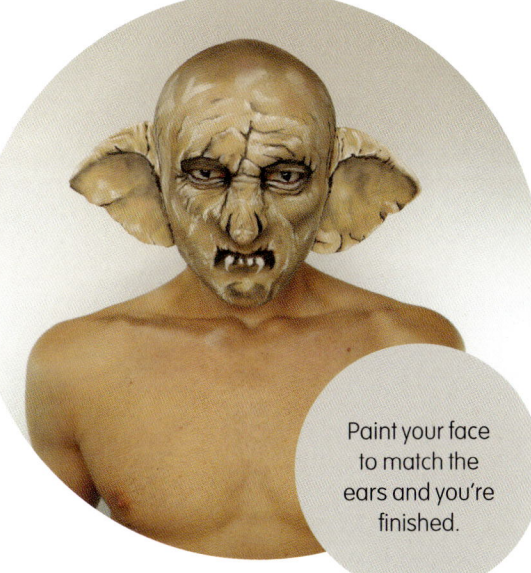

Paint your face to match the ears and you're finished.

Origami

You can also use paper to create origami elements to incorporate into your look. It's worth doing a Google search to see if there's a design for what you're looking to create. You'd be amazed by what some people have come up with that you could follow a tutorial for! I've created all sorts, including tiny hats, bow ties, and roses!

HOW TO CREATE A WITCH'S NOSE AND CHIN FROM SLIME

STEP BY STEP

BOHS White Squishy Slime is a great product I use to mold temporary prosthetics. It's a super malleable clay-like material you can mold into any shape and it will retain its shape. This product can be heavy, so if you're looking to create larger pieces, build them onto a thin layer of cardboard, which will provide a lighter, sturdier base.

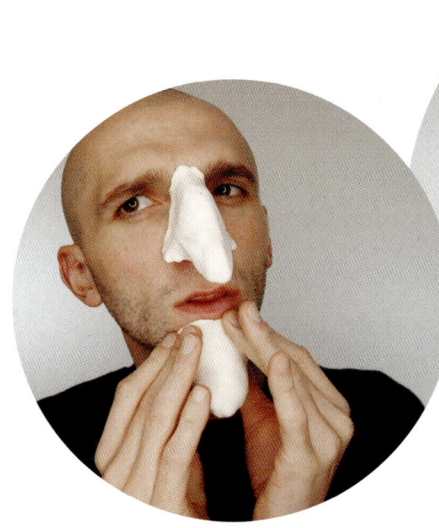

Step 1
Mold nose and chin directly onto your face or face cast.

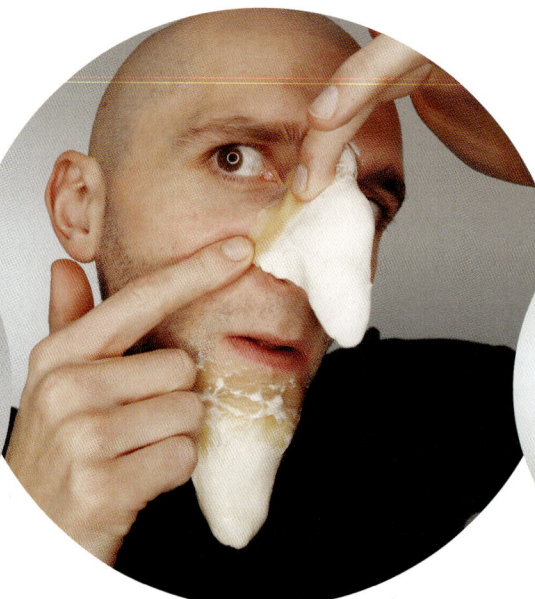

Step 2
Blend the edges out into the skin. You can use SynWax and petroleum jelly to get a seamless finish, then cover with liquid latex.

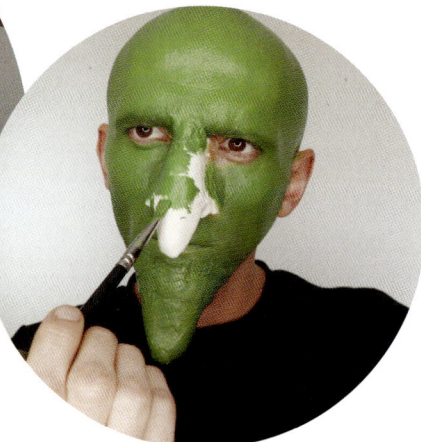

Step 3
Powder and paint your whole face green including the prosthetics.

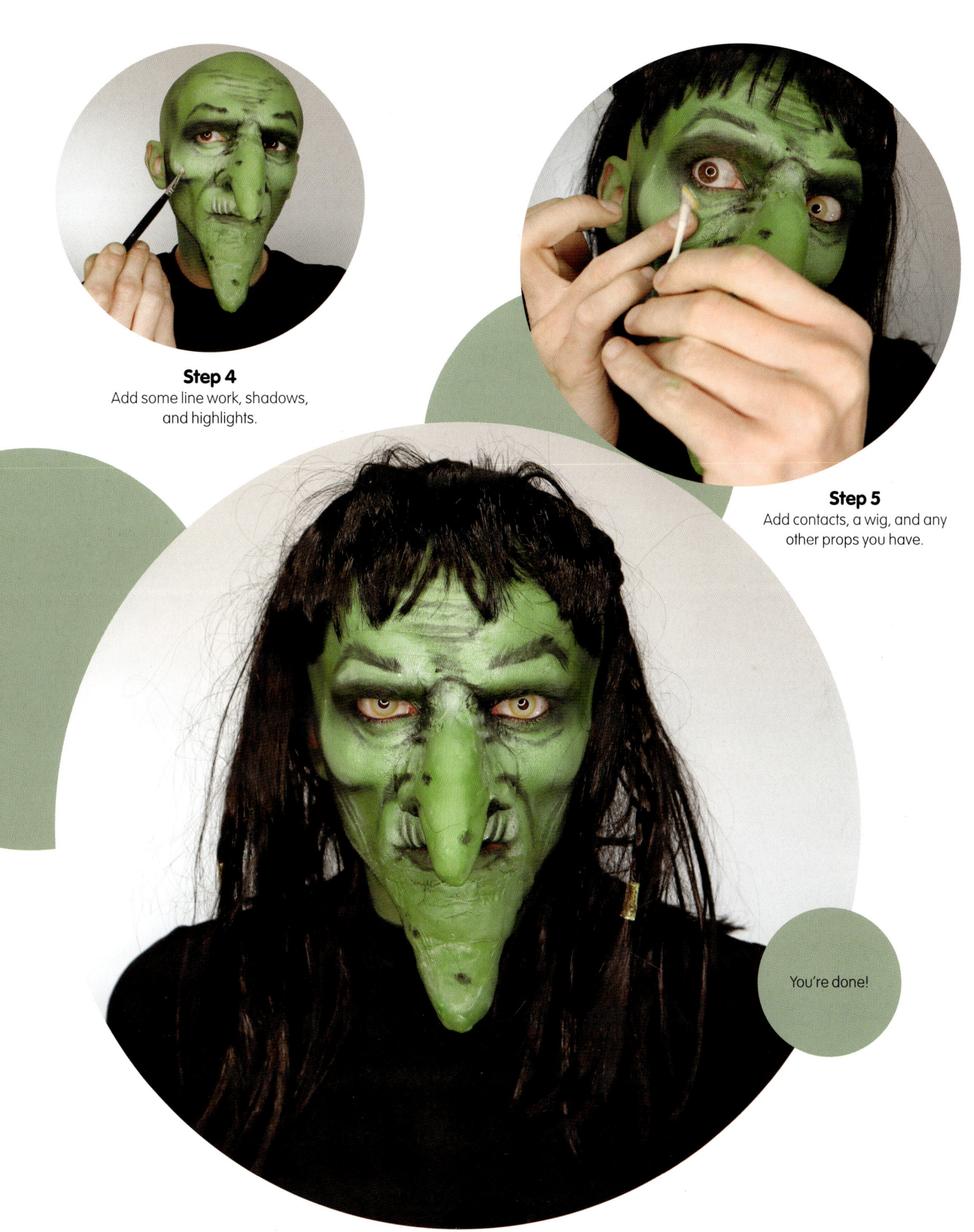

Step 4
Add some line work, shadows, and highlights.

Step 5
Add contacts, a wig, and any other props you have.

You're done!

HOW TO BUILD YOUR OWN HEAD PIECE

STEP BY STEP

Building your own headpiece is really easy and can look super effective. In this example, I used a plain headband, cable ties, small black roses, gold paint, gold leaf, and cheap jewelry. The bigger you go with this, the heavier that headpiece, so you might need to pin this to your hair (if you have any) for it to stand up.

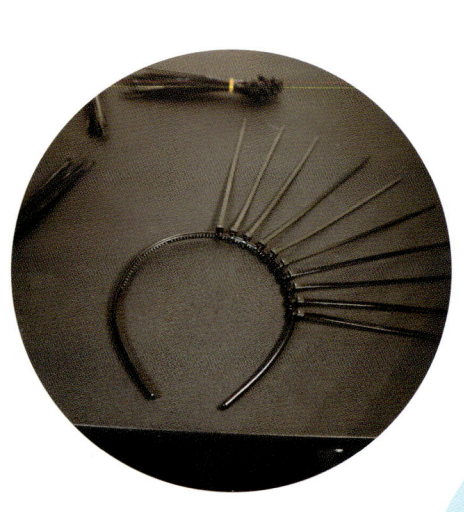

Step 1
Tie cable ties to the headband making sure they are all facing the same direction.

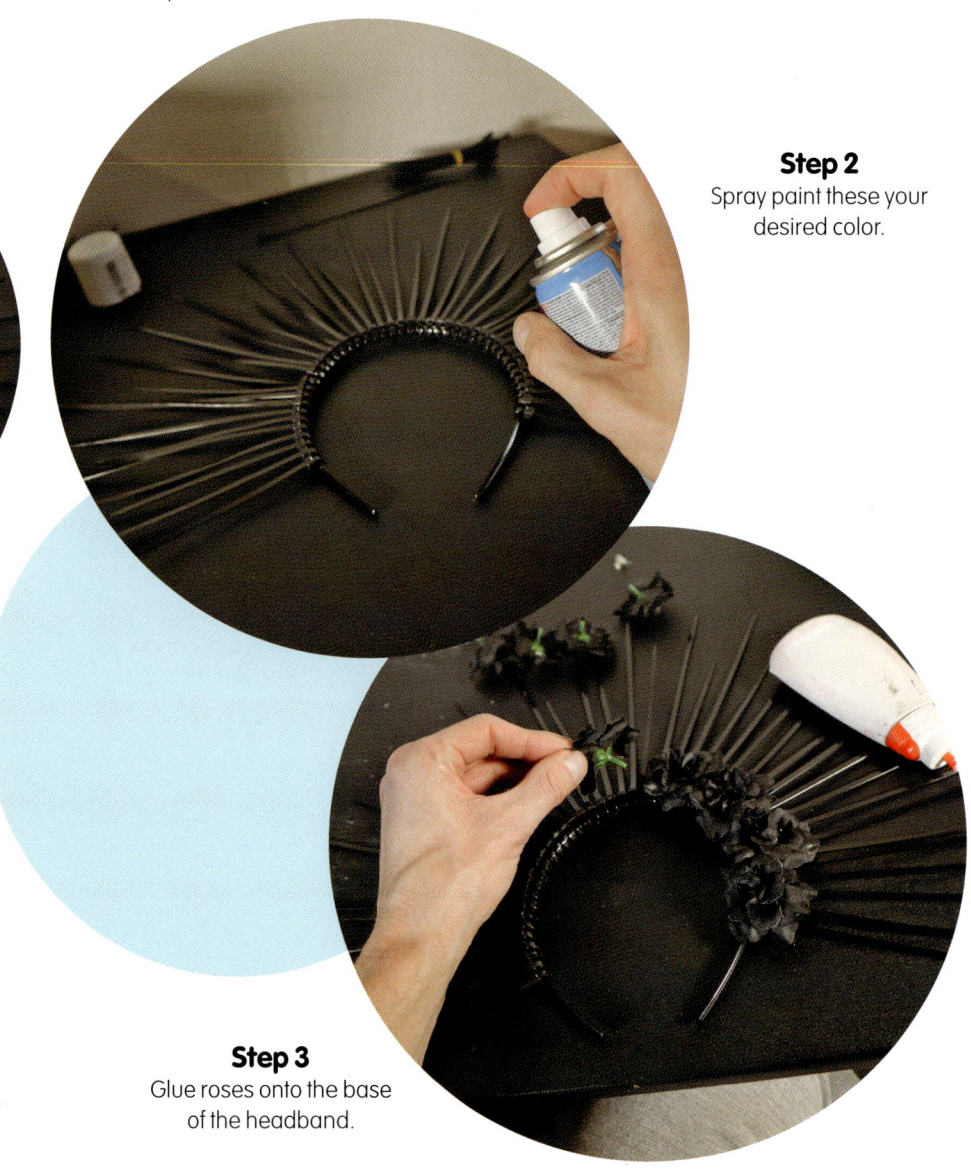

Step 2
Spray paint these your desired color.

Step 3
Glue roses onto the base of the headband.

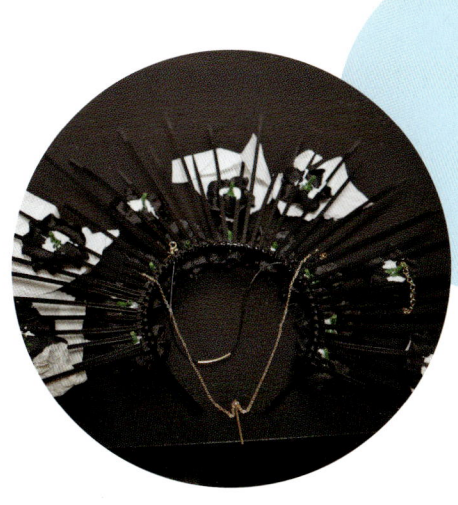

Step 4
Add any jewels and a few more roses.

Step 5
Paint the flowers with some gold paint and gold leaf.

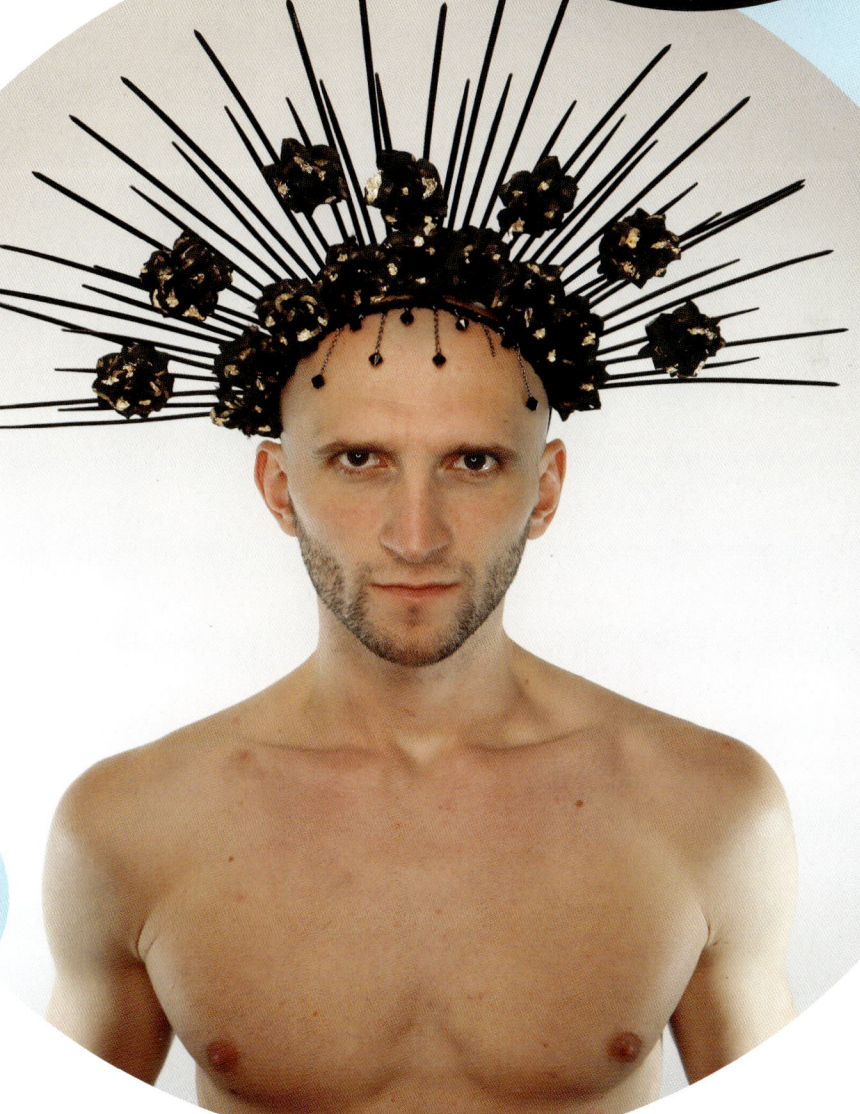

Your DIY headpiece is done!

HOW TO BUILD DIRECTLY ONTO A MASK
STEP BY STEP

Sometimes it's helpful to be able to reuse your creations repeatedly, but if you build them directly onto your face, then when it's time to peel them off it ruins the prosthetic. A clever way around this is to build it on a mask. Then when you put the mask on, it looks like it's been built onto your face, but you can easily remove and reuse it.

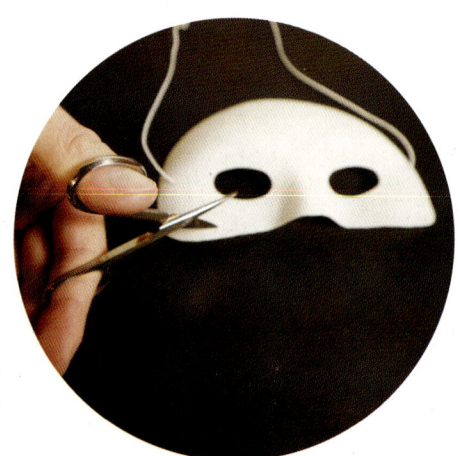

Step 1
I cut my face mask in half, but you can use a full-sized face mask if desired.

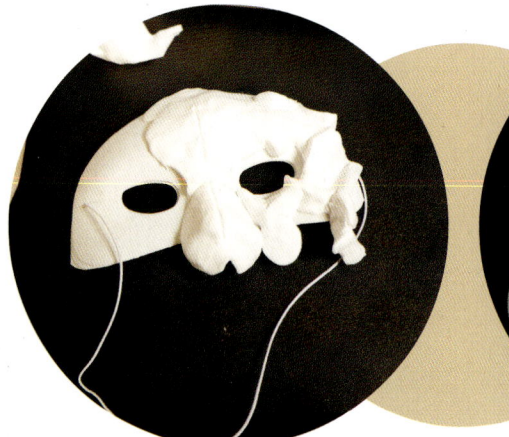

Step 2
Start building clay up directly onto the mask.

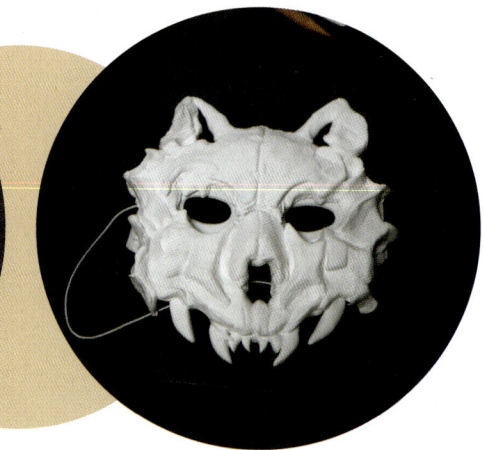

Step 3
Build up layers of detail. Don't worry about extending this further than the mask.

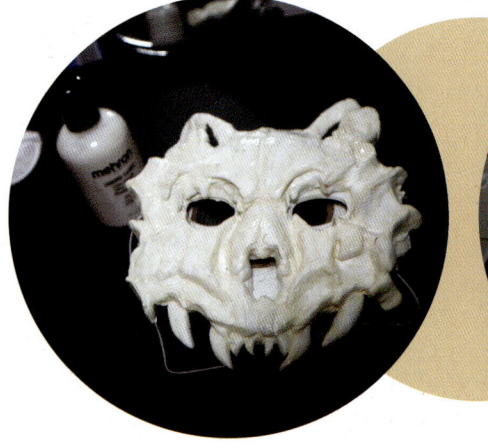

Step 4
Let the clay dry or cover it in layer of liquid to prevent the clay from cracking.

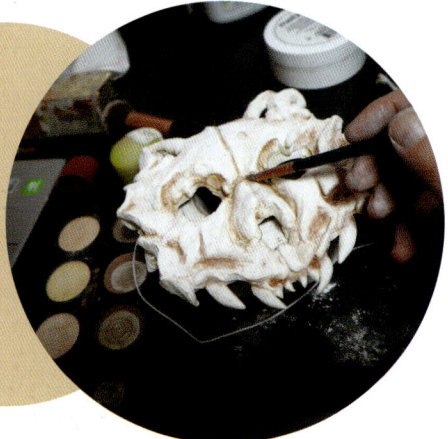

Step 5
Decorate with cream paint and eyeshadows.

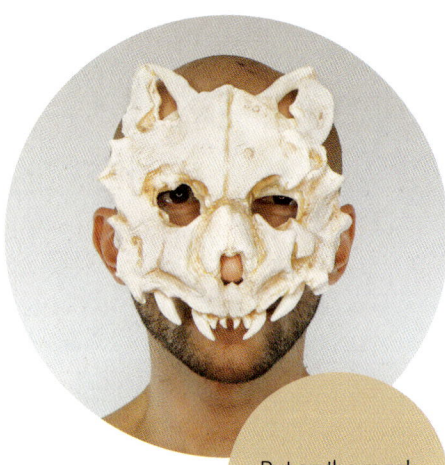

Put on the mask and you're done!

HOW TO MAKE HORNS OUT OF FOIL
STEP BY STEP

Foil can be a great tool when it comes to creating prosthetic pieces, because its super lightweight, very easy to manipulate, and it retains its shape well. I've used cable tape to cover the horns below, but depending on what you are creating, you can use other materials such as tissue paper, cotton balls, or even the BOHS White Squishy Slime we used to create the witch nose on page 108. If you don't want to tape your hair directly, you can use a swim cap, bald cap, or simply wrap your head up in cling wrap and then start the process from there!

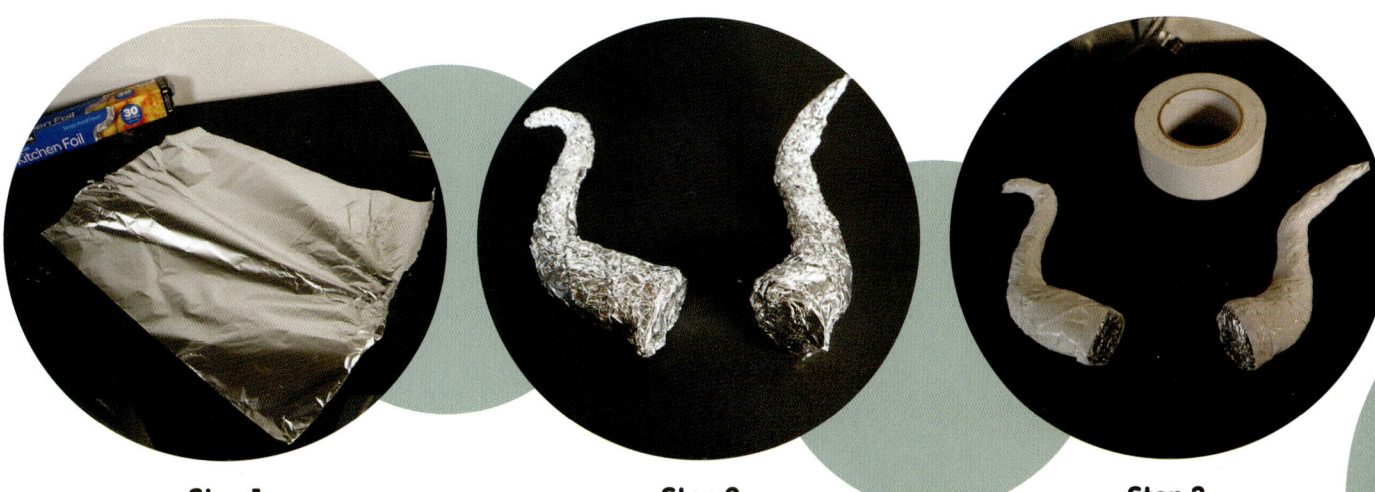

Step 1
Tear off a few long sheets of foil.

Step 2
Scrunch up foil into horn-like shape.

Step 3
Cover horns in white tape.

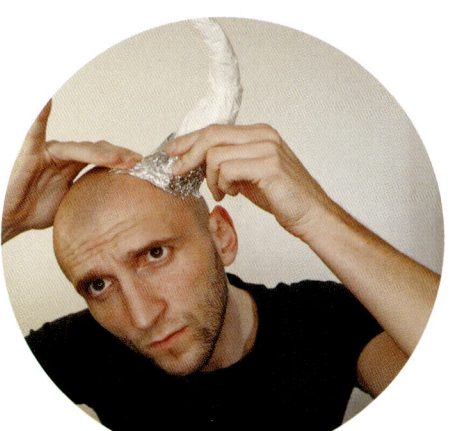

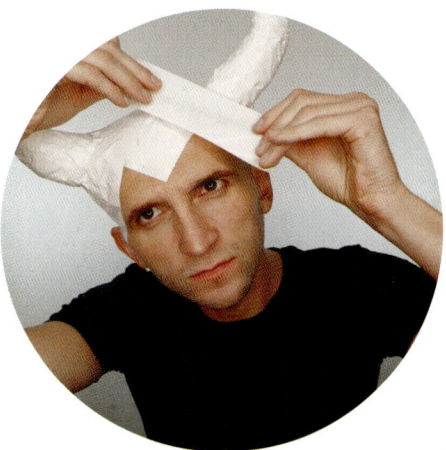

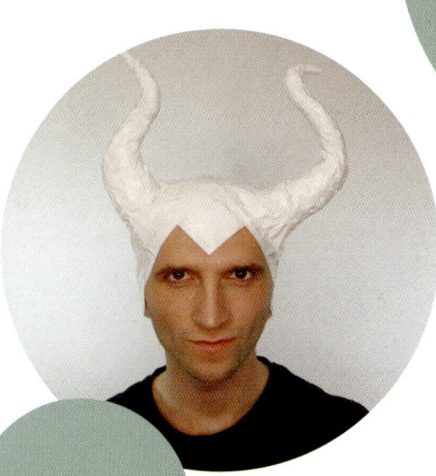

Step 4
Create a wider base and mold it to the shape of your head.

Step 5
With the same white tape, tape the horns to your head.

Enjoy your pair of DIY horns.

WORKING WITH WHAT MAKES YOU YOU!

In this section, we're going to go through how you can work with what you've got to make the most engaging content. We've all got limitations but we also have traits worth celebrating. Learning how to embrace them and work with them will set you apart.

Every face is unique, and you can learn to work with your physical characteristics to best enhance your features. I remember when I first started out, I tried to replicate certain details around my eyes, but as my eyes are so set back, I found it impossible.

Regardless of how much time I spend and paint I use it will never look right. On the plus side, I've also learned that because my eyes are so set back, if I want to create a spooky black eye, it really stands out! So rather than trying to create really detailed looks around my eyelids, I've found a more effective way of working with my natural face shape.

It's all about being realistic and not letting other people's standards warp your idea of reality. For instance, I'm 6 foot 2 and have a large nose, large ears, broad shoulders, and never-ending forehead. So, I'm probably not going to be able to turn myself into a character who is small and petite. But if you have difficulty transforming into a person or character because of significant physical differences, but you want to do it anyway, go for it! Refer to it as "makeup inspired by the character/person." Don't let others tell you what you should or shouldn't do!

Skin color is also another important factor to consider. Find products that are suitable for your skin tone. This may not be as necessary if you're working with face and body paint, and you're turning yourself completely red. However, it is for creative makeup which involves contouring and highlighting or painting on your own muscles. You need to find a shade that is darker than your natural skin tone to apply contour, and lighter than your natural skin tone to add any highlights. Don't be afraid to ask makeup store employees to help find the right shade, or use the tester products. It's all about finding the right product for you!

Everyone's skin is also completely unique as to how it reacts to certain products. If a specific product irritates your skin, don't keep using it just because a friend or someone on the Internet recommends it.

Over time you'll find the products best for you. A prime example of this is how everyone online swears by Mehron's Clown White paint. Any video you watch online recommends it for long-lasting, perfectly white coverage. But when I tried it, I used the product itself was too sticky so I used an alternative. Mehron actually has a Clown White Lite product which applies more easily, is less sticky and greasy, and still gives a solid coverage to build upon.

Hair as well! If you've got a huge, bushy afro, or long red hair, or absolutely no hair at all like me, make it work for you! Embrace it! Ingrain it into your online personality, and people will end up loving you for it! People warm to people online if they feel like they are being genuinely themselves. If trolls start to pick up on an insecurity of yours, they're going to double down because they're vicious creatures. If you learn to love the way you look, the comments online won't hurt you!

Working with what you've got and being authentically you, can be inspiration enough to give someone confidence to pick up a paintbrush, or do something they've never done before. You never know who is watching your videos and is really going to resonate with how you are portraying yourself!

So, celebrate your achievements, look back on what you've achieved over the past twelve months, compare your current work to your previous work, and see how much progress you've made in such a short period of time!

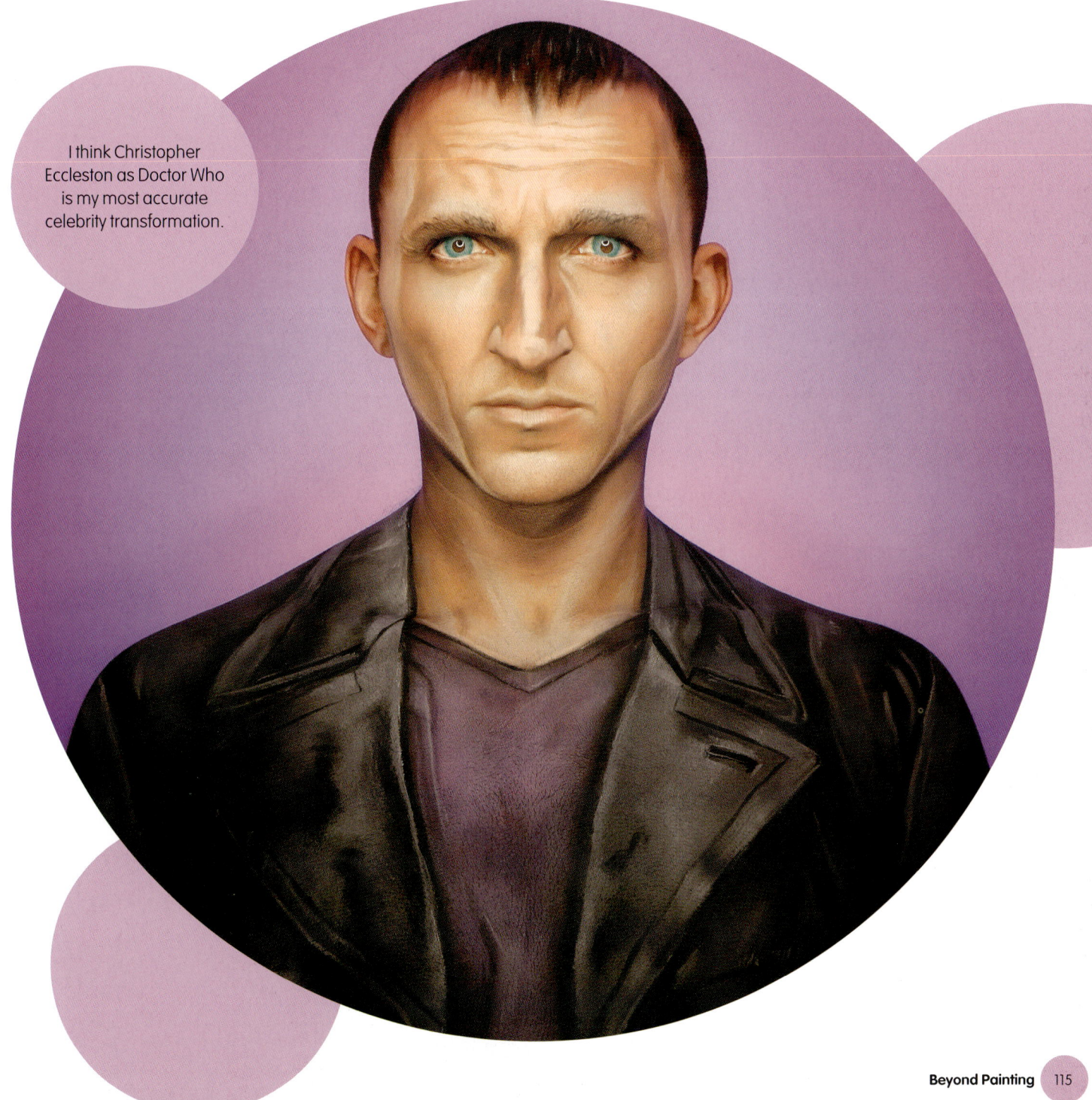

I think Christopher Eccleston as Doctor Who is my most accurate celebrity transformation.

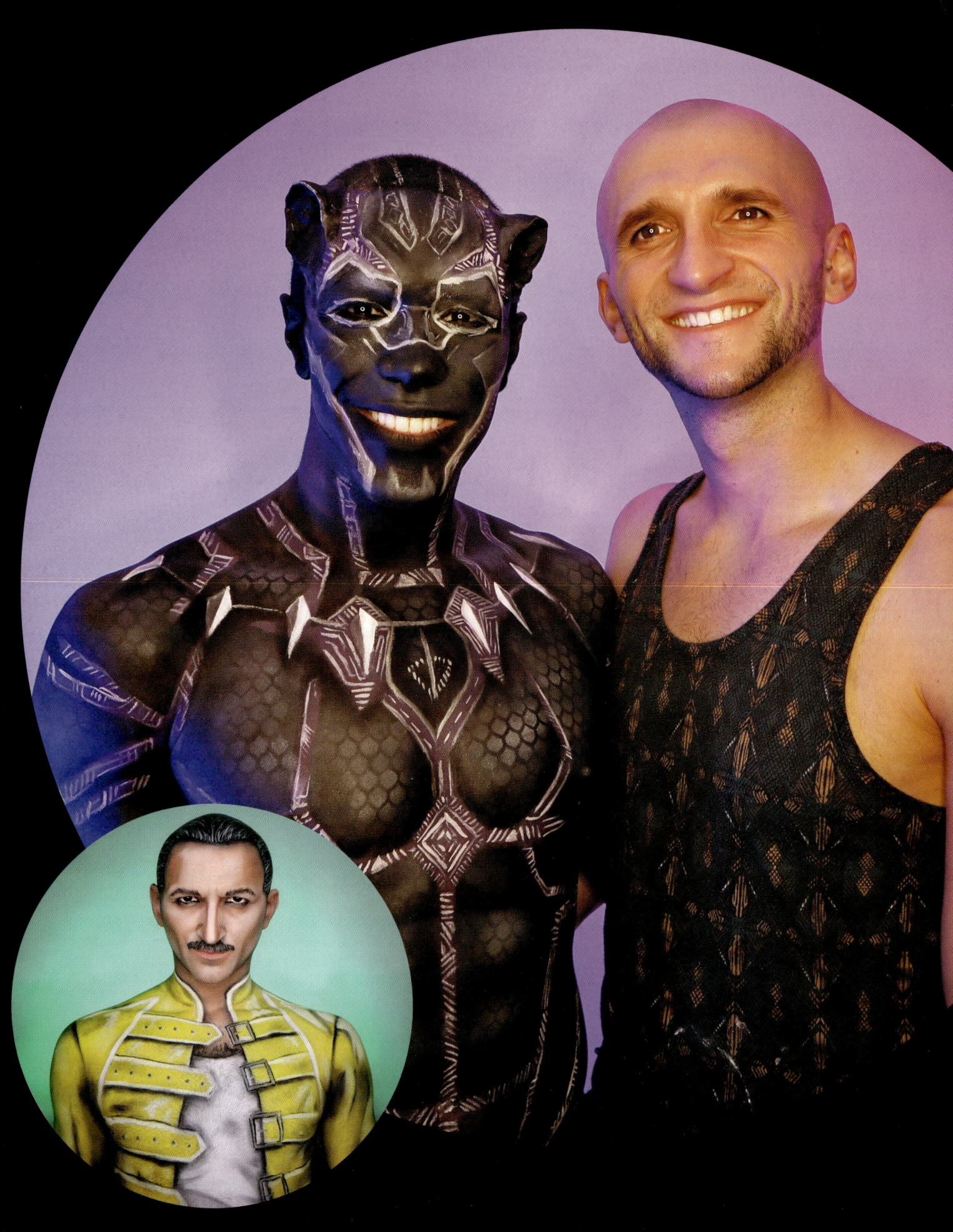

PART 3

BECOMING A SOCIAL MEDIA CONTENT CREATOR

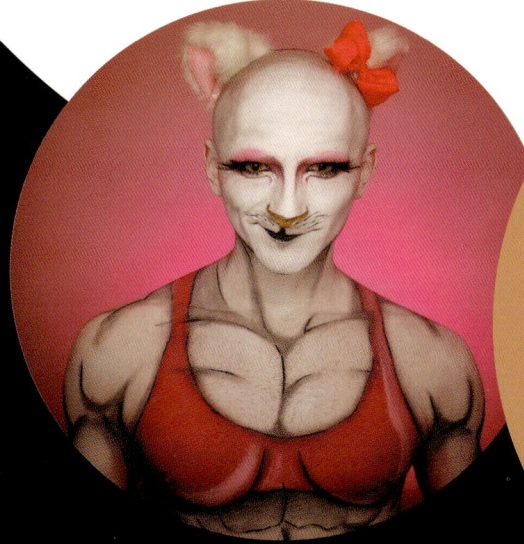

In this next section, we explore what it's *actually* like being a content creator, rather than the glitz and glam of what 95% of influencers lead you to believe. I'll share my top tips and best kept secrets for how you can grow your social media following and develop a stellar social media strategy!

FINDING YOUR CREATIVE INSPIRATION

A big part of being a content creator is being able to think up content to keep posting on a regular basis. Sometimes even daily! Coming up with new ideas that are engaging and relevant can be difficult, so here's how I do it.

I take my inspiration from my followers.

Why? Because my followers are exactly who will be watching my videos, and I always notice a huge difference in engagement when I decide to do a character I chose versus a character my followers picked for me. Some of my most-watched videos have been characters and memes I'd never even heard of!

If you're thinking, "Chris I don't get many comments on my videos" this is where you need to get creative. Identify an account you admire that creates similar content to yours and immerse yourself in their comments sections to see what people are requesting they create. The longer you spend in their comments, the more you'll understand what people *want* and reach that audience.

Once I've decided on what character to paint, I gather reference pictures, finding photos of the character in different positions, so I can understand how they look from all angles.

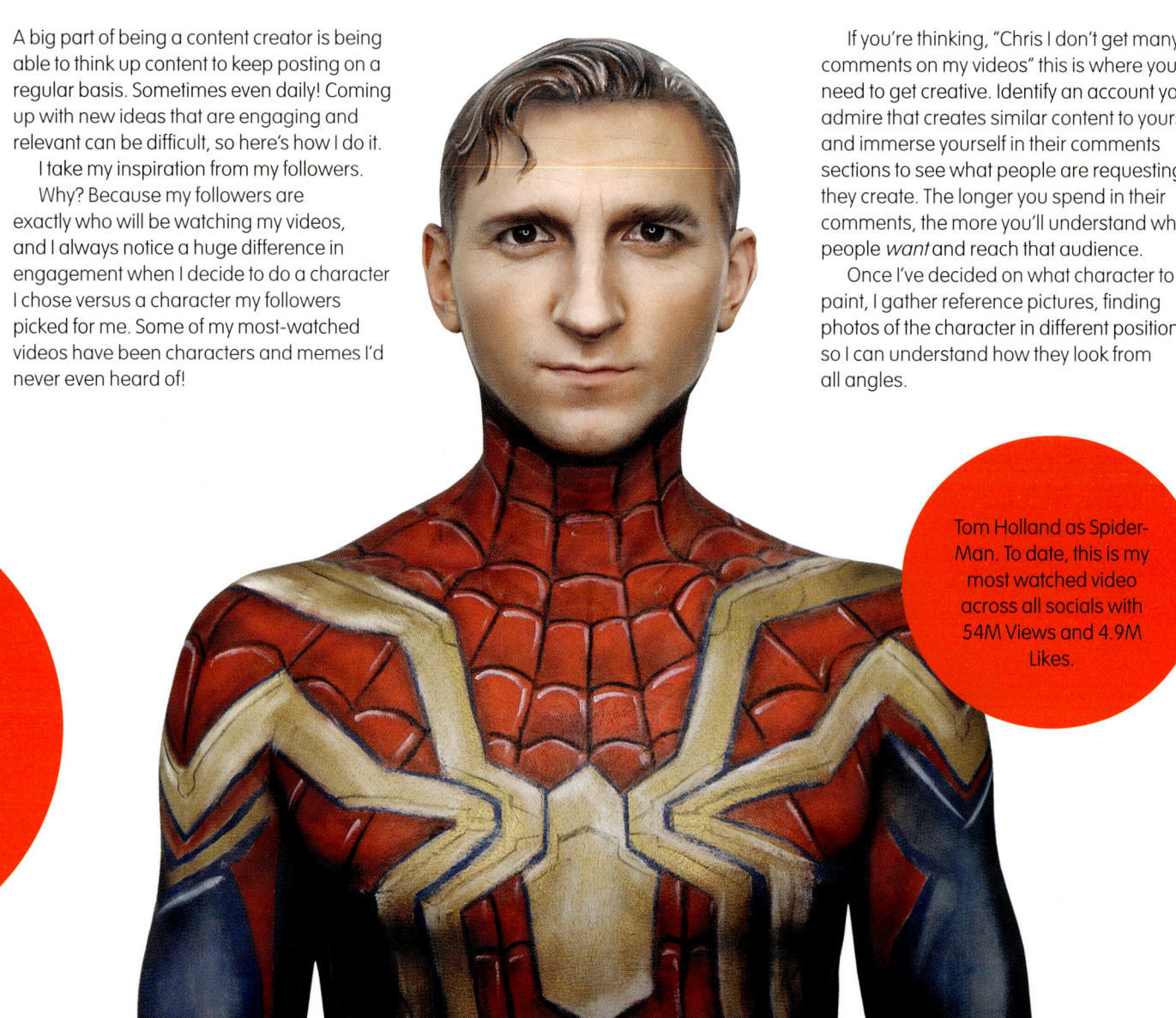

Tom Holland as Spider-Man. To date, this is my most watched video across all socials with 54M Views and 4.9M Likes.

CHOOSING THE RIGHT SOUND

If you want to become a content creator, you need to understand the importance of trending sounds and using the right sound. Doing this puts your video in front of the audience the platform knows will enjoy this sound. The perfect example of this was when I posted a video, and I didn't use the original sound of the trend. I used a sound that sounded exactly the same as the original, but the original sound hadn't been tagged in the video. I posted a video using this non-original sound and my video got around 2K views, which was much lower than I was usually getting at the time. I then came across the original sound and posted the video again. This time it got 15.7M views.

MANAGING YOUR TIME

As a content creator you'll find that there are never enough hours in the day to get everything done! You're expected to stay on top of the constantly changing current trends. There's never going to be a point where you'll sit back and think, "I'm all done." There's always more you can do. More research, more replying to comments, more answering Direct Messages, more content to create. The list is endless.

I manage my time by sitting down at the start of the week to schedule what I'm focusing on for each day that week. I break each day down into morning and afternoon. In the morning I do market research and scroll socials. Then in the afternoon I might prepare for my next makeup look, make sure I have all my products, and pre-record videos. On a painting day, I break the day down into chunks and give myself a deadline to meet at a certain point in the painting process.

As a social media content creator, you create your own targets and goals. With so much freedom to do whatever you like, you need to plan your time efficiently to be able to meet those goals.

So, how do you find the right sound?

There are a few things I've picked up over the years.

How many videos are there using this sound? Anywhere from 1,000 to 100,000 videos is a good sign. Any lower means that sound isn't appearing enough in the algorithm to get in front of enough people. Any higher and you run the risk of this sound being oversaturated and your video getting lost.

How well have the top performing videos done using this sound? You want to see those videos getting hundreds of thousands of likes, if not millions.

How recently has this video been uploaded? If the top performing videos did well two years ago, chances are this is no longer a trending sound. You want recent video that has performed well within the last three to four weeks.

What is the general theme trend behind this sound, and does your content fit into this? There is an expectation from viewers that the sound is accompanied by a certain trend, so try to stay true to that trend as best you can.

It's important to do this for each social media platform separately. Just because a sound is trending on TikTok, doesn't mean it will be on Instagram and YouTube. For the best success using this technique, follow this same process for each platform.

UPLOADING CONTENT SMARTER

It's important to think about posting the right content to the right platforms in the *right* way. These platforms are programmed to pick up any other social media watermarks, or features, in the video themselves and will actively *suppress* views to them. If you download your video from TikTok and upload it to Instagram or Snapchat, they deliberately limit the views as they don't want to be seen promoting a video made for an alternative social media platform.

When it comes to the physical act of uploading content itself, utilize the scheduling feature as much as possible. Not all social media platforms allow you to schedule videos or posts but, for the ones that do, make sure you take advantage of this. This allows you to plan your content a lot more effectively and essentially not have to worry about remembering to upload to that platform at the prime time for your audience.

Scheduling posts is also a super helpful tip when it comes to taking a break from social media and going on a vacation. It's important to make sure your schedule is consistent, so social media knows that you're committed to posting to their platform.

Spend some time in your analytics to work out where your followers are based and then you can work out the best time to post.

EVERY SOCIAL PLATFORM IS DIFFERENT

As a content creator, it's important to spread your following across multiple platforms, because know never know whether a platform will even exist in two years. Remember MySpace?

You might assume what works well on one social media platform is bound to work well across other platforms as well, right? I assumed this, and a video I spent ages on did well on TikTok but flopped on Snapchat. Through consistently posting to multiple social media platforms I started to understand why.

Firstly, each platform has its own algorithm, which may share similarities, but fundamentally, are completely different. Secondly, each platform is likely to have a different demographic of people, and you've got to tailor your content to meet their requirements.

So, if you're on Instagram, TikTok, YouTube, and Snapchat, you have four entirely different audiences that all want something different out of you. It's *your* job as a content creator to make what they are looking for.

To better understand a platform, spend time on it, figure out how it works, and find out what the majority of people use the platform for. For instance, Stories are an integral part of Snapchat and Instagram.

While they are a feature on YouTube and TikTok, not as many people use them in the same way. However, you can get real success out of using Community posts on YouTube, which is something you can't do on any other platforms.

Going live is an interesting opportunity, and I've found it really helped boost my engagement on some platforms, but not on others. For instance, TikTok pushes your livestream based on the amount of engagement a particular live gets to non-followers. However, Instagram **only** shows your livestream to your followers. There is no discoverability element on Instagram live.

You can elevate your growth if you spend time providing a tailored approach to each social media platform.

START THE DAY PREPARED!

As a content creator, you have so much freedom to do what you want that you don't need to stick to a nine to five work day. But I find it really important to have a plan and be prepared for the day and week ahead! This is especially true when it comes to body painting and creative makeup. My content takes so long to produce and demands so much of my brainpower and concentration if I don't prepare, I know I will mess up.

If you are using a sound associated with a particular trend, make sure you understand the type of transition that is relevant to it. People expect to see that type of transition if everyone else is using it. You don't need to reinvent the wheel.

Keep in mind transitions are a skill in itself. Don't expect to be amazing at them straightaway. If I scroll back two years in my content and look at the transitions I was doing then compared to the transitions I'm doing now, I've come a very long way.

The way I plan out my transitions is something along these lines:

Sounds

Nothing/ Outline / Base colors / Finished look

Paint splatter / Finished look

I have it written on a piece of paper so I know how I've broken the video up into different transitions and what stage of the paint I need to be at when I'm filming that transition. Each slash mark indicates where a transition needs to be. I then tick each section off when I've filmed that transition so I know exactly where I am.

It's important to make sure that when you go into a video you have every product you need to complete that look. I can tell you from experience that the worst thing is to reach for a product in the middle of a video and realize it's run out. Be sure to check your makeup kit regularly!

To prepare, I like to sit in front of my reference picture and think through the process of how I'm going to create that paint. I decide which colors I'm going to need to lay down first, where I'm going to put the shadows, how I'm going to do the details, and so on. Visualizing the whole process means you know exactly which products you're going to need.

This step is also important to marry up with your transition plan because if you are doing a progression video that has transitions at different points of the process, you will need to remember to stop painting at a certain point to record the next part of your video. Even if this wouldn't be a natural way of painting that character, it's important to build this into your plan.

My planning goes as far as writing out exactly which photos and videos I need to edit after I finish painting, where I need to post each video, and even a reminder to clean my brushes and tidy my workstation. This might be over planning for some people, but I know my brain works well when I have a list of things in front of me I need to complete, which is why I put even the small tasks on my list.

I collaborated with champion swimmer Michael Gunning to raise awareness for Black History Month and painted him as Black Panther.

USING REFERENCE PICTURES

Most people have a reference picture they copy when it comes to creative makeup. Here's a tip when it comes to making your content unique. Think about creating your makeup look like a Build-A-Bear toy. Pick and choose elements from different reference pictures and put them into one. This adds your personal touch to your content.

When copying other people's work, you need to be careful not to plagiarize them. Use their work as inspiration, rather than something to replicate. There's a fine line behind taking inspiration from someone's work and copying, which is why I find having multiple reference pictures handy.

I've been on both sides of the argument. I used to mimic other makeup artists designs and put them on myself. The trouble with doing this is you're taking on *their* persona, whereas you want to develop your own unique style. If you're trying to be someone else, then why would people want to follow you? It's like going to watch a tribute act perform. You might enjoy watching them once, but would you go back? Probably not.

You need to find what makes you stand out and makes you different.

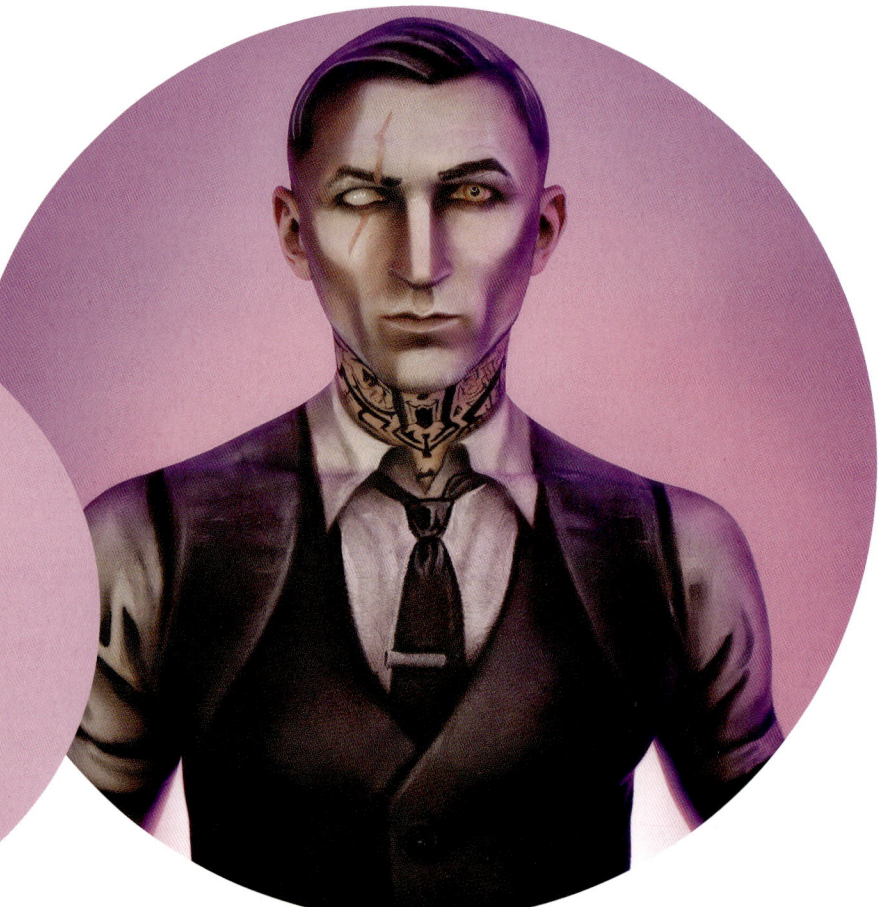

I painted Midas from *Fortnite* live on TikTok and my live was screen recorded. It was then stolen and used for the next three months everyday on TikTok Live, fooled everyone into thinking I was constantly live, and who knows how much money they made from live gifting. I had to complete about 10 copyright infringement forms, and TikTok did absolutely nothing about it. The account using my video gained over 30K followers from using my content!

MY PERSONAL PAINTING SETUP

Every content creator has a different setup, but I want to share what mine is like in case you're starting from scratch and need some tips. My painting setup consists of three things: makeup kit, computer display, and lighting.

I paint standing up in front of a ring light. Inside that ring light I have a small circular mirror and my phone in selfie mode. The reason I have my phone always pointing at me is because the paint can sometimes look different on camera than in real life, and we only care what the paint looks like on camera.

Generally, the camera can be forgiving so you might find that in real life it looks a bit messy, but if it looks good on camera you don't necessarily need to spend the time tidying it up.

For lighting, I have LED floodlights that can change color, which I shine on the back wall to alter the color of the background. To the left of my ring light, I have a computer stand where I have all my reference pictures in front of me while I paint. This stand also has a tiny shelf for my water pot and paintbrushes. A small table to the left of me holds excess paint, makeup brushes, eyeshadow palettes, sponges, and makeup wipes.

My makeup kit is foldable with four shelves. There is no right way to set up your makeup kit; just keep things relatively organized when painting because it's going to get messy! What's the phrase? Tidy desk, tidy mind. It makes a big difference.

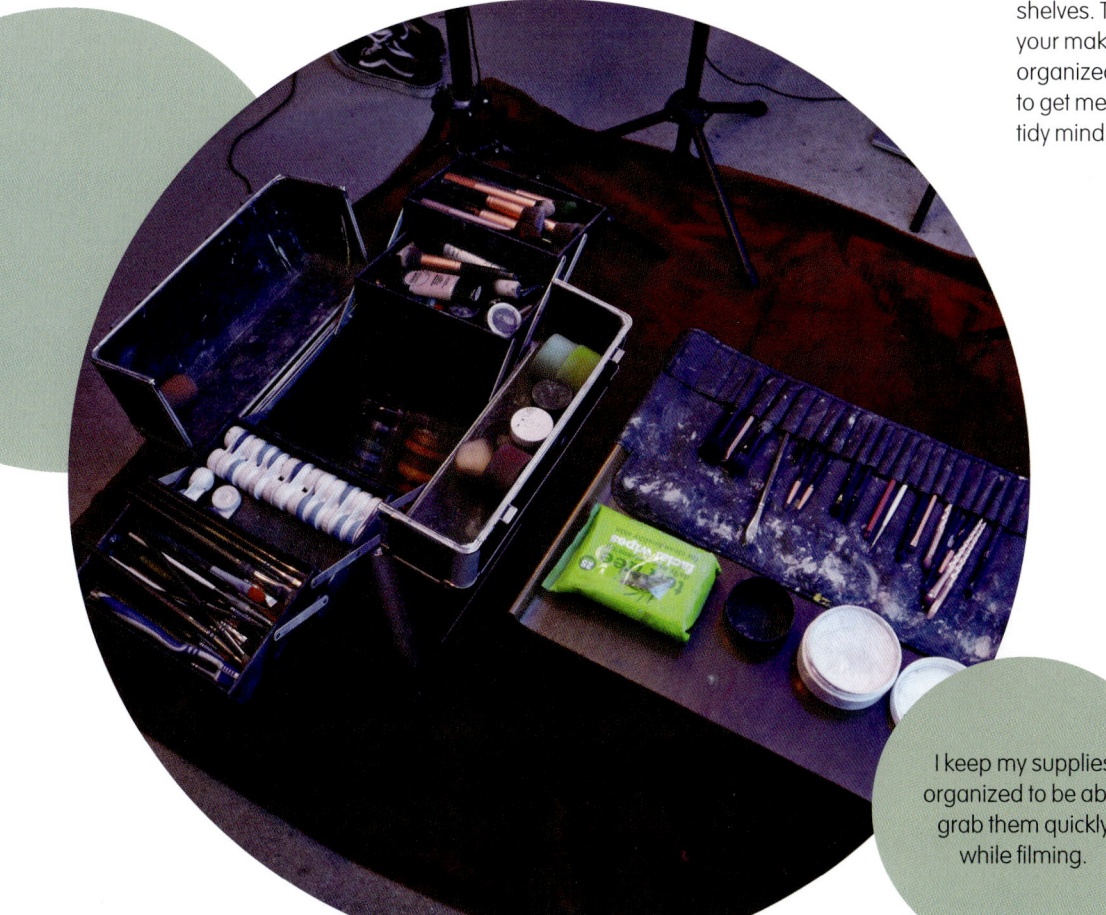

I keep my supplies organized to be able grab them quickly while filming.

THE IMPORTANCE OF GOOD QUALITY LIGHTING

Lighting is key for any content creator! I know I have fallen short on this in the past, but it's so true for many creators out there. Obviously, this depends on the purpose of your videos. If you're filming full HD quality for YouTube then yes you will need a good camera, but for social media, a lot of the platforms aren't compatible with 4K footage, and reduce the file quality to 1080p, so there is no need for the best camera out there. But what you can do to improve your quality is invest into your lighting. It's also much cheaper than a brand-new shiny phone or camera.

Having a set way you do lighting is important for building your personal brand and aesthetic for your videos. People will start to recognize your videos based on the way they're lit so being consistent with your lighting is important.

You can use lighting to highlight a specific part of your video and help draw the attention of the audience to where you want it to be.

In terms of different types of lighting, some people swear by a ring light, others choose to use the big box lights, or LED alternatives. I use a mixture of them all.

I have three big LED flood lights that change color so I can change the backdrop to match the feel of the video. I tend to position at least one of them directly behind me for the videos. I paint into a ring light, and I like it to shine directly at my face, illuminating everything, so there are no shadows cast at all.

However, if you're looking for a more natural effect, you might want to opt for the three-point lighting technique. This consists of:

Backlight: This light is shining from above and behind the person, pointing at them to make a distinction between the subject and background.

Key light: This is your main source of light for the video. It should be the most powerful light and closest to you or the subject of the video. It should be placed to one side of the camera, so this can create some natural shadows on the face.

Fill light: This should be placed on the opposite side of the key light and should be set to a dimmer intensity. If you can't change the intensity, just move the light further away.

We've spoken a lot about artificial lighting, but nothing can beat natural lighting, so if you can utilize this in your videos, go for it!

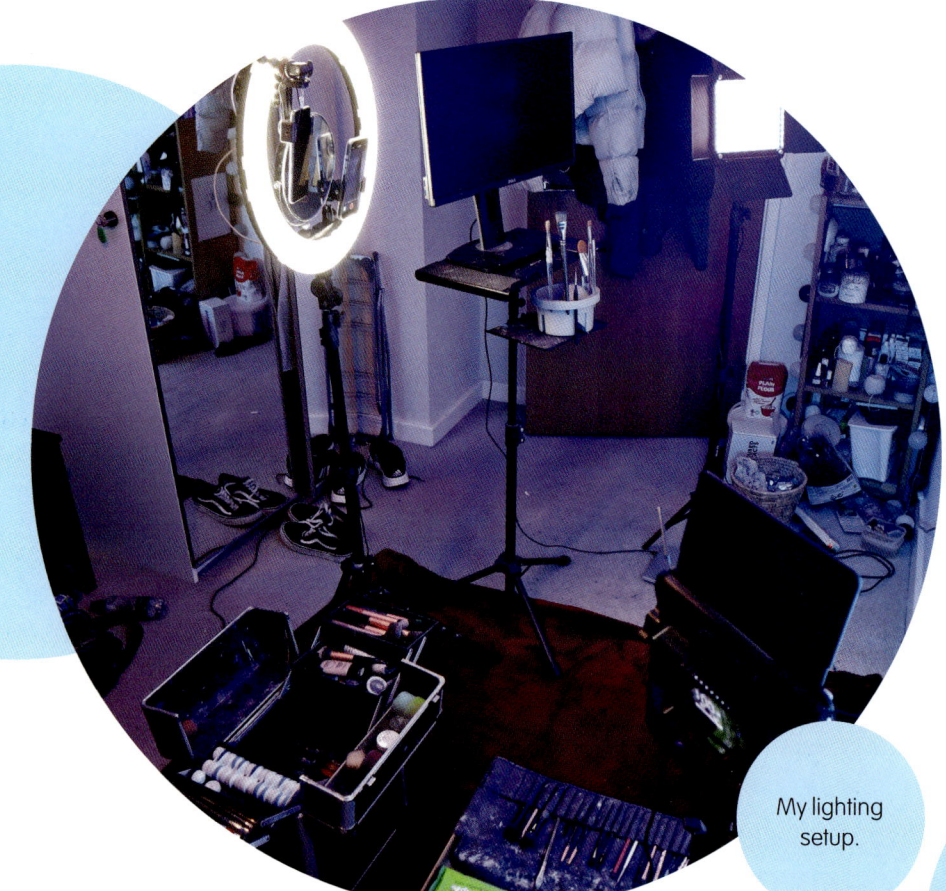

My lighting setup.

VIDEO EDITING TIPS

This isn't a step by step section on how to edit videos, but my exclusive tips that will make your life easier and videos more professional.

I edit my videos on free software on my phone, so 95% of the time I use the app InShot, but if there are certain effects I want to use that aren't available on Inshot I use Capcut, or Videoleap. They are all free to use with in-app purchases to unlock additional features.

There is more professional software you can use on a computer such as Premier Pro, which might be preferable if you shoot in 4K using a camera.

My first tip is to work smarter not harder. Repurpose your content across multiple platforms so you're reaching as many people as possible. The best way to do this is to film all your content offline from any social media apps. That way when you export your video, there will be no social media watermark, and you can post the same video to all platforms without worrying about getting your views suppressed by the app.

A useful tool to help with this is the "extract audio" feature. Every editing app will have one. Say you've found the sound you want to use. Download this video and then from that, extract the sound directly into the video editing app. Then when you overlay your own filmed content, you can ensure your transitions match the audio perfectly.

I've always found it much easier getting a smooth transition offline. You have more control over how finely you can snip a video down in the editing apps. A great tip for making sure your position remains constant from clip to clip, is to crop the video, or zoom in to enlarge the video until your outline matches. Do this for both sections until the before and after transition are aligned perfectly. This will result in a smoother transition.

Another helpful tip is to use the "speed" feature. Slow the timings down for a small chunk to make sure it matches with the sound. I sometimes use this when I want to repurpose a video using a new trending sound, and I want the original transitions to match up perfectly. So rather than re-recording, I either speed up or slow the videos down until it fits. See? Smarter, not harder!

UNDERSTANDING YOUR CAMERA ANGLES

Spending time understanding your camera angles can really elevate your videos. Simply changing the camera angle alone can be helpful in creating a story with your video. It's something I use in my videos all the time to change up the dynamic. For example, if the camera angle is peering down on someone, this tends to indicate that the person in the video is small or weak. The opposite is true if the camera angle is pointing up at someone. That generally indicates that character is strong and powerful.

Swapping the camera angles every now and then can add diversity to your content. If the viewer is seeing the same camera angle from you again and again, then they could get bored. Keep your audience guessing. Utilizing different camera angles can make your content much more engaging.

I like to use camera angles as a time-saving exercise when it comes to my body-painting videos. You might be thinking, "What an earth are you on about, Chris?" In the majority of my videos I'm painting half of my body and it usually takes me about eight hours. It's a lot, I know! So, I adjust the camera angle so it's facing directly in front of me and take a step closer to the camera. This way it still can capture all the details of the face and chest, but anything below the chest isn't visible on camera. Using this trick alone can sometimes save me hours worth of painting time, and most people still see it as a half body paint.

TOP 10 TIPS
TO BECOME A SOCIAL MEDIA INFLUENCER

If you've made it this far, and *still* want to be a content creator, in this next section I'm sharing some of my closest kept secrets. Why? Because I'm a strong believer that everyone should have the knowledge to succeed. If you know what I know, it doesn't mean I'm going to be less successful. You're still going to need to put in the time and effort. If you have a mindset of "Instagram hates me," or "TikTok shadowbanned me," then you're bound to get frustrated and quit. If you accept that the algorithm is constantly changing, and what worked for you six months ago might not necessarily work for you now, and that **you** will have to adapt and evolve with the times, then you're ready to be a content creator.

Let's get into it…

#1 Understanding the Importance of Trolls

You won't find a social media guide written by a so-called "social media expert" talking about trolls as a viable and actually quite reliable method of boosting your engagement. But if you completely immerse yourself in your comments section, you can start to build an extensive profile on what really makes social media users tick, and how to benefit from that. You start to develop sneaky little tactics that can really set you apart from other content creators in your space, but we'll come to that in a bit.

We all want people to like the content we post; we want people to think we're funny, talented, entertaining, whatever. But the reality is there will always be people who have something negative to say about

it. Unfortunately social media nurtures an environment where it's okay to share unfiltered thoughts no matter how nasty or vicious they could be because there are likely zero consequences for what you put online as an observer. The reality is you'll need to develop a coping mechanism.

I don't want to come across as supporting trolls. I'm all for strict community guidelines in order to provide a safer space on the internet to share content. What I hope to do is change your mindset on trolls, which will hopefully make reading those inevitable comments much more manageable to stomach.

Someone once said to me, "If your haters aren't hating, then you're doing something wrong," and I'm inclined to agree with this statement. You're always going to have people who like you and people who don't, and that's okay. You just can't take it personally. You need to be confident in your content, know where you want to go, and let the trolls come on that journey with you. If you build up a thick enough skin to not let the comments bother you and think of them as aid towards your bigger goal, then you'll nail it. For me, this process was a very quick learning curve. My first viral video had over 50,000 hate comments in the space of twelve hours, and it was intense. But I powered through it, got better, and eventually turned a lot of those trolls into fans. But still to this day, I pull on those nostalgic strings to generate views, and because I've been able to do that, I've generated millions of additional views out of what was quite a traumatic experience for me, and turned into something which is continuously benefiting my social media journey.

I've been making content for my trolls for years. Now this might seem a bit backwards, surely. I should be making content for my followers, as they're the ones who have chosen to follow me, and I do. It is important to keep your audience entertained and satisfied, but the reason why I make content specifically targeting my trolls is because I want their engagement to boost my views, so more people see my video. The best thing about it is they don't even realize I'm doing this intentionally. I like to see it as a game of cat and mouse: the trolls think they're the cat and I'm the mouse. By leaving a hateful comment they feel great about themselves, and that's what I want them to believe. The reality is, I've orchestrated that video to encourage them to comment, share, and troll. But why?

I want you to think of your favorite creator. You love watching their content, you might have a couple of friends who love their videos as well, but when they release a new video, do you send it to 10 of your friends consistently? Or is it more likely you're going to like, comment, and maybe share to 1 or 2 friends if it's a particularly good one, but generally you will just keep enjoying their content quietly?

Trolls like to make noise, they like to be heard, and in doing so can send a video super viral. If a troll finds your video funny, or cringeworthy, or for some reason takes a disliking to it, they will share this video with ten of their friends, encouraging them to laugh and comment on the post, boosting your engagement, who will then in turn share to another ten of their friends. Suddenly the algorithm is pushing your video because

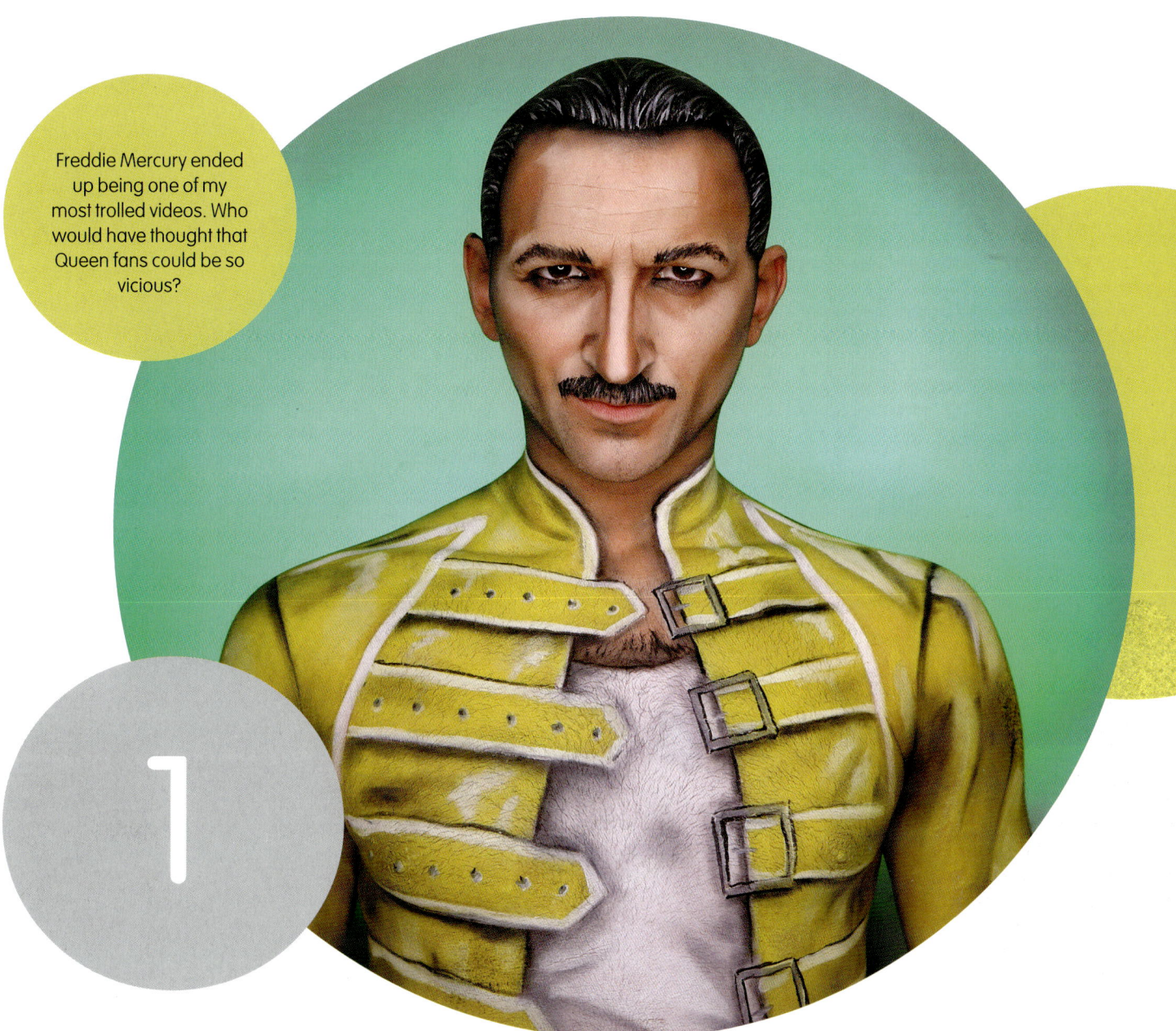

Freddie Mercury ended up being one of my most trolled videos. Who would have thought that Queen fans could be so vicious?

1

you're getting high engagement. If you were to look through your comments, a majority of them might be negative, but you should also be confident in the knowledge that for every troll's feed you reach, you can reach another twenty people who end up liking your content and choose to follow.

If I've managed to convince you this is a viable strategy to pursue, let's discuss how we can achieve it. This can be something as simple of deliberately making a spelling mistake in a video/caption. I can guarantee there will always be at least one person (but likely many) out there who feels it's *their* duty to correct you, which does what? Boosts *your* engagement.

What also works quite well is leaving something questionable, or funny in the background of your videos, and ignoring

it's there. This is something the eagle-eyed viewers will pick up on and comment on. The main source of your engagement should come from the video itself, but if you've put something in the background which sparks conversation in the comment section you've now got two sources of engagement for that video. Some people watch the video may not notice what was in the background, but when they open the comments and see the most liked comment is referring to this funny object, they will have to rewatch the video to see it.

You might be thinking though, wouldn't this sort of deliberate behavior start to grate on your followers? From my experience, what tends to happen is the complete opposite. The more they get to know you as a creator, and the content you make, they realize you're

doing it deliberately and start to go along with the joke as well. So, you've now got a community of people who are all in on the joke, and essentially poking fun at the trolls who think they're doing the most to bring you down by leaving a smart comment.

There are loads of different ways you can put this into practice, and you've got to find a way that works well with the style of your content. Let me tell you, it can be an absolute game changer when you've mastered "trolling your trolls."

#2 Keep Going When You Feel Like It's Pointless Carrying On

This tip is super important, and I think I might just have a different outlook than other social media gurus.

I'll be the first one to admit that it sounds totally cliché to recommend posting consistently, having a schedule and keeping to it, blah blah blah, but if you ask any content creator who's grown a large following, this will likely be their #1 tip, and they will probably say something along the lines of "If you're not posting content, then how do you expect to grow?" That is only just scratching the surface of why consistency is so important.

When I refer to consistently posting, I'm not referring to posting every day for a month and if you haven't gotten anywhere then

giving up. That is exactly the time you need to be doubling down with your content creation. And if you're wondering how long you need to be consistent before you see success, then you're asking the wrong question. Consistency means constantly showing up UNTIL it works, not giving up when you feel like you're not getting anywhere. Why? Because you never know if that next video you post might be the one that changes your life and gets 50M views overnight!

But consistency means more than just having a consistent posting schedule. This also refers to being consistent with the time and effort you put into researching, creating, and preparing your videos. Being consistent in editing your videos to a certain quality, with replying to comments, engaging with your audience, building that community.

Consistently looking to improve yourself and become the best content creator you can be.

When most people hear the advice about needing to be consistent, they assume it's all about them, and what they can do to make this work. And while this is all true, it's the next concept that really drove home the importance of being consistent for me.

To understand this, we need to think about how consistency can coincide with the social media platforms themselves. We need to move away from the mindset of there being this evil algorithm looming over us all that is constantly changing and never favors our content. Every social media platform has its own algorithm to prioritize content and keep as many people on the app as possible. But it's also responsible for figuring out which audience is suitable for

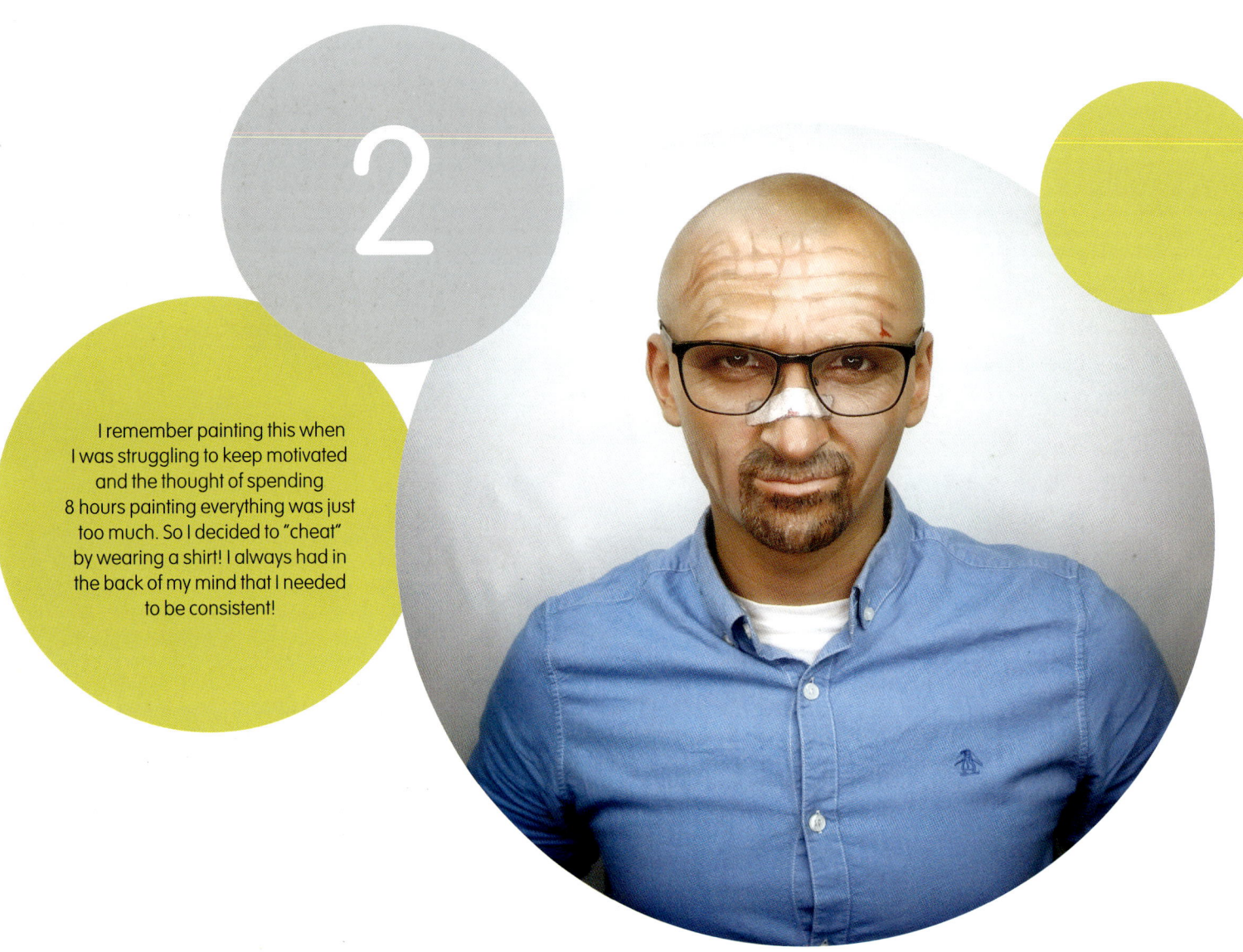

I remember painting this when I was struggling to keep motivated and the thought of spending 8 hours painting everything was just too much. So I decided to "cheat" by wearing a shirt! I always had in the back of my mind that I needed to be consistent!

your content. If you post gaming content, but your videos end up in the feed of someone who favors book reviews, they're not going to engage with your content. This is all information the algorithm retains and takes into consideration next time you post. The algorithm wants you to reach as many people as you can, because if your content keeps people on the platform then the platform makes more money. They'll group certain users together who have similar interests and trial your content on their news feeds until it finds a group of people who have shown greater interest in your content, people who watch your video, like, comment, share, and follow. The algorithm learns from that and pushes your content to that group of people in future to try and retain their engagement. If you only post one video, you've given the platform

one chance to find your ideal audience. How can you expect the platform to get it right the first time? What you need to do is give each platform enough information to be able to find the right audience for your content. That could take weeks, months, or years, but the more information you give the platform (i.e. the more you post) the more iterations of the algorithm your account has been through to find an ideal audience for your content.

I want to share this graph of my own YouTube analytics which shows my views since starting my YouTube account in June 2020. You can see I was posting for nearly two years before I even started to gain any sort of traction. If I'd given up at 1 month, 6 months, 1 year or even 2 years, I would have missed out on the huge growth I've seen from July 2022 onward.

My YouTube Analytics
Posting dates by number of views

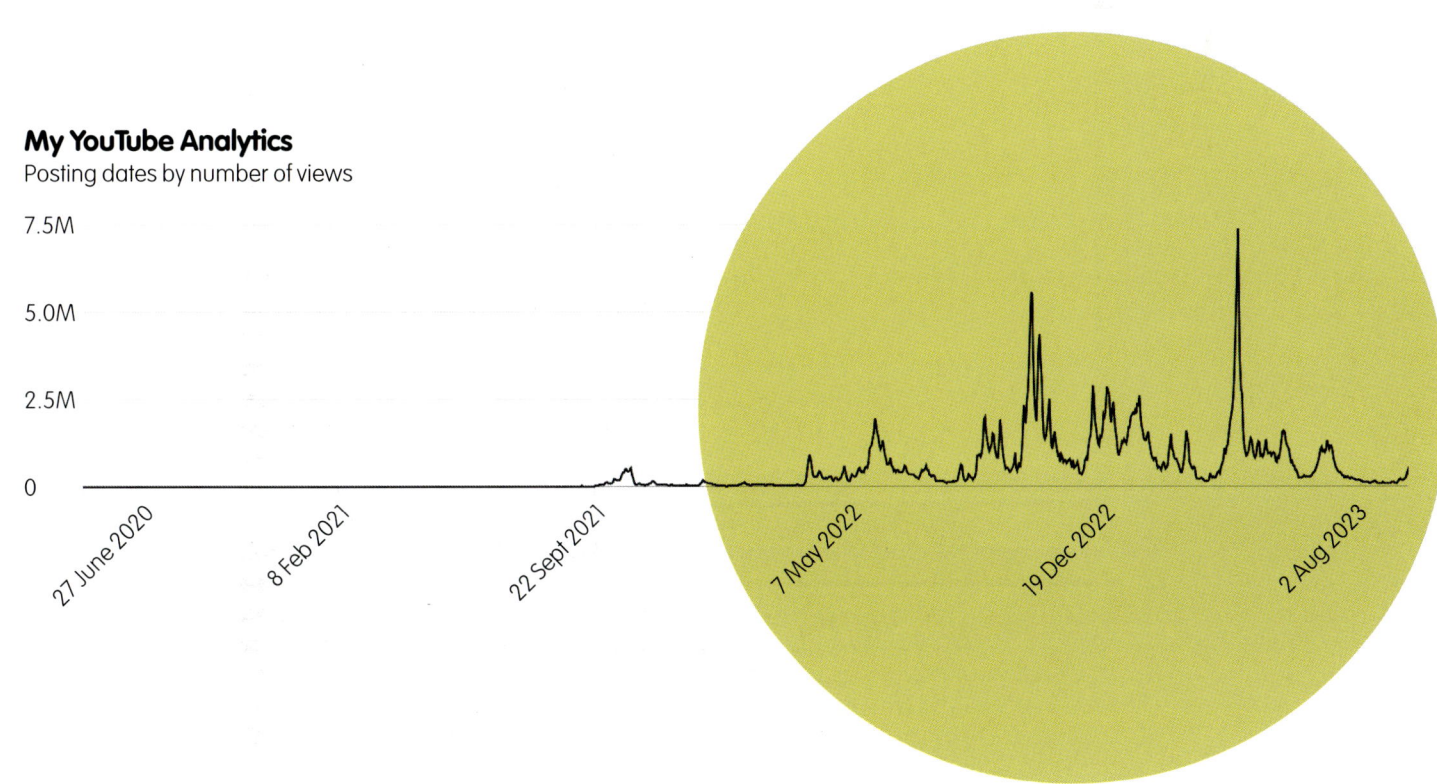

7.5M

5.0M

2.5M

0

27 June 2020   8 Feb 2021   22 Sept 2021   7 May 2022   19 Dec 2022   2 Aug 2023

#3 The Chicken or the Egg: Quality Vs. Quantity

It's the age-old question, isn't it? What came first, the chicken or the egg? Do you focus on quantity or quality? You might think it's obvious. Quality, right? But it's a bit more complicated than that. Consider: do you want to spend hours and hours creating the perfect video because quality is what is going to get your video seen? Or do you go down the route of producing as much content as possible, with the hope that some of it sticks?

The reality is both strategies are correct, but it's important to be aware of when to use them and why this will differ depending on what stage of the journey you're in.

My recommendation for anyone starting out is to begin with quantity and focus on quality later. There's nothing worse than spending hours and hours on a super high quality video and getting only 200 views. It's soul destroying! My videos take on average eight hours to create! Despite the quality, it may not translate to views because this video simply wasn't what your audience wanted to watch. So, this is where quantity comes into play. Work out what your audience wants to watch before dedicating the time and effort into quality. The logic behind this is if you throw enough content out there some of it will stick, and once you find it you can double down on quality.

This is exactly what I did when I first started on TikTok. I painted a look and created eight to ten different videos using that look with different lip sync sounds, transitions, and funny clips, and then when I eventually had a video that went viral, I stuck with that concept, and repeated it. It's about finding your unique selling point. You may have it real clear in your head what you think that should be, but chances are social media is going to steer you in a completely different direction, and it's up to you whether you choose to listen or not.

It's so easy to get caught up in the type of content *you* want to create, and if you're creating for fun, then by all means make whatever you like! But if your goal is to make this a full-time career, then you need to listen and take action from what your followers want from you.

My early viral videos were always ones in which I painted on my own hair, not out of artistic preference, but out of laziness as I didn't want to buy a wig for every character I made. It ended up being the focus in my comment section. My audience either loved it or they hated it! Was this an intentional move by me? Absolutely not. Pure fluke. What wasn't fluke though, was tuning into those comments and in future videos intentionally painting on hair to achieve the same result. With this knowledge I was able to produce better quality videos and reduce the quantity I was pushing out.

The more you post, the more you'll learn what works and what doesn't. That way you can start to fine-tune your content.

Finally, the larger your following gets, the more you will need to find a balance that works for you between quantity and quality. My advice is that once you've built up a large following, less is more is a good strategy. But this could differ depending on your content! If you've built a following doing daily vlogs, then continue to post daily! You need to start to think of your account along the lines of a portfolio. Does it work well together as a whole? If not, then make sure you are more deliberate about the type of content you're making. You might need to go back to trying to understand what your followers want to see and hone in on this.

3

The Joker from *Batman* was actually created as a paid collaboration, but the brand decided they were going to pull out and refused to pay me. I posted the video anyway and it generated over 2M views. I think it's fair to say they were kicking themselves after they saw this.

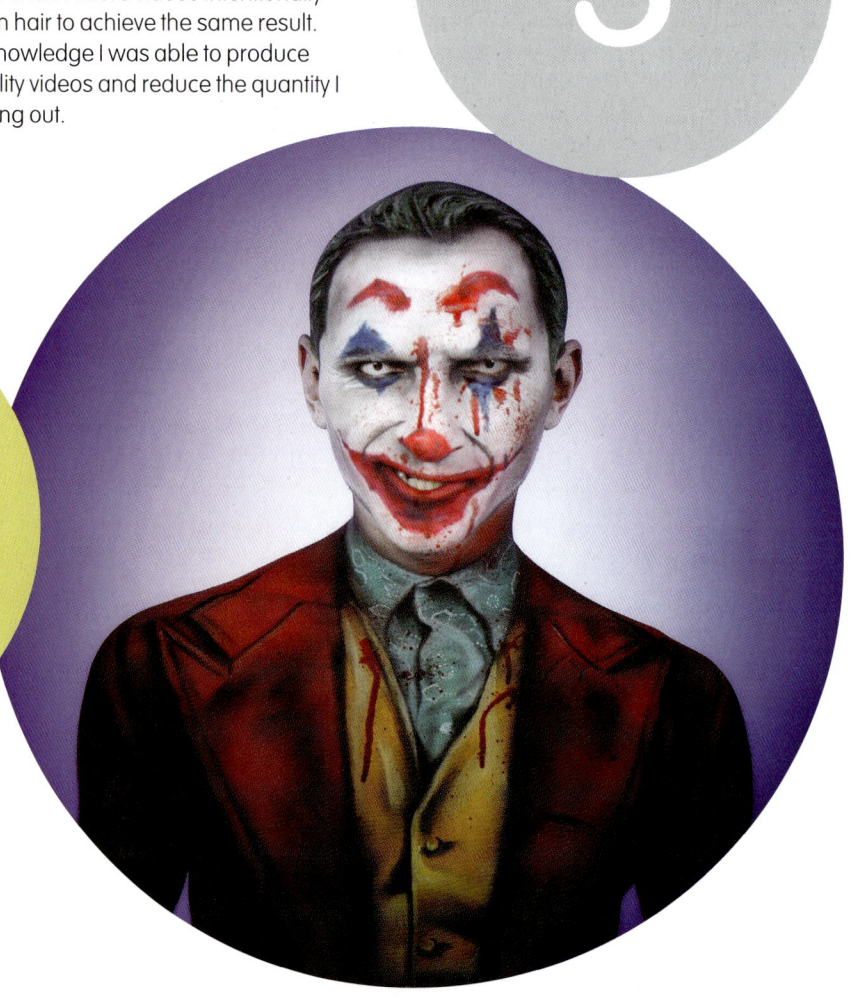

#4 Listen Loudly to Your Followers

How exactly do you develop an understanding of your audience? The way to do this is to be fully immersed in your own channel. Go in the comments, reply and talk to your followers, ask them questions, and put up polls on your story or community page. It's demanding and can take some time but it's invaluable!

If you think about it this way, it will actually save you a lot of time in the future as you'll be creating more tailored content, rather than putting effort into creating content that is going to flop. Marketing agencies pay thousands to get this sort of marketing insight so they can make informed decisions on products to release, but you've got all this information for free if you just look and listen.

If you understand what your audience wants to see, then you can tailor every video you make to address their needs. This is much easier said than done, but there is a way around this, and we've already discussed it!

Remember when I said to find a creator in your niche who already has a large following? Apply this logic again and spend time in their comment section. If you spend the time understanding what their audience wants to see from them, then you can make your content tailored to that in the hope you reach that audience.

You can do this with multiple creators within your niche, until you've built a following of your own. It's by no means foolproof but once you've built a following of your own and are getting more comments come through, then you can analyze tailored requests specifically aimed at you.

Two more benefits of understanding your audience are that replying to comments creates a sense of community where your followers can come to interact with you and each other, and it's easier to monetize your following. This is something we will touch on in greater detail later.

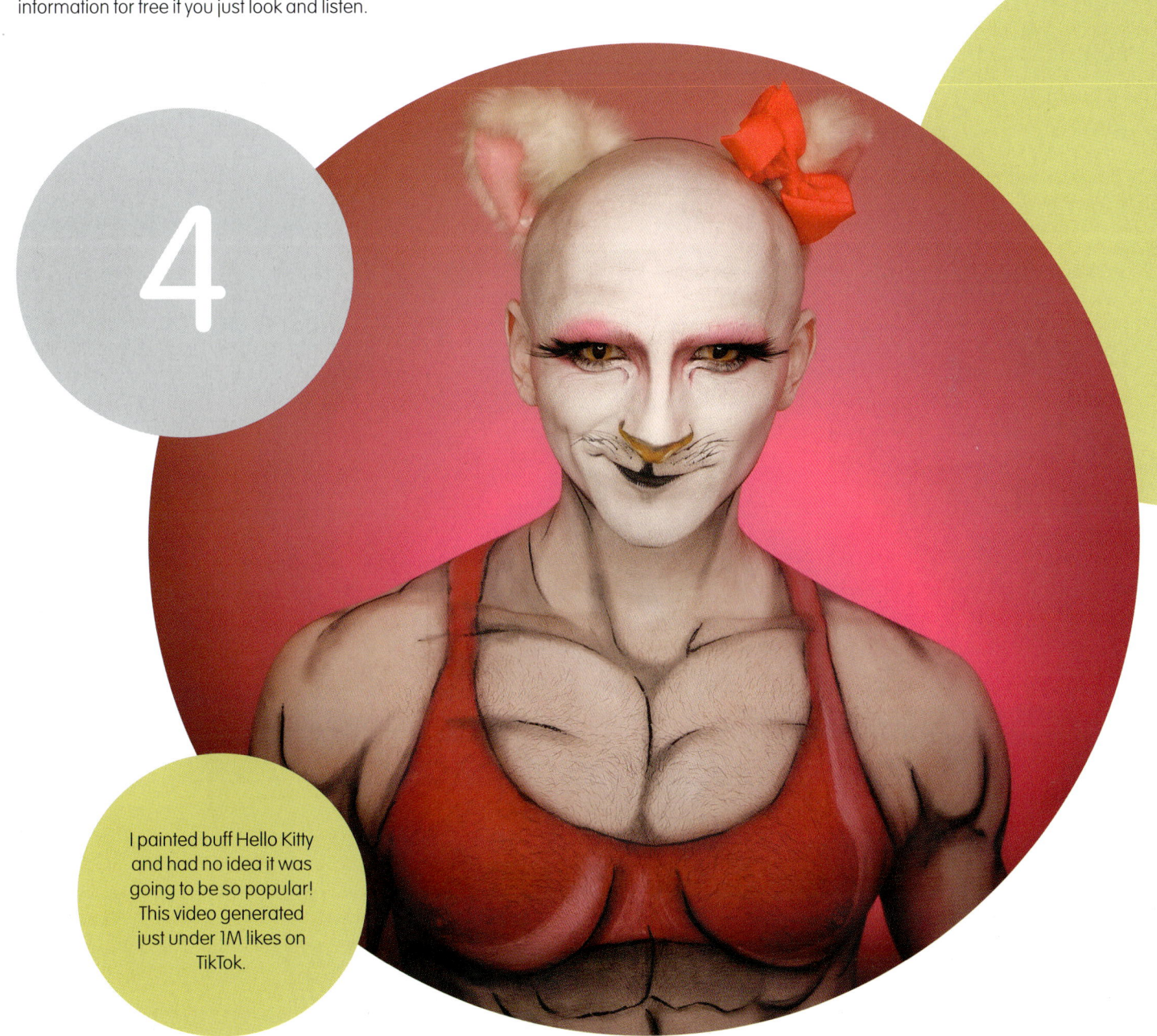

4

I painted buff Hello Kitty and had no idea it was going to be so popular! This video generated just under 1M likes on TikTok.

#5 Become Besties With Your Analytics

You can get SO much useful information from your analytics that will help steer your content going forward if you just spend a bit of time looking at it. In my opinion, not enough people know how to use the analytics!

It will take some time to get your head around what each platform has to offer. YouTube has its own app or you can access it online. With TikTok it is all in an app. With Instagram you can access in the app but you can also access additional information from the Facebook business suite. If you don't have access to your analytics, you might have to change your account to a professional account. If you do have access to your analytics, spend ten minutes looking through them, click through all the different options, play around with the dates, and try to immerse yourself in them before reading the rest of this section.

Did you notice anything interesting? Have you picked out something that will help guide your content going forward? If not, then no worries we'll go through some specific things to look out for.

There are different ways you can look at your analytics. You can look at them for your whole account and for specific posts and videos. I highly recommend looking at all your most watched videos individually to understand where the views came from and the average watch time. Then you can compare this to videos which haven't done so well.

You might find that your average watch time dropped three seconds in, so now you know you need to make that first three seconds more engaging to retain watch time. Or it may have been something you did or said at three seconds which make people scroll. Try to understand what the analytics are showing you rather than just looking at the number on the screen.

Apply what the number is saying and always ask why. Why is this number so low? Why does this video get a greater average watch time than others? You'll start to piece a puzzle together, and you'll see similarities between multiple videos. Whether that is the style, sound, theme, or character you chose. These are all things you can utilize to make future decision with your content.

It's easy to look at your total followers and only worry about growing them, but I think that's in direct opposition to the way you *should* be looking at your analytics. Instead, focus on views and engagement rather than follower growth. If you build your engagement, then *this* will bring followers.

The longer you spend in your analytics the quicker you'll start to pick up on trends, for instance when is the best time to post, what type of content performs better, and where views are coming from. If you have a particularly strong audience in France, for example, then that could help steer the type of content you make and you can tailor your next video to that particular nationality.

The more comfortable you are in your analytics, the easier you'll be able to deduce exactly what type of content encourages more shares, more comments, and higher views when planning future content.

There are also free tools that look at this on a much broader scale, such as Google trends. This brilliant tool tells you what is currently trending on Google. You can also break this down to what's trending on YouTube. Type in words or phrases which are relevant to your content and Google trends will tell you if it is trending or not. It will also provide you with related terms that are trending, which you might find helpful.

If you know, for instance, that 70% of your audience is from the United States, you can filter down by location, so it only shows you what is trending there. Use your personal analytics to input data into Google trends to help guide your content.

You can filter it down by timeframe as well. It's always useful to compare if something is trending within the last twenty-four hours, whether it's still trending days later because this might encourage you to create a whole series around a particular topic, or if it's a one-off you can turn your attention elsewhere.

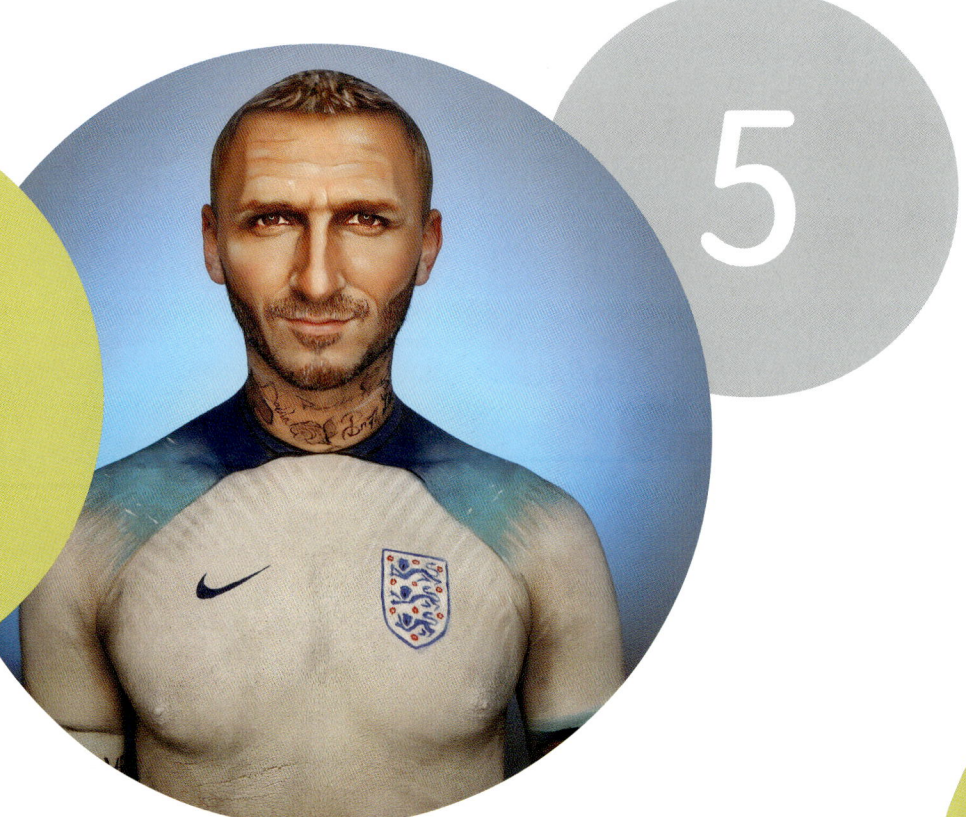

I was getting a load of comments to paint a footballer (soccer). I'm not really a football fan, so had no idea who most of these people were I was being asked to paint! So, I decided to go with probably the most recognizable football player there is: David Beckham. I'd never painted a football player before, so it was unknown territory for me, but being steered by your comments is the only way to truly understand what your audience wants to see!

#6 Stick to What Works…

You may have been posting for weeks, months, years and seen no success, but when you have a video do well, learn from it! Make it your mission to understand why and make it your online persona. I don't want you to worry about boring your audience with the same content either. If you look at the video analytics, you'll see many videos that go viral on social media have a fresh faced, new audience. As many as 97% of viewers will be seeing your content for the first time. If you want to grow your following, you need to reach this new audience all the time!

Most content creators with a large following will be able to pinpoint an exact video of theirs which blew up the internet and brought in a load of followers.

My very first viral video was flooded with hate. I painted a Fortnite character and within the time it took me to go to bed that night and wake up the morning after, I had 50,000 hate comments. I became an internet meme overnight. It was rough and looking back on it I understand why it happened (the paint was awful) but that initial video opened the world of painting Fortnite characters for me and I was able to build my following to over 1 million from Fortnite videos alone on TikTok. I found something that worked, and stuck to it.

It's so easy to fall into a trap of just creating content you want to create. You might find that sometimes your content isn't necessarily what the masses want to see, but if you want content creation to be your profession you need to produce content people want to see, as that's essential to monetize this job.

You might find that a particular style of video has worked for you in the past, but it's no longer getting you views. If it stops working, then stop making that content, and stick to what does work! You have to keep repeating this cycle again and again.

The algorithm across all social media platform is constantly changing, and it's your job as a content creator to change with it. The most successful content creators stick to what works, and understand their audience better than anyone else on the planet. They know exactly what their audience wants to see, understand how to engage them, and give them what they want in a way that is entertaining.

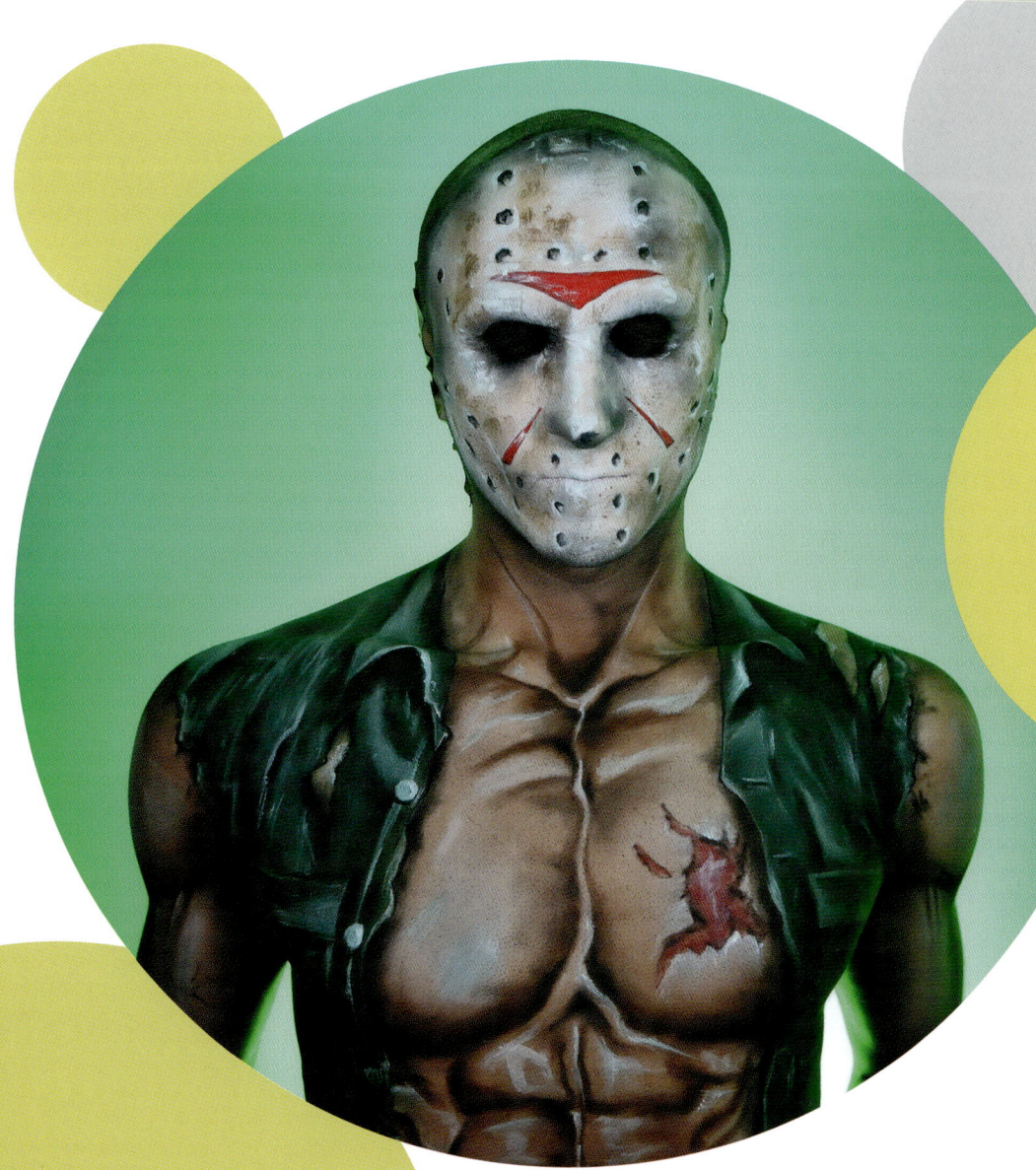

6

The video I created for this character was a social media trend: a Halloween makeup transition trend using a knife. I adapted it to use a paint brush instead of a knife, and transformed into Jason Voorhees. I ended up using this sound for 6 different characters and all of them generated over 1M views.

#7 …But Also, Don't Be Afraid to Try New Things

I've said it before and I'll say it again. Social media is fickle, so you've got to be constantly on your toes, looking for the next big thing. Try new pieces of content. Whether that's a new style of video, new theme, new topic to talk about, or new feature the platform released. Try everything, while still remaining loyal to your iconic content. You still need to appeal to your core audience, but trying new things is what is going to bring a newer audience in and help you appeal to fresh faces.

Think of it like this: Imagine you're the brand Doritos and you have your loyal fan who only eats Chilli Heatwave, but you've also got a casual user who sometimes eats Doritos but sometimes goes for competitor products because they like variety. You're never going to win that customer over if you just keep trying to sell them Chilli Heatwave (core flavor). You need to give them variety with new and exciting flavors to bring them back into buying Doritos. Treat your social media following the same way. You've got your core audience who are loyal to your videos and avid fans. But you might have viewers who have seen *some* of your videos, but you haven't managed to convert them into a follower yet. This is when trying new material comes into play. This material might be enough to convert them into a follower. You can do this all while still producing your core material to appeal to your main audience.

If you only do what you're comfortable with, then there is no room to grow and develop as a content creator. You'll just get stuck in a rut and eventually get bored of creating your own content, and then viewers will get bored watching it because it's nothing they haven't seen a hundred times before.

Creators who are willing to change with the times stick around longest. Those stuck in their ways of what worked once quickly die off. You've got to find a way to create the type of content the algorithm wants to see, and then it will reward you with views. Regardless of how many followers you have, it's all about each individual video and how well that video performs against the algorithm's metrics.

You might try a load of different ideas and they all flop, but that's okay; you've got to throw enough at the wall for some of it to stick. You don't know if it will work until you try! *Insert inspirational quote about how the more you fail the more you learn and are more likely to succeed in the future.*

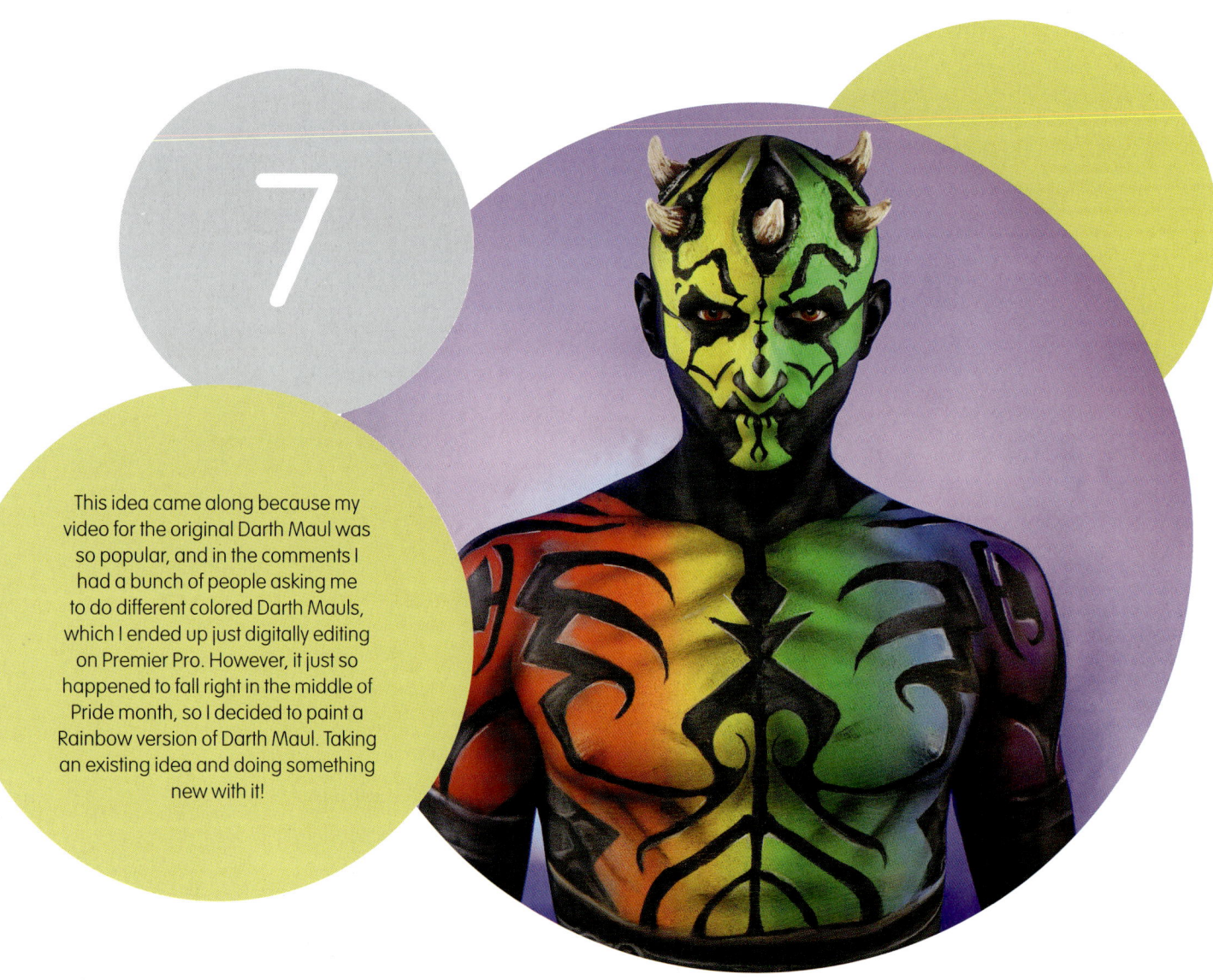

7

This idea came along because my video for the original Darth Maul was so popular, and in the comments I had a bunch of people asking me to do different colored Darth Mauls, which I ended up just digitally editing on Premier Pro. However, it just so happened to fall right in the middle of Pride month, so I decided to paint a Rainbow version of Darth Maul. Taking an existing idea and doing something new with it!

#8 You Grab That Attention… and You Keep It.

If you think about the purpose of a social media algorithm, from a social media platform perspective, they want to prioritize videos that keep viewers on the platform. So, bearing that in mind, watch time is king. But to achieve a decent watch time, you need to grab attention within the first two seconds! Yes, it's as brutal as that. You have literally two seconds to engage the audience, or else they scroll to the next video.

Experiment with different engaging hooks. You don't want to waste those first two seconds introducing yourself. Get right into the action! This can be done with music, visual impact, overlay text, asking a thought-provoking question, addressing a common problem people want to fix, or even something completely random that will spark a discussion in the comments section. Humor works well in a hook. Throw all your best and funniest clips at the start to get people hooked to watch the build-up in your video through the end. I cannot stress this enough when it comes to watch time.

One thing I would say though, is to try and keep your hook relevant to your video. Don't promise to deliver something you have no intention on following through with. This will frustrate and discourage viewers from watching your future videos.

Once you've mastered how to grab attention from the start, you need to shift your focus onto *keeping* that attention throughout your entire video. Keep the video moving quickly with short clips. Keep in the back of your mind that two-second attention span. Every two seconds of your video is just as important as the next.

Other ways you can keep people's attention is by replying to comments in a video and to requests. An additional benefit to this is if you produce content which enables follower engagement with you directly, that will boost your follower loyalty, and will positively impact your video engagement for your future videos! People **want** to hear from you and get to know you. They like to be able to talk directly to and build a relationship with a creator. If you can successfully do that, then these followers are going to stick around forever.

My last tip for increasing your overall watch time is to create loops to your videos. Specifically seamless transitions from the last clip of your video to the start of your video so viewers easily watch the video twice. You'll lock in a watch time of over 100% which will bring your overall average up. This will be flagged as a positive and social media platforms will start to recommend your videos to others as the algorithm can see your watch time is above average!

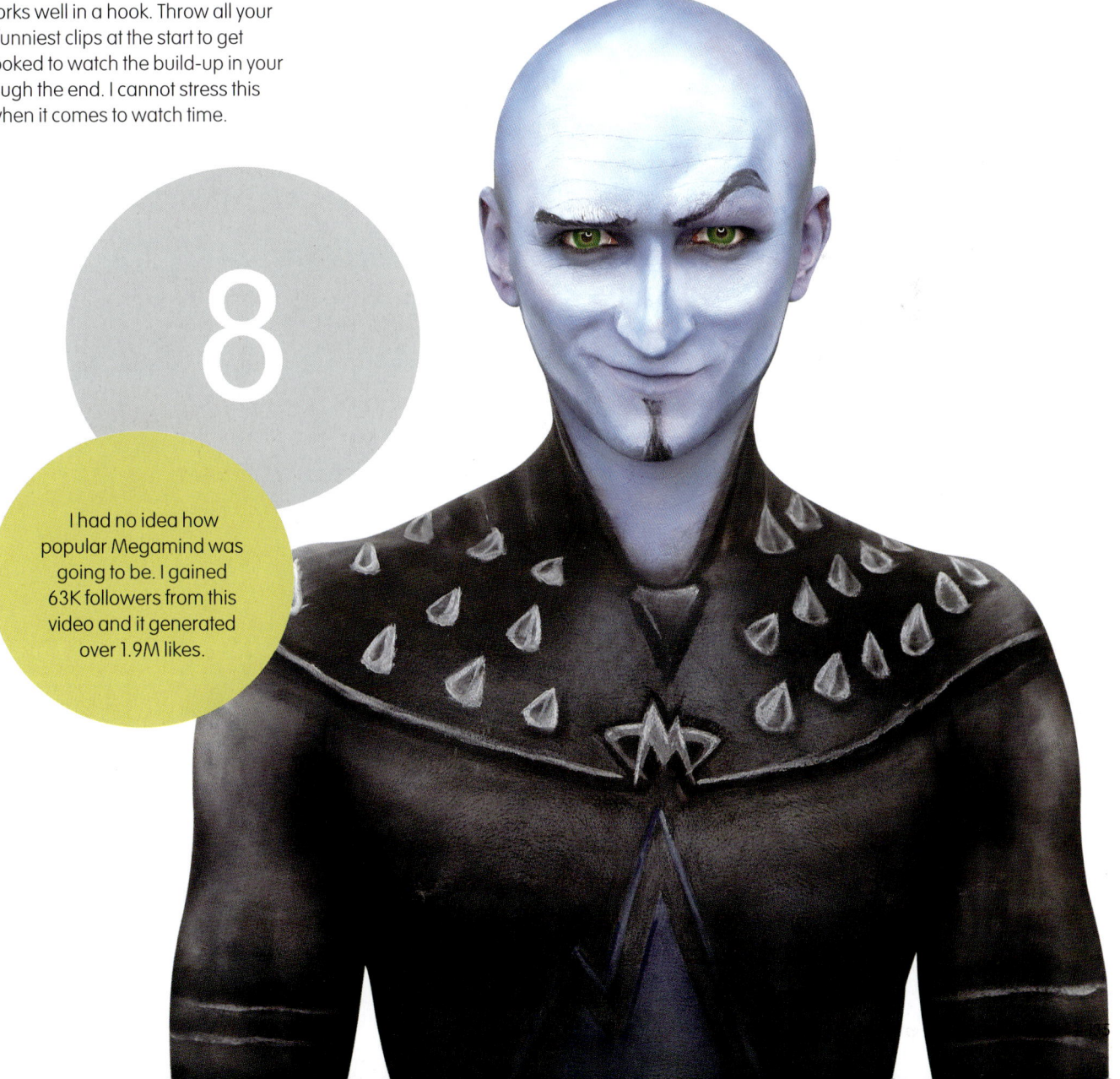

8

I had no idea how popular Megamind was going to be. I gained 63K followers from this video and it generated over 1.9M likes.

#9 Be On Top of the Trends

Whether you *like* to follow social media trends or not, unfortunately this is a necessity of the job. Jumping on a trend, or even just using a trending sound can really boost your engagement. Social media moves so quickly these days you need to be all over the trends as soon as they're blowing up. In a matter of days trends come and go. If you're late to a trend, then that sound is most likely saturated, no one is watching, people are bored of it, and your video will get lost. Social media platforms prioritize certain sounds and push videos using that sound to users who have previously engaged and liked video using this sound before. The earlier you get on a trend, the more likely your video will be one of the ones which gets picked up and goes viral.

Be aware not all trends would be suitable for your content. Try to understand what is trending in your wider niche, and if and how you can tweak a trend to suit your content.

The longer you spend scrolling social media, the more you'll start to realize certain sounds and certain trends are being pushed to your newsfeed. When you start to connect those pieces and notice a particular sound is being pushed a lot more than other sounds, that is a sign that this sound has been picked up by the algorithm as something you personally would like to watch. If the platform has noticed this for you, then there's a strong chance that you're not going to be the only one who wants to see that.

Look for patterns then work out the best way to engage that audience. Think about it like this. If you've been selected by TikTok as someone who would want to watch this type of content, ask why. What do you like, and what can you put into your videos which others are going to enjoy. It's difficult to know exactly how these algorithms work but generally they group people together who have similar interests and create pools of content each group of users would enjoy.

It's your job to work out what group your content fits within and how best to engage with them!

You might find that a trend doesn't work for you, and that's okay. There have been hundreds of trends I've tried to take part in, and my videos flopped. But I wouldn't have known if I hadn't tried.

On the flip side I've taken part in other trends and became the #1 watched video for the sound, gained thousands of followers, and generated millions of views! Social media is not an exact science, but if you're posting content constantly and understand what is trending around you, you have the best chances of going viral!

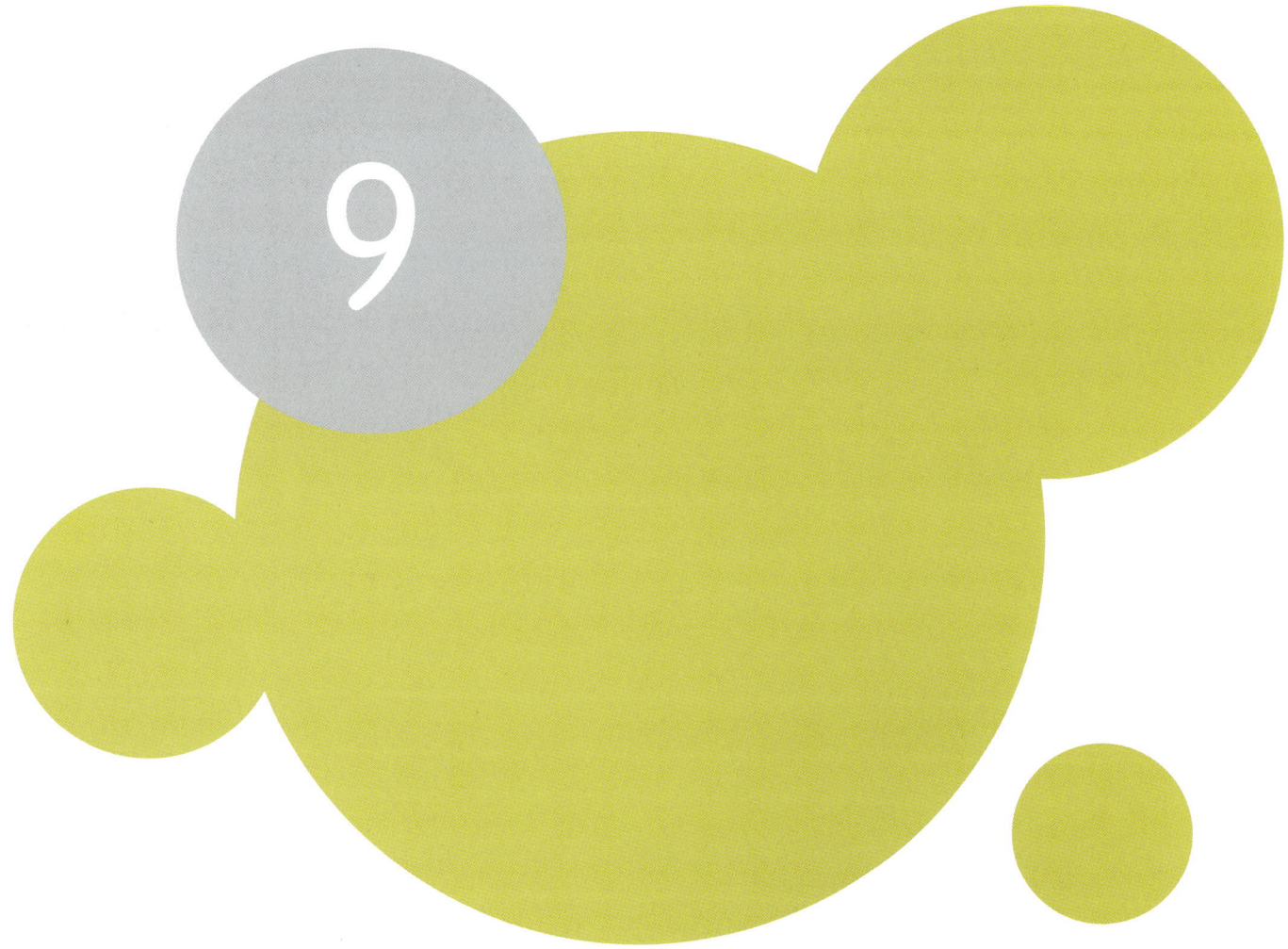

9

#10 Have Fun!!!

Most importantly of all, and it's going to sound a bit cliché, have fun with it! Being a content creator is such an amazing job. It gives you freedom to be creative, have a great work-life balance, and make a living off doing something you're genuinely passionate about.

If you're having fun with your content, it will come through in your videos. It's super difficult to fake it on social media. Even the best actors would struggle coming across genuine twenty-four seven! If you're putting on an act it will show, which is why it's so important to find a topic you genuinely care about and enjoy. You don't need to be an expert, but you need to have enough interest in it to be able to produce engaging content for the people who share that same interest.

If you get to a point in your content journey where you're not enjoying the content you make anymore, that is absolutely okay. You are allowed to not enjoy the content the same way that you used to when you first started creating it. This might just be a sign that you need to change it up a bit. You are naturally going to get bored of creating the same thing again and again and again.

You can show a lot more of yourself in the content you create if you enjoy the content you create, as opposed to just churning out content for the sake of it.

A lot of people think social media is a super easy job, but the reality is it's constant. So sometimes that means taking a break. Try shutting your phone off for a week or going on holiday and taking time away from social media. No matter how much you love your job, everyone needs a break from it every now and then. Sometimes you'll find when you come back from your holiday the ideas will be flowing! Taking time away from thinking about work can give you a new perspective and suddenly you might get the best idea you've ever thought of.

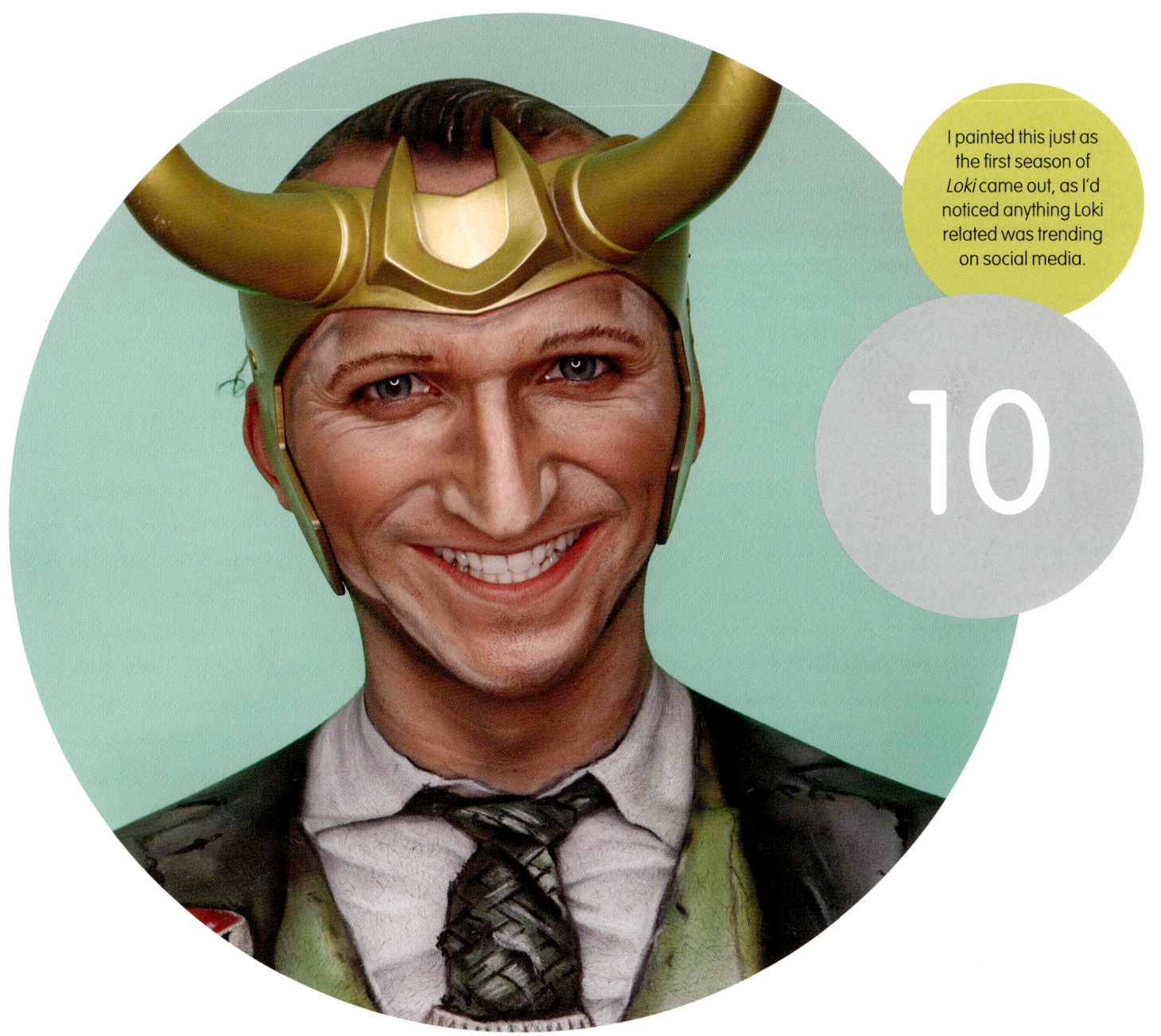

I painted this just as the first season of *Loki* came out, as I'd noticed anything Loki related was trending on social media.

10

MONETIZING YOUR CONTENT

There's a bunch of different ways you can monetize your content online, from being paid to create content by social media platforms themselves, to being sponsored by large corporations to advertise their product, to starting your own brand. In this section, I'll discuss all the different ways you can make money through social media and touch on how you can tailor this to your specific audience to generate the most income. Let's start with the different types of monetization.

Advertising Revenue

This is generated from the social media platforms themselves. Some platforms offer ad revenue shares, and some are more lucrative than others. The most famous and lucrative at the moment is YouTube. However, I'd be cautious about relying solely on this for your income as it's dependent on views, and if you create short form content, it's much less lucrative. Longer form videos where you can place advertisements before **and** during your video earn much more money.

Affiliate Marketing

This is where a company or brand creates a unique discount code or link that you share to your followers. By promoting a particular product as an affiliate you get a commission from all sales made from that code or link. Commission rates vary depending on what market you are in but generally they are anywhere between 5–25%.

Selling Your Own Products

This can be anything from branded merchandise to creating a product from scratch that you know your followers would enjoy and benefit from. There are loads of companies out there to manage the whole product creation, payment and logistics. Influencers often take this approach.

Sponsored Content

This is essentially influencer marketing and a company's alternative to traditional marketing. This involves working closely with a brand to come up with a concept which suits your style but also meets the requirements of the brand to advertise a certain product or service.

Gifting and Donations

This can be anything from being sent gifts on TikTok live, to asking for donations directly. This strategy tends to work well if you have a clear reason why. Be careful because if you don't use that money for what you promised you would, it can quickly flip into cancel culture. It's best if you have a genuine reason for needing to raise money, like for a medical reason, or tuition fees. Asking for money so you can buy the latest Gucci bag won't go down so well.

Freelance Work

If you have a skill that can be transferred into a paid service, for instance if you are a makeup artist or personal trainer, you can advertise your services on social media so people can hire you directly.

Sponsorship Models

These types of services come from websites such as Patreon and OnlyFans. Your followers pay a monthly fee to subscribe to your content and get access to all the additional content that has been posted behind a pay wall. They are paying for the privilege of any exclusive content which hasn't been shared publicly. Most social media platforms offer a subscription service as well.

MONETIZING YOUR SPECIFIC AUDIENCE

We've discussed a bunch of ways you can monetize your content, but you might have read some of those and thought "Nah, this just wouldn't work for me." If you can't see it working, then chances are you are right, it won't. Some of the methods won't lend themselves well to your style of content and that is okay!

In this section, let's look at a detailed overview of all the different ways you can make money, and you can decide what works best for you.

Let's think about this practically. Imagine you create baking videos online, and one of your videos, which was a vegan recipe, went viral and you gained a load of new followers. If you're business-minded you'll create more videos with vegan recipes, as chances are all of those followers are looking for more.

You can take this steps further and work on creating a vegan cookbook you could sell directly to your followers, reach out to large vegan baking brands to see if they would sponsor a video, and collaborate with smaller independent vegan food businesses to offer an affiliate program and earn commissions.

What I *wouldn't* do if I was this person is create a generic cookbook without vegan recipes or make basic merchandise like t-shirts. It's all about being in tune with what your audience wants to see, and if you can provide them with a clear benefit, they will buy it.

As long as you stay true to yourself and don't sell out for the money, your followers will come with you, and will happily spend money to support you. Your followers have built a connection with you and know they can trust you.

If you create a subpar product which comes across as a cash grab, you'll lose the trust in your audience, and may even lose followers and never be able to sell to them again. Provide them with a good quality product which has value and benefits them, they will come back for more and be around forever.

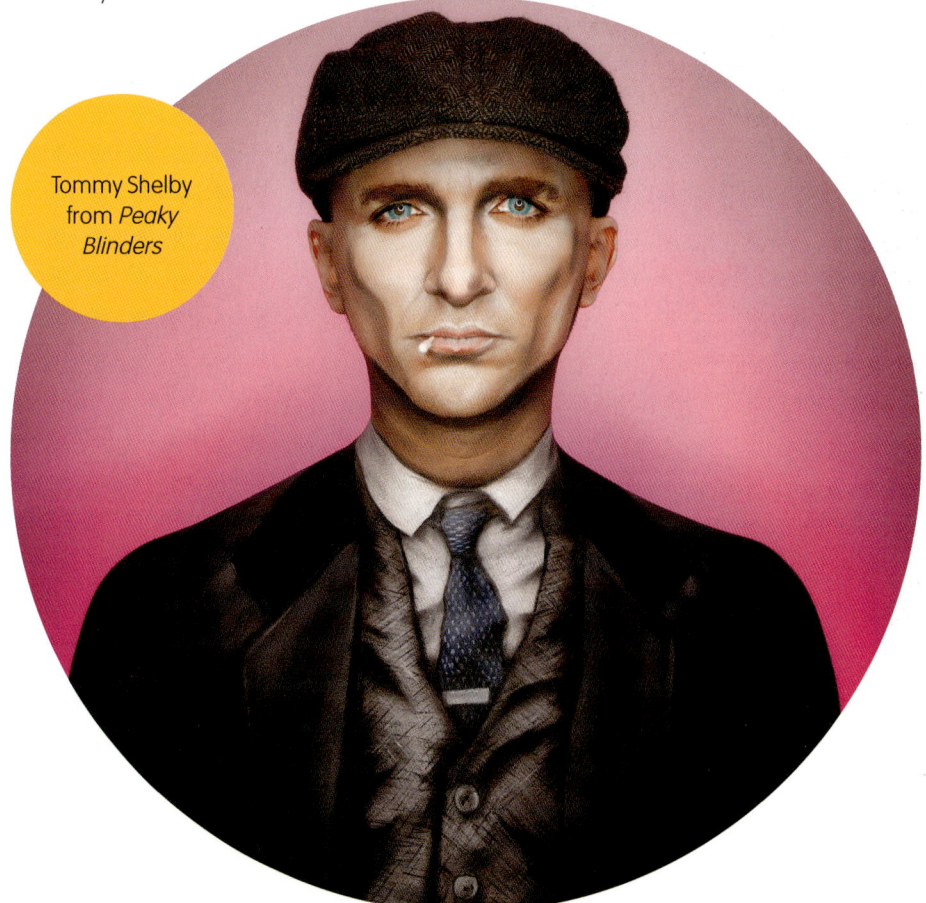

Tommy Shelby from *Peaky Blinders*

RESOURCES

There are many products on the market that work great for cosplay, including ones you can find at drugstore and craft store chains. You may already have some that you can use for the techniques in this book. The companies listed here sell the makeup and other supplies that I use most. When you're ready to purchase new supplies, you might want to give them a try. See what works best for you!

Mehron Makeup
https://www.mehron.com/
All water-activated face paint, fake blood, Syn Wax, liquid latex, rigid collodion, charred ash powder, spirit gum remover, fixative "A," color-setting powder, brushes, sponges, and spatulas

Coloured Contacts
https://www.colouredcontacts.com/
Contact lenses

Kryolan Professional Makeup
https://us.kryolan.com/
Black tooth enamel

Ben Nye
https://www.bennye.com/
Fake blood effects gel

NYX Professional Makeup
https://www.nyxcosmetics.co.uk/
Contour palette

Sleek
https://visitstore.bio/sleek/
Cream contour

E.L.F. Cosmetics
https://www.elfcosmetics.com/
Concealer and liquid foundation

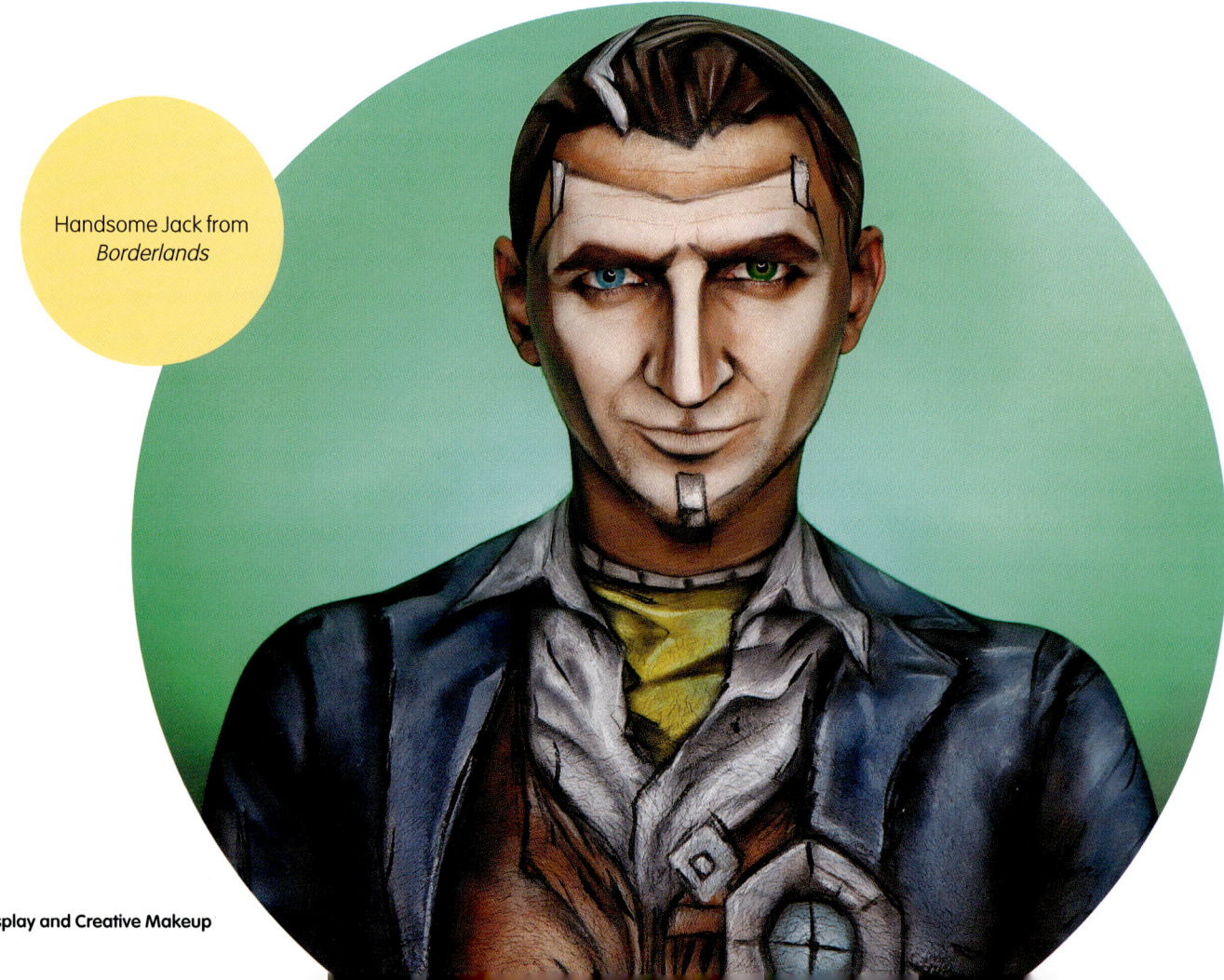

Handsome Jack from *Borderlands*

ABOUT THE AUTHOR

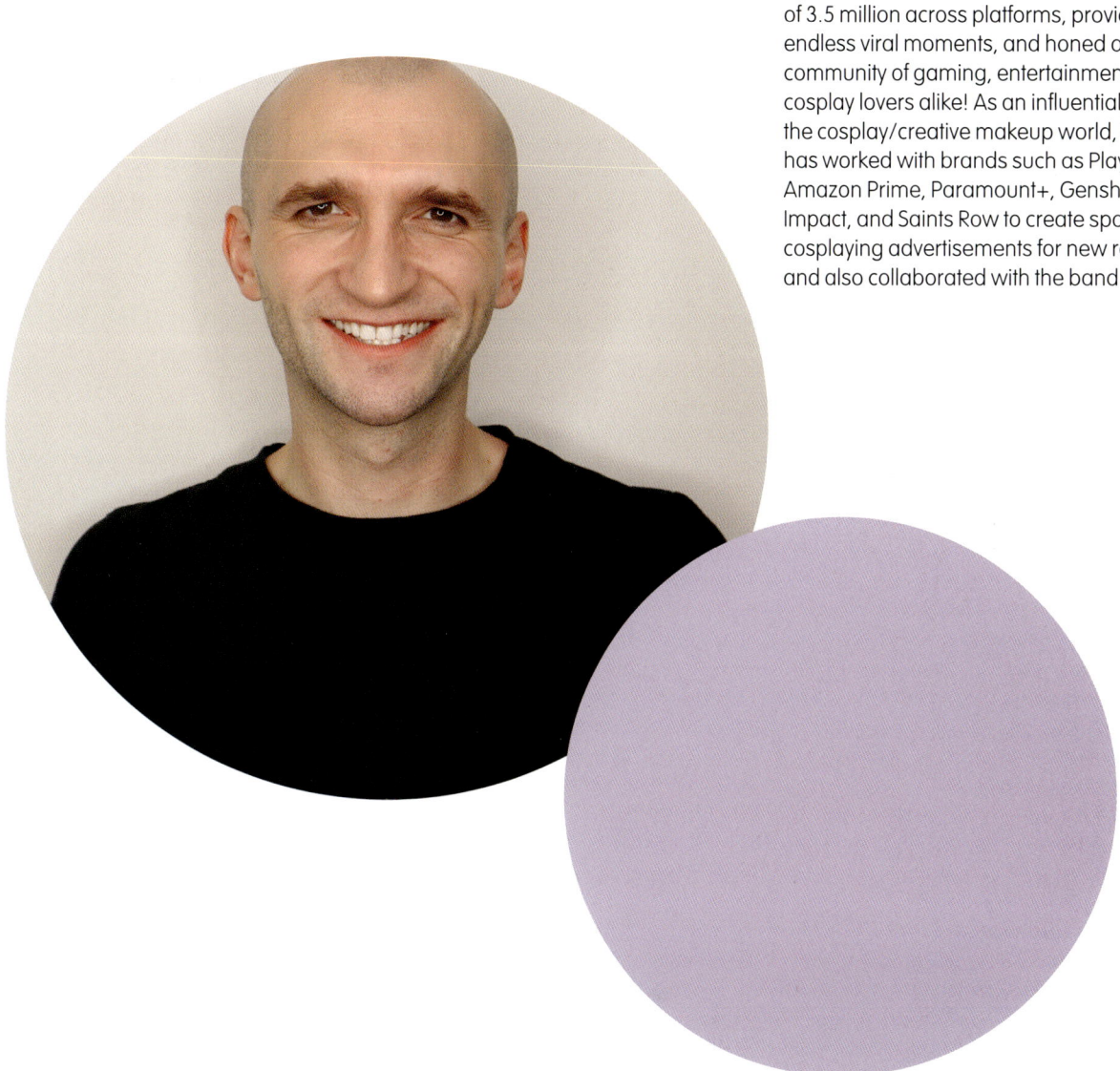

Chris Peck, a.k.a. **Rainbowskinz** on social media, is a creative shape shifter with a makeup brush. Based in London, United Kingdon, but with a global audience, he creates amazingly creative and entertaining videos that showcase his creative makeup and body painting skills. Chris's transformations have amassed a following of 3.5 million across platforms, provided endless viral moments, and honed a strong community of gaming, entertainment, and cosplay lovers alike! As an influential face in the cosplay/creative makeup world, Chris has worked with brands such as PlayStation, Amazon Prime, Paramount+, Genshin Impact, and Saints Row to create sponsored cosplaying advertisements for new releases and also collaborated with the band Gorillaz.

INDEX